WINDRUSH
A SHIP THROUGH TIME

PAUL ARNOTT

The
History
Press

Cover image: Empire Windrush on arrival at the Port of Tilbury on the River Thames on 22 June 1948. © Contraband Collection / Alamy Stock Photo

First published 2019
This paperback edition first published 2021

The History Press
97 St George's Place, Cheltenham,
Gloucestershire, GL50 3QB
www.thehistorypress.co.uk

British Library Cataloguing in Publication Data.
A catalogue record for this book is available from the British Library.

ISBN 978 0 7509 9745 4

Typesetting and origination by The History Press
Printed and bound in Great Britain by TJ Books Limited

Trees for Life

CONTENTS

Introduction: A Hostile Environment   7

1   An Equivocal Name   13
2   The Five Sisters   21
3   Eldorado   29
4   Bad Seeds   37
5   'Strength Through Joy'   47
6   A Warning for the World   57
7   On the Meridian Line   69
8   Norway Falls   79
9   Moses and Aaron   87
10   The Beast   101
11   Fire in the Chimney   109
12   Max Manus   121
13   The Tyskerpiger   131
14   War Prize?   147
15   Sore Spots   157
16   The Poles   169
17   The Mother Country   177
18   The Forgotten War   187
19   A Cold Premonition   201

20	A Celtic Cross	211
21	The Final Voyage	223
22	Letters to Father	237
23	A Very British Inquiry	245
Afterword: At 37°00′N 02°11′E		255

Notes	259
Bibliography	273
Acknowledgements	277
Index	280

INTRODUCTION

A HOSTILE ENVIRONMENT

'A state is called the coldest of all cold monsters. Coldly lieth it also, and this lie creepeth from its mouth: I, the state, am the people.'

Friedrich Nietzsche, *Also Sprach Zarathustra*

On Sunday 30 September 2018, the United Kingdom's Prime Minister, the Right Honourable Theresa May MP, was warming up for her Conservative Party's annual conference beginning the next day in Birmingham. It is too soon to be certain how history will record the success or otherwise of that event. For now, it will be remembered as the occasion when someone advised her to follow her two outbreaks of dancing the month before on a trade mission to Africa with giving the people some more. This time, for her leader's keynote speech, she jerked on to the stage to Abba's 'Dancing Queen', arms and legs agonisingly out of sync. When the toadies in the crowd faked ecstasy in response, she gave them another burst. Elsewhere in the country, spirits slumped.

That Sunday morning there would be no opportunities for dancing for May. BBC television journalist Andrew Marr[1] was about to pin her forensically to a chair in a television studio near the conference hall. Marr's reputation is as a courteous interviewer without fear or favour, but here before him sat the Prime Minister, whose intention was to take this opportunity to boast of her achievements before a week of being cheered by the party faithful. This gave Marr the journalistic justification to fire some tricky questions about her whole record. These ranged from austerity and the covert privatisation of the National Health Service to the subject of the hour, the United Kingdom's efforts to leave the European Union, colloquially known as 'Brexit'. Dodging and weaving, May fended Marr off for about fifteen minutes knowing there were only a few more hits to survive. If it had been a boxing match, the scorecards stood at even.

That was when Andrew Marr took off his gloves. Glancing at his notes, he reminded her of her pronouncement, when she'd first entered Downing Street as Prime Minister on 13 July 2016, that her foremost mission would be to tackle 'burning injustices':

Let me bring you to what a lot of people would regard as a 'burning injustice'. The treatment of all those people who came here in the 1950s and 1960s to work, people from the Caribbean and elsewhere. We brought them to this country, and as a result of your 'hostile environment' policy their lives have been turned upside down. I am talking of course of the Windrush generation. Do you not think that was a 'burning injustice'?

For the next five minutes May repeatedly pulled that extraordinary face when the corners of her mouth reflexively stretch down as she prepares a dissembling response, like a tell from a poor poker player. Marr was bowling her one bouncer after another: did she know how many Windrush people had lost their homes as a result of her policies? How many had been refused medical treatment they were due under the National Health Service? How many had lost their jobs?

Then Marr did something still relatively unusual in an interview with a UK Prime Minister: he ambushed her with some video. Footage appeared on a large television screen placed between them, and May could not escape from watching a minute of interview with 57-year-old Sarah O'Connor. What had happened to Sarah had become infamous throughout 2018. Just ten days earlier she had died.

Sarah O'Connor had arrived in England from Jamaica in 1967 as a 6-year-old, had got married, raised four British children, worked in a computer shop for sixteen years and, when that closed, was told she was ineligible for state benefits unless she 'proved' she was British. All this happened to her even though she'd been to state primary and secondary schools, and paid national insurance and tax all her working life. The records were there – the government's own records. Yet suddenly, she was rendered a non-person. Stateless.

Sarah began on the video:

I lost my job last July. I couldn't work because I hadn't got the right documents. You go and try and get some sort of help from the Unemployment and get told, no, you're not entitled to anything. Apologies are all good and well but an apology doesn't help the things that the Windrush people have gone through.

The video snapped shut and Marr turned to May. She looked as if she had just seen a ghost.

'What's your message to her family?' said Marr.

'Well. I hear what Sarah said about apologies but I can only apologise for what Sarah went through and for what her family went through. This shouldn't have happened.'

'There's apologies saying you regret that bad things happened,' said Marr, 'and there are apologies which say, do you know, it was my policies which made these bad things happen and it was my policy which was wrong and I'm sorry for it. Are you prepared to say that to the Windrush generation?'

For the next minute May wriggled on the hook. Marr knew what he was doing. Each time she pulled that inverted rictus grin he jerked the line again. Until she said it, the biggest whopper of them all, the ultimate deflection from what had really happened, the message to every member of the party faithful and arrogant Little Englander in the country. It was a brilliant, patented elision of two entirely different issues, a smokescreen, an insult to every Windrush victim:

Well I just want to explain the policy, Andrew. The point of the policy was to ensure that those people who were here in the United Kingdom illegally were identified and that appropriate action was taken …

What went wrong was that people from the Windrush generation who were here legally who had every right to be here – who had helped to build our great institutions – found themselves unable to show that through documentation and got caught up in that but I think for most people, and I'm sorry Andrew, but most people do want to know that the government is taking action against those people who come to this country illegally or stay in this country illegally. What we need to do is make sure that in doing that we don't find people who have every right to be here being caught up in it. That's what went wrong in Windrush.

Marr tried one more time:

But this policy went, as we have just demonstrated, catastrophically wrong. And I'm asking you again, as Home Secretary during many of their experiences it was in effect your policy, Theresa May's policy. The Council for the Welfare of Immigrants say 'This lady died after a long period of terrible stress as a result of Theresa May's Immigration Act. The buck stops with the Prime Minister.' Will you apologise for the policy?

The Prime Minister responded:

The policy, the purpose of the policy – it was to ensure and maintain the compliant environment policy. The purpose of the policy is to ensure that those people who are here illegally are identified and appropriate action is taken. I apologise for the fact that some people who should not have been caught up in that were caught up in that with, in some cases as we have just seen, tragic results.

It is perhaps part of the tragedy of individual human beings finding themselves unable to avoid being victims of knee-jerk, populist immigration policies that when it all goes horribly wrong, as in Sarah O'Connor's case, they then fall victim once again. This time their lives are traduced by the Orwellian doublespeak of the very person who caused their suffering. Because, when she was Home Secretary in 2014, and was piloting the Immigration Act 2014 through Parliament, Theresa May was making 'every Briton – doctor, landlord, or teacher – into a border guard, and every migrant, whether they have a right to be here or not, into a suspect'.[2]

Fearful of a resurgent, soft-racist, United Kingdom Independence Party (UKIP), and its cheerleaders in the press, only eighteen Members of Parliament voted against that policy. Labour MP Diane Abbot, one of the eighteen, asked May on 30 January 2014 if she had thought through 'the effect that her measures, that are designed to crack down on illegal immigrants, could have on people who are British nationals, but appear as if they might be immigrants'.

Abbot's question was waved away.

Thus, the record shows not only that the 'hostile environment' policy was deliberate, and racist in those it must inevitably effect, but that it had been explicitly predicted and warned about by Abbot and others, and nonetheless pressed ahead with. As Sarah O'Connor was left to lament in the final months of her life, 'Prejudice has come back, when I thought we'd stamped that out years ago.'[3]

2018 repeatedly showed how far there was still to go. That spring, Professor David Olusoga[4] noted the unfortunate confluence of historical anniversaries falling within a few weeks of each other. Seventy years before, the British Nationality Act had been passed, which allowed British subjects from the Commonwealth to migrate to the UK. Fifty years before, Enoch Powell had delivered his 'Rivers of Blood' speech. Twenty-five years before, a teenaged Steven Lawrence had been murdered in Eltham, south-east London, by racists.

Olusoga writes:

> We know that those arriving faced appalling discrimination, but we also want to believe that in the end it all worked out and we became the inclusive, diverse nation that we like to believe we are. Rather, as the story of abolition has come to obscure the story of two centuries of slavery that preceded it, an overtly rosy version of the Windrush story risks standing in the way of us taking a real hard look at the politics of race and migration in the period in which the Windrush generation arrived.

1

AN EQUIVOCAL NAME

Thus, in 2018, the name 'Windrush' acquired a new and unwelcome meaning. How had everything soured so badly since 1998, just twenty years earlier, when Prince Charles joined celebrations to recognise the fiftieth anniversary of the arrival at Tilbury Docks on 22 June 1948 of 600 migrants from the Caribbean, paying tribute to all they had contributed to the life of the nation ever since? A superb book was written at the time to coincide with this celebration by Mike and Trevor Phillips,[1] and the former Brixton Oval open area near the Ritzy Cinema was renamed 'Windrush Square', adjacent to which now sits the Black Cultural Archives.

In the new millennium, what the *Windrush* now healthily symbolised was presented by a proud nation to the global television audience in director Danny Boyle's opening ceremony for the 2012 London Olympics. A *Times* editorial lavishly praised the event and said that 'the depiction of immigrants from the Caribbean arriving off the *Empire Windrush* at Tilbury in 1948 was affecting and profound'.[2] *The Times* also took a steady aim at the 'foolish and inflammatory comment' from 'Adrian Burley, a Conservative MP, [who] coarsely derided its purposefully "leftie multicultural nature"'.

However, just six years after the wonderful Olympic summer – and, in reality, tardily following up on many years of neglected coverage already run in the UK's black press – *The Guardian* newspaper picked up on rumbling concerns of what had been happening to the Windrush generation. It began to take up the stories of people like Vernon Vandiel.

Vernon Vandiel had come from Jamaica as a 5-year-old in 1962 and grown up to become a well-regarded welterweight boxer, once topping the bill at the Royal Albert Hall. He retired with a final victory in October 1982 witnessed by a 'loyal army of fans'.[3] It's not as if nobody knew who he was: he had been feted in the press many times, a contemporary of well-known British boxers like Lloyd Honeyghan and Charlie Magri.

In 2005, Vernon travelled to see a son in Jamaica and out of the blue was told during his stay that he would only be permitted to return to the country which was his home on a temporary visa. When Harold Macmillan was still Prime Minister, Vernon had arrived on his mother's passport with a brother and three sisters. Now he was another Briton of Caribbean origin rendered stateless.

Vernon eked out an existence in Jamaica until in 2018, thirteen years later, a guilty Home Office arranged for him to be flown home to Tottenham. 'I love the United Kingdom, this is my country,' Vernon said, 'but I feel unwanted really, and uncared for, unloved …'[4]

It is still unclear how many others have been affected in this way. It is known to be at least hundreds, perhaps thousands, and that many of these British people died in exile.

Thus, the Windrush name, made in 1998 and 2012 into something of which the entire country could feel proud and positive – a beacon for the potential of a nation belatedly learning about its own conflicted history – became a by-word in 2018 for one of the greatest injustices enacted against its own people by any British government. Theresa May was not alone in culpability, of course, but she was consistently at the wheel throughout the worst of it all.

The legitimate question arises: how could a Windrush victim not now wonder if there was, after all, real racism in play? Because elsewhere in May's in-tray, marked 'Brexit', was the more recent issue of how much a person whose origin was within the European Union would have to pay to establish their settled status in the United Kingdom after the UK's departure. This amount was set at £65, with half that for a child. Faced with anger in the context of Parliamentary battles over 'Brexit', in 2019 May even cancelled that £65.

Yet British members of the Windrush generation, missing some paperwork through no fault of their own, were forced to apply for a biometric card costing £1,300, which many of them have found genuinely unaffordable. May had been Home Secretary and Prime Minister across all of this.

Leaving the injustice of it to one side, a person of black origin might be forgiven for wondering 'would a white person be treated like this?' This was no longer an academic question. No, they wouldn't, and they weren't.

One aim of this book is, by telling the story of the life and soul of a single ship, to equip the Windrush generation with some more ammunition for their cause. This may prove necessary. Unfortunately, as their own drama continues to play out and much-delayed compensation is awarded, it is inevitable that they will be ghettoised by certain sections of the press, made out to be whingers and depicted as an ungrateful few. It is just a matter of time before the victim-blaming begins in our often bigoted and intolerant public discourse.

In truth, other BAME people know how this script goes already. Stephen Lawrence's mother, Lady Doreen, can tell the Windrush victims how the British government likes to work in such matters when it comes to victim-blaming. In June 2013 she had met Theresa May, then Home Secretary, to complain of a smear campaign against her and others that had come to light. It had allegedly been coordinated by undercover police officers who'd infiltrated the Lawrence campaign group over many years gathering details about both her and her ex-husband, Neville. Police resources, rather than trawling for evidence to convict Stephen's alleged murderers, were allegedly spent instead on spying on his grieving family. In July 2015, after much soft soap, May announced an inquiry.

In February 2019, Lady Lawrence lamented to a Parliamentary committee both that this inquiry had neither reported yet and was still clearly years from doing so, and that it had not yet taken any evidence at all, either from the alleged police spies or their innocent targets. She delivered a stinging rebuke. The inquiry had cost £13 million so far, £8 million of it on staffing and legal fees. 'For me 25 years, coming up to 26 years, and this to be still going on!' she commented.

It may yet prove important, then, for those for whom the word 'Windrush' is part of their personal identity, that they may claim ownership of a much greater story than just those of 1948, 1998 and 2018. Certainly, without their involvement at all these times, the name *Windrush* would have no currency whatsoever. Instead it is now up there, with the *Mayflower* and the *Titanic*, as a name which stands for both a period of time and a social phenomenon.

So guilty was the British government when caught out in 2018 persecuting these people that it finally recognised this deep significance. On 22 June 2019, the nation first celebrated an officially endorsed annual Windrush Day. This is welcome, but, to tabloid columnists emboldened in the era of Trump, this annual celebration will also present an opportunity for reflex disdain. Now the Windrush is to be a 'brand' for the foreseeable future, and the price of maintaining its integrity will be eternal vigilance.

Perhaps, then, those whose lives and suffering have given one ship's name its potency might feel further empowered by the potent undercurrents in the entire tale of the *Windrush* ship herself – something of an epic adventure from her creation as a German transatlantic liner in 1931 to her controversial explosion and sinking twenty-three years later off the coast of Algeria. In all of this story there is a great deal of related hard truth to be divined – almost none of it uttered by the powers that be.

This wider story shows that the 1948, 1998 and 2018 generations were not the first, or even the most unfortunate, to have cause to look back in anger at their relationship to the *Windrush*. In June 1948, a generation of migrants voluntarily arrived, but a mere four years earlier, stepping down the very same gangplanks at gunpoint on to the quayside at Hamburg, were hundreds of Norwegian Jews. They had been forcibly transported from Oslo.

These innocent Jewish people were then herded inhumanely on to a wagon train bound for Auschwitz, from which none of them returned. They were victim-blamed too, by the most evil regime ever to emerge in Europe, which, deploying the 'Big Lie' principle, blamed it on someone else.

In the words of Hitler, adapted by Joseph Goebbels: 'The essential English leadership secret does not depend on particular intelligence. Rather, it depends on a remarkably stupid thick-headedness. The English follow the principle that when one lies, one should lie big, and stick to it. They keep up their lies, even at the risk of looking ridiculous.'[5] The repellent Goebbels, who also had a personal connection to the *Windrush*, may or may not have been right in his analysis of history; he did believe, though, that he had learned the toxic lesson of the 'Big Lie' from the master practitioners.

The question arises of what to call the *Windrush* for the purposes of the voyage ahead, and in this context it is worth thinking of one of the many superstitions affecting seafaring people. Whistling on board, for example, brings bad luck. A dolphin swimming alongside is thought highly propitious. In days gone by, some crewmen were so persecuted when a ship was marooned in the doldrums that they were called albatrosses and forced overboard for the common good.

Another of these well-recorded superstitions is to do with a ship's name, and it first appears in nautical literature when overheard by young Jim Hawkins hiding in an apple barrel on board the *Hispaniola* as it approached Treasure Island.[6] Jim had jumped into the barrel to try to scrump one of the few remaining apples when Long John Silver himself hobbled over and, leaning his weight on the seasoned wood, began to talk conspiratorially about 'gentlemen of fortune' such as him. It did not take long for young Jim to realise that his erstwhile chum and protector was using the phrase to describe what the old fraud and half the crew truly were – pirates.

'Now, what a ship is christened, so let her stay, I says,' said Long John Silver, a few inches from the cowering Jim, before reeling off a list of ships that had changed their names only to come to sticky ends, mostly at the hands of his fellow pirates. He plainly had his own plans for the *Hispaniola*, but was too wise to the superstitions of the sea for anything as crass as a mere name change once it fell under his command.

So, it must be declared at this point that SS *Empire Windrush* was not born with that name at all, and was not even the first British ship to bear it. One of the least-known stories of the D-Day invasion in June 1944 concerns her predecessor, HMS *Windrush*, a troop carrier carrying hundreds of men towards the beaches of Normandy. Floating alongside her that day just off Omaha beach was the US troop carrier *Thomas Jefferson*, and in between the two much larger ships was a landing craft already filled with American troops waiting for the signal to proceed.

Getting ready for the off, this small command group boat for the 1st Battalion, 116th Regiment, became wedged beneath *Windrush's* 'head' (toilet outlet), where it remained stuck for thirty minutes, unable to move forward or aft.

Executive Officer Major Thomas Dallas remembered:

During this half hour, the bowels of the *Windrush's* company made the most of an opportunity which Englishmen had sought since 1776. Streams, colored everything from canary yellow to sienna brown and olive green continued to flush into the command group, decorating every man on the boat. We cursed, we cried and we laughed, but it kept coming. When we started for the shore, we were covered in shit.[7]

The decommissioning of this muck sprayer of a ship after the Second World War left the name available for the subject of this book. But even then she was not a new ship when she was given the name. When she became the *Windrush* in 1946, she was actually MV *Monte Rosa* – a German ship put to sea in Hamburg in 1931 and not then re-christened until a year after her capture by the British at Kiel as a war prize in 1945, when she became SS *Empire Windrush*.

To break her name into component parts, her SS prefix stood for 'Single-screw Ship (or Steamship)'. The designation of *Empire* at the time was optimistic as the British Empire referred to was shrinking by the month. There was a scintilla of the British class system at work here too. To be designated HMS like her namesake she would have to have been part of the senior service, the Royal Navy. This *Windrush* was a mere merchant ship, but an important one. So, she had to settle for *Empire*.

Windrush itself is a 35-mile-long river that rises in the Cotswolds and joins the Thames near Newbridge in Oxfordshire. Anglo-Saxon documents variously have it as Wænric, Wenric or Wenris. But Windrush is also a small village in Gloucestershire, which, by circumstances of fate, in the first decade of the twenty-first century, found itself in the pale of the 'Chipping Norton' set – a group of right-of-centre politicians and celebrities enjoying weekend homes off the M4 out of London.

One of the set, Andrew Cooper – an amiable man in his fifties originally from Reigate in Surrey – was a policy adviser and lead pollster to David Cameron's government. It is unfortunate for him that his company's polling prediction on the day of the 2016 referendum showed 'Remain' 10 per cent ahead, and was afterwards said by some to have persuaded Remainers not to bother to vote.[8] It is for readers to judge if it is also unfortunate, perhaps thoughtless of other meanings and sensitivities, that when Cameron wished to elevate his pollster to the House of Lords nobody wondered if he might not pause before choosing to call himself Baron Cooper of Windrush.

So, what must we call the *Windrush/Monte Rosa* in telling her full tale today?

Plainly it will be confusing to call her by both names. For example, generations of adopted people now know that they were born with a different name, but even if they find it out later they usually retain the given name to which they have become used – including this author.[9]

Moreover, the only reason so many of us know of the *Windrush* name today is and always will be that single voyage from the Caribbean in June 1948. That 1948 *Windrush* had already been, and would be again, involved in many more adventures and misadventures in her near quarter of a century at sea. Yet in the present day, the name *Windrush* chimes for so many today only because of that one crucial trip from Kingston, Jamaica.

The experiences of those people in June 1948 may be seen to symbolise both the historic events and, latterly, the grotesque injustices that were inflicted on so many who travelled on the ship's hundred or so journeys around the globe in her lifetime. As much as anything, the *Windrush* story is about the displaced. The particular plight of the 1948 and after generation towards the end of the second decade of the twenty-first century was not an immigration issue: it was banishment, malicious exile and heartless eviction to another part of the world – the theft of both national identity and a place to call home. But in this ship's tale, they were not alone in meeting that fate.

So, we'll call her the *Windrush* then, from her birth to her extraordinary demise in March 1954.

2

THE FIVE SISTERS

Every ship has a reason to be built: a blend of commodity, need and, perhaps too often, nationalist ambition. To understand the *Windrush*'s origin tale, it may be salutary to take a tourist's trip along the Rhine, and to disembark at the town of Rüdesheim.

Arriving there is like a slap across the chops with a leather glove. Immediately on landing, assorted billboards offer entertainment ranging from Siegfried's Mechanical Museum to the Museum of Medieval Torture. At first sight, therefore, Rüdesheim presents itself merely as the quintessence of *Chitty Chitty Bang Bang* German kitsch: all half-timbered houses and turrets, dirndl and lederhosen hanging behind panes of glass in tidy shop windows.

Once these museums and shops have been enjoyed, however, visitors can then take a cable car high above the Rhine valley, the vineyards below bursting with grapes cultivated for white wine. As they climb further, they can look back across miles of vines as far as the eye can see. The urge – rare perhaps in the stereotypical British person – to acquire a chilled glass of Riesling to toast the view is overwhelming. But that is not the point of this ascent, which is to see the immense monument on the summit above the town.

Because for anyone wishing to understand why, sixty years after the monument was erected, thousands of tons of Norwegian pig iron would be smelted to form the steel to make the *Windrush*, the Rüdesheim peak is as good a place as any to take a clear-eyed view. The *Windrush*, as much as anything else, was built because of German pride and the desire to carry the German Fatherland across the high seas thousands of miles beyond Europe.

As you walk the final yards from the cable car, it appears before you: the Niederwalddenkmal monument. It's a marble stunner, with winged angels blowing horns, topped with a statue of Germania – the German equivalent of Britannia – a proud woman, with a crown raised in her right hand and the hilt of a sword grasped in her left. This is no mere civic adornment to the hill. It is the principal monument in Germany to its victory in the Franco-Prussian War of 1870 – a war prosecuted by the French under Napoleon III to prevent the expansionist ambitions of the Prussian Chancellor, Otto von Bismarck.

European mainland history, not deeply studied in Britain unfortunately, records that this initiative by Napoleon III backfired epically, and within a year the Prussian states had merged with areas claimed to be German-speaking, from the west in France to the far east in Poland. Thus, modern German history, as we understand it today, with those resounding dates of 1914 and 1939 occluding our perspective, really began.[1]

The vast Niederwalddenkmal monument is both triumphalist and, in its many allegories of peace depicted in its statuary and friezes, a statement of the aspiration that 1870 would be the war to end all wars. Ironically, upon the abdication of Germany's last monarch, Kaiser Wilhelm II, in 1918, and his replacement as head of state with the new role of President under the Weimar Republic, the monument became yesterday's news – a tourist's curio.[2]

It was with this unification of the German state that the construction of the *Windrush*, and dozens of ships like her, became inevitable. For the entire span of the nineteenth century, German merchants and ship-owners had been obliged to hire or buy ships from British shipbuilders. Unification changed all that, and before long the two countries would be involved in a mercantile marine arms race, which would descend ultimately to the tragedy of the First World War and the virtual elimination of the German merchant fleet.

During this torrid period, one German shipbuilder survived and flourished, and could be found by taking a boat north from Rüdesheim along the Rhine and then heading west along the Weser. A passenger would then arrive in the greatest of German ports, Hamburg. Here, on 5 April 1877, on the island of Kuhwerder a mile or so south of the city, two craftsmen, Hermann Blohm and Ernst Voss, built a wooden workshop in the harbour and began to offer boat repairs.

Their timing was good. The new Germany wanted to order ships from its own domestic yards, while Blohm & Voss adapted early to working with steel, at first for hulls of vessels still propelled by sail and wind, but at the turn of the century by steam engines. Half a century after its founding, their company built the *Windrush*.

Founding a new enterprise in Hamburg was complex; it was a city of attitudinal contrasts. There was a placidity at its heart with the Alster Lake, and then a surging mercantilism driven through its immense tidal artery coursing out into the North Sea. Like the seaboard cities of many other nations, this made Hamburg outward looking, and by comparison with the German interior relatively progressive.

Its internationalism had been long ago established between the eleventh and the fifteenth centuries when Hamburg was geographically at the centre of trading routes dominated by the cities and towns of the Hanseatic League. This route stretched from London in the west to the far reaches of the eastern Baltic at Novgorod, with trading points at Bruges, Hamburg, Lubeck, Falsterbo, Danzig, Visby and Riga – all of which drew goods to the coast from many miles inland.

Unfortunately, in the twentieth century that same renown as the hub of the long-gone Hanseatic League also bred both arrogance and a misplaced nostalgia, as well as a tendency to masonic standards of transparency left from the obsessive secretiveness of the Hanseatic network, which often operated within a hostile local governance. There lurked a nationalist and racist longing which was heavily influenced by Hamburg's position looking north to Scandinavia and

beyond, and to their ancient legends, with Wagner shamelessly pur-
loining the old Icelandic dragon-slaying stories of the Nibelung for
the *Ring* cycle.

In the nineteenth century, August Vilmar, a German theologian and
linguist, promoted the rediscovered Saxon poem *Heliand*, a ninth-
century retelling of the gospels as a North Sea epic. Vilmar finessed these
into a pan-Germanic myth in which Christ and Bismarck had a moral
equivalence, relishing the rude remarks throughout the text about the
'sluggish' peoples of the 'South'. These were mostly identified as Jews like
Messrs Blohm and Voss – inferior, it was oft repeated, to the 'Germanic'
disciples of the Lord.

Vilmar's reading persisted throughout the First World War when
the *Heliand* gospels retold in Saxon verse became a 'pithy story of
German manhood'.[3] Most Christian homes in Hamburg had imbibed
this stuff.

However, at Blohm and Voss' yard on Kuhwerder island, their
employment of Jews was overlooked. There was a burgeoning
demand for whatever they could build. They had synchronicity on
their side too. Also being founded in Hamburg at the same time
with the end of the Franco-Prussian War – by a joint-stock company formed of representatives of eleven Hamburg merchant houses
– was the shipping line company, Hamburg Südamerikanische
Dampfschifffahrts-Gesellschaft.

This became known, thankfully, as Hamburg Süd for short. In the
context of the various levels of dominance of the British, French,
Spanish and American empires in the late nineteenth century, Hamburg
Süd's first enterprises as part of the newly unified Germany were to
make inroads into South America. The other powers had colonised and
become *in situ* governors of all the inhabited continents in the world,
and doggedly reserved all rights of migration for their own peoples, or
those indentured from their colonies to make other colonies more prof-
itable. This was true of South America too, but the imperial writ did
not have as much of a stranglehold as elsewhere. This historical anomaly
would drive the early years of the *Windrush*.

In the 1880s, Hamburg Süd had established monthly voyages to Brazil, stopping at Bahia, Rio de Janeiro and Santo, as well as to Buenos Aires and the River Plate in Argentina. By far the greatest number of passengers were emigrants from Germany itself and from Eastern Europe. (This flow continued, only interrupted by world conflicts, until the verge of the Second World War.)[4]

After the First World War, and with the depression in Germany worsened by the world economic crash of 1926, this flight of migrants to South America experienced a resurgence. This had been exacerbated by new immigration controls into the United States of America cutting off access there to a new generation of Germans. Hamburg Süd wanted to provide the transport to South America, and the dominant directors, John Eggert and Thomas Amsinck, authorised a massive investment to commission Blohm and Voss to construct a new class of ship to be known as the Montes.

In the ten years between 1924 and 1934, five of these Monte-class ships were launched: *Monte Sarmiento* (1924), *Monte Olivia* (1924), *Monte Cervantes* (1927), *Monte Pascoal* (1930) and finally, launched on 13 December 1930, *Monte Rosa*, or, as we shall know her, *Windrush*.[5]

These ships became known as the Monte sisters and Blohm & Voss made their international reputation with these functional but comfortably furnished and equipped new liners. Alas, under the proprietorship of Hamburg Süd this did not guarantee good fortune. Other than the *Windrush*, the Montes all seemed to have fallen under a curse.

The first of the five sisters to perish was the *Monte Cervantes*. In July 1928, just a few months after her maiden voyage, she was severely damaged by ice during a cruise to the Arctic and nearly sank. Then on 22 January 1930 she was holed under the waterline by submerged rocks during a cruise from Buenos Aires to the southernmost tip of South America at Tierra del Fuego. Her 1,117 passengers were put off in boats and she was driven on to the Eclaireur Reef. Two days later, she suddenly turned turtle and sank, taking her master down with her. Only her propellers, rudder and bottom remained above the surface. There she stayed wedged for fifteen years until an effort to salvage her by an Italian company resulted in her slipping into the deep.[6]

The outbreak of the Second World War greatly increased the risk to shipping, but for an oft-defenceless merchant fleet it was particularly unlucky. The *Monte Sarmiento* was bombed in harbour and sunk during an Allied raid on Kiel on 26 February 1942. The *Monte Olivia* was bombed and set ablaze in Kiel during another Allied raid on 3 April 1945. The next day she sank. The *Monte Pascoal* had been bombed and damaged in February 1944 at Wilhelmshaven, was salvaged, and then after capture by the British was loaded with materials intended for chemical warfare and deliberately sunk at Skagerrak, the strait running between Norway and the south-west coast of Sweden.[7]

Only the *Monte Rosa* – the *Windrush* – survived beyond the Second World War. Nevertheless, her own demise would prove to be the most mysterious of them all.

An immense amount of the history of the early German years of the Windrush was lost in the saturation bombing of Hamburg in the Second World War. There was nothing at all left of either Blohm & Voss or Hamburg Süd when war ended in Europe on 8 May 1945. RAF Bomber Command had dropped 22,853 tonnes of bombs on Hamburg, and the USAAF 15,736 tonnes – a total of 38,589 tonnes. Hamburg Fire Department calculated after the war that 48,572 people had been killed between 1940 and 1945.[8] It seems petty in that context to comment that as a consequence there are few archival remains of the *Windrush*, but it is the case. Indeed, neither Blohm & Voss nor Hamburg Süd, extant and flourishing today, would even exist without the investment and benevolent political decisions made by America, Britain and France in the years after the war to rebuild Germany from the ground up.

It is possible, however, from statements provided at the inquiry into the *Windrush*'s final days, to relate the basic specifications which described her in her lifetime:

The *Empire Windrush* was a twin screw motorship and the total number of passengers and crew for which a Safety Certificate was issued was 1,541. She was 501 feet long; her beam was 65.7 feet; her depth 37.87 feet; she had a gross tonnage of 14,651 and a net tonnage of 8,305.[9] She was built of steel and had five decks up to and including the uppermost complete deck. Above this were the promenade deck, the foredeck and the Navigating Bridge deck. The ship was divided by watertight bulkheads, extending to the uppermost complete deck.[10]

Fortunately, too, back in the City of London, we can find out where the *Windrush* sailed for almost her entire life. Next to the church of St Lawrence, Jewry, which was itself severely damaged by German bombs in the Blitz of December 1940, is the Guildhall Library. There, tucked away in the stacks, are the *Windrush*'s voyage cards originally maintained by Lloyd's, the London shipping insurers.

These index cards were completed with information published in the daily *Lloyd's List*, recording shipping movements and industry news from anywhere that Lloyd's insured – in essence the entire world. On these voyage cards, and throughout the ship's entire history, someone was writing in black and red ink the dates and ports of call of every journey ever made by the *Windrush*. Sailings are written in black, arrivals in red.

Thus, we know that the *Windrush* was launched 'New At Hamburg' on 13 December 1930. We know that, at the end of March 1931, she was testing her engines in sea trials steaming north-west up the River Elbe towards Heligoland and the open sea, and then back. This must have gone well, because on 28 March 1931 she took to the high seas on her maiden cruise, and would not be back in Hamburg until 22 June, nearly three months later. Then, for reasons that would prove crucial fifteen years later, she began her cruises to South America.

3

ELDORADO

The *Windrush*'s first recorded Hamburg Süd Line voyage to South America left Germany on 24 August 1932.[1] The final voyage arrived home nearly seven years later on 4 August 1939, just a month before the outbreak of the Second World War. In that time, she made the 14,000-mile return journey on more than twenty occasions, carrying up to 30,000 Germans to Brazil, Uruguay and Argentina who never returned.

In the years since the First World War, German migration to South America had intensified after major parts of the German economy were ruined. The heavy industrial sector, which had been bent towards mass arms manufacturing, was left without purpose. Although Germany still had the coal reserves to power industry, it lacked the foreign currency to import the crucial raw materials from Scandinavia and elsewhere.

This was the primary economic damage left by the war, but there was secondary chaos in the rural agricultural sector. With the economy in crisis and enduring sporadic hyperinflation, demand for food was suppressed, and there were scant prospects for young farmers on the land – and none at all in the cities.

Because of this, the 1930s migrants who took to the *Windrush* at Hamburg bound for South America were more various than the stereotype of workless urban dwellers exiting industrial heartlands might suggest. There were thousands of rural migrants too; to them, the prospect of acquiring land in what they thought of as a still relatively unexploited continent was a compelling lure.

By the early 1930s, 140,000 Germans in total had migrated to South America.[2] Many of them might have wished to go to the United States, but it had closed its doors to Germans entirely until 1921, and thereafter only let in a tiny annual quota; the German governments of the 1920s and '30s were not overly disappointed by this. In the nineteenth and early twentieth centuries, German migrants to the USA had assimilated so well that their home nation worried they were no longer Germans at all. It was feared they could not be relied upon beyond the first generation to support German causes internationally, as the USA's entry into the First World War eventually proved.

Yet in South America, where German settlement had always been more rural, migrants usually bunched in tight communities and remained loyal to their cultural heritage for many generations. German politicians also perceived weaker political structures in South America than in the USA, providing a potential opportunity to dominate, and perhaps even make up for the colonies lost through the Treaty of Versailles.

Meanwhile, the Brazilian government, for example, had hundreds of thousands of acres of uncultivated land and was keen to welcome German skilled agricultural workers. It even subsidised migration on ships such as the *Windrush*, although for many this did not end well. Some succeeded, but others ended up in coffee plantations as little more than indentured labourers, one rung up from slaves. These people pledged their labour in exchange for room and board but were paid so little that they could never escape. Many wished to return to Germany but were unable to afford the fare. Living hundreds of miles from big cities like Rio and São Paulo, where there were vibrant migrant support networks, they disappeared from the record.

Sharing space on board the *Windrush* with the urban and rural migrants was another group too: the political and religious refugees. Ironically, some of the most successful German migrants to Brazil were Jews who, with anti-fascist Catholics, moved to remote areas such as Rolândia, 250 miles south of São Paulo.

Both communities brought a respectful appreciation of their differences with them, and the Brazilian government's prohibition of running religious services in anything other than the Portuguese language served to make the Jews, for example, resist blending in with older local Jewish communities and so retain the Germanic Jewish customs they brought with them. This semi-assimilation was a lasting success.

Yet for their rural Protestant countrymen lost to indentured labour, such success would always elude them. For these migrants, it was a tragic outcome, but they were not the first Germans to meet disaster by chasing their dreams to South America.

The virulent German strain of anti-Semitism long predated Hitler. In the half-century before the *Windrush* transported them to South America in their thousands, other German zealots had been responsible for transmitting the racist virus from struggling Mittel Europe to the still inchoate societies of places like Paraguay.

Prominent in this movement was Elisabeth Nietzsche, sister to the great philosopher Friedrich. Before leaving on a deranged mission to found a New Germany in Paraguay in the 1880s, she spent months writing press releases, advertisements and finally a book promoting the idea with the enthusiastic collaboration of her obsessed husband, Bernhard Förster.

However, even before the couple left Germany to cross the Atlantic Ocean, Elisabeth's mother and especially her famous brother were profoundly concerned at their suitability for such an ambitious enterprise. The Försters' idea was to found some kind of new Eldorado in sparsely populated Paraguay, where they wished to attract co-shareholders to a 50,000-acre location – roughly the size of a German dukedom – comprising virgin land and forest.

To find the necessary investors, who'd need to stump up 100,000 marks each, Bernhard Förster toured Germany speaking to Wagnerian societies, colonial clubs, civic groups and farmers' and workers' associations. His theme was always the same. He warned his countrymen of the impending loss of their national heritage, for which he blamed 'international Jewry'.

His anti-Semitic shtick won the support of some regional papers but was ridiculed elsewhere, not least by his brother-in-law Friedrich Nietzsche.[3] However, Förster's supporters included many German academics who, fifty years before Hitler's prime, were demanding Lebensraum[4] for Germany's expanding population in the warm afterglow of trouncing the French in the Franco-Prussian war.

Fifty years before the *Windrush* would arrive in Uruguay at Montevideo, Elisabeth and Bernhard arrived there, and then proceeded – just as Joseph Conrad might have done – on a paddle steamer upriver to Asunción, Paraguay's capital. They disembarked after five sultry days in a state of some horror. The city buildings were pockmarked by evidence of many previous revolutions, and the imperial palace was abandoned and overgrown.

The couple's determination was relentless. For more than a year, Bernhard identified land and did deals with the government, while Elisabeth travelled back to Germany to continue the struggle to attract investors. When this did not prove as fruitful as she'd hoped, she blamed 'Jewish intrigue'.[5]

Returning to Paraguay again, Elisabeth arrived in Neue Germania to find that the dream of Eldorado had become a living nightmare. There was a continuing lack of investors, some early colonists were already returning to Germany and her husband was apparently starting to have a nervous breakdown under the stress of it all. Clearing the forests and attempting to till the heavy clay soil broke Bernhard's back, while the demand for the return of the investments by departing pioneers from a now non-existent fund broke his spirits. Meanwhile, the government of Paraguay, hearing that the project was failing, refused to hand over the freehold on the land to Neue Germania as it had promised.

To twist the knife, one disgruntled settler – a tailor called Julius Klingbeil – recouped some of his losses by releasing a tell-all book, *Revelations Concerning Dr Bernhard Förster's Colony New Germany in Paraguay*. It was a bestseller. This is a typical quote regarding Bernhard and Elisabeth:

If it were not for the fact that his actions show cunning and calculation, as I shall have occasion to prove, you might think that the man was crazy. It is revolting to witness how he endures the tyranny of his domineering wife, who insists that she and her husband are the rulers of the small principality, as she calls the colony.[6]

The publication of the book accelerated Förster's ruin. He already suspected he'd married a martinet and to have that dawning realisation as well as his supine role confirmed in print for all to read was devastating to him. The slurs against the colony's finances alarmed existing investors and blocked the prospect of any new ones. Then, little more than a year after he had arrived, Bernhard Förster was found dead, widely rumoured to have taken poison, just as the sceptical Klingbeil predicted he inevitably would in his disloyal book.

For a few years, Elisabeth attempted to assert control over the colony but she seems to have been unbearable, and the previously loyal *Colonial News* published in Asunción printed a damning letter, albeit reluctantly. The editor commented that 'German colonial policy has made so many serious mistakes that necessity and not delicacy must now govern our actions'.

Elisabeth was out, but this did not prevent her continuing to justify herself in the press back in Germany: 'I must say farewell to all colonial affairs because another great task now waits me – the care of my dear and only brother, the philosopher Friedrich Nietzsche.'[7]

Elisabeth Nietzsche died fifty years later with her brother's legacy assured and a library in his honour funded by the Nazis. In November 1935, Adolf Hitler attended her funeral. Today, a few thousand people still live in New Germany, and about 10 per cent are thought to be descended from the Nietzschean pioneers.

The path the *Windrush* took to South America, half a century after Elisabeth Nietzsche's first attempt to build Germany a new *Heimat* overseas, would have been familiar to Elisabeth. The ship's many 7,000-mile voyages to South America in the 1930s usually followed the same outward route, with some variance on the return voyage.

First, the *Windrush* would leave Hamburg, pass Heligoland, and sail west into the North Sea with the Frisian Islands to her port side. Then, on past Holland and Belgium, entering the English Channel via the Straits of Dover. A day and a half later she'd pass the lighthouse at Ushant, an island off the North West coast of Brittany, then turn due south through the Bay of Biscay and south-west along the coast of Portugal, where she would dock for the first time at Lisbon. After a day, she'd go south again with the coast of Morocco to port, pulling in after another two days at Las Palmas in the Canary Islands. This was her last chance to take on fresh water and food.

It took another ten days to reach the coast of Brazil at Rio de Janeiro, and after disembarking passengers there and picking up local travellers she'd drop down to Santos, Rio Grande, Montevideo and finally Buenos Aires, which she'd reach a week after leaving Rio.

The return leg retraced much of the route, but she might add a stop at Salvador in northern Brazil, then pull in at Madeira instead of Las Palmas on her way back to Europe. Sometimes she even pulled in at Dover to pick up travellers making for Germany.

Like any cruise liner, to keep her passengers happy the *Windrush* had to feed and water them as best as could be managed. Dining was not her strongest suit. Present-day British opinion of German food has perhaps been prejudiced by what travellers to beer festivals and Christmas markets have found on offer, even though some of the finest cooking in the world now comes with a Germanic twist. The Steirereck on the edge of Vienna's Stadt Park, for example, deserves its regular place in the world's top fifty restaurants. It is astonishing what can be done with a wiener schnitzel. Unfortunately, although British cuisine in the 1930s did not require many pages itself in *Larousse Gastronomique*, its German equivalent had an even less appealing reputation.

This is a typical day's *Speisenfolge*, or menu, served on the *Windrush* as the voyagers left the continent of Europe behind them sailing west. It is far from the all-you-can-eat, all-day binge of cruise ships today.

Passengers began, of course, with *Fruhstück*, possibly the best meal of the day served between 7 and 9 a.m. To drink, there was apple juice, coffee, decaffeinated coffee, tea and Germany's answer to coke – *Mate*. This was a caffeinated fluid newly popular then, which today is the German hipster's cocktail base of choice, into which rum, lime and ice are liberally added. Toast and honey were available, as well as boiled eggs, pancakes with cranberry sauce, rice pudding with sugar and cinnamon, and porridge. To help all this along, there were stewed prunes.

Passengers had to wait only until 11.30 a.m. to be able to tuck into their lunch. There were two soups: *Jackson suppe*, which was leek and potato, or *Apfelkaltschale mit Korinthen*, which was a cold apple soup with currants. Once the bowls had been taken away, waiters approached the tables with *Steinbutt gesotten, Zerlassene Butter, Gurkensalat* and *Kartoffeln*. This was boiled turbot with melted butter, cucumber salad and boiled potatoes. To round off lunch, there was the German staple *Gemischtes Kompott*, a mixed bowl of cooked pears and peaches in elderberry syrup.

If a passenger felt peckish in the afternoon, they were able to summon a steward to whichever lounge they were in. They would be brought coffee, decaffeinated coffee, tea and *Mate* as at breakfast time, but this time with an assortment of marzipan treats and butter cookies.

At dinner between 7 and 8 p.m. every night, passengers on these transatlantic crossings were expected to dress smartly but not formally – perhaps the captain might have felt awkward asking them to get into penguin suits for what there was on offer. The evening began with spinach topped with fried egg, and an absolute favourite German cheese, *Rahmkartoffein*. This came in oblong bars which were sliced, each slice having a pungent rim and a gelatinous interior. The idea came from the Belgians, and in Walloon it is called *Remoudo*, meaning 're-milk', as it is always made from the second daily milking of a cow. This was then followed with *Sardellenwurst*. As any tourist to Germany knows, there is a multiplicity of speciality *Würste* of varying appeal. The *Windrush*'s offering was pork sausage meat – as might be anticipated – to which anchovies had been added. Again, to the British palate this might seem a surprise choice as the *Windrush* rolled from side to side on the heaving ocean – especially as it was served with blood pudding, sardines in tomato sauce, Dutch hard cheese and a soft German cheese called *Romardurkse*.

In the event that a passenger elected to eat this, they could then wash it all down with more tea and, of course, a bottle of *Mate*. This would give them time to think as they saw the coast of South America come into view. Depending on which country they were bound for, the Germany they brought with them would be very different.

4

BAD SEEDS

That so many Nazis fled to South America after the Second World War has fascinated cinemagoers to the present day. In 2013, the Argentinian film industry produced *Wakolda*, known as *The German Doctor* in English[1], about Josef Mengele recommencing his evil experiments in a small town in Patagonia. In 2018, Sir Ben Kingsley starred as Adolf Eichmann in *Operation Finale*,[2] dramatising Eichmann's kidnapping to Israel by Mossad agents from an anonymous house in an industrial area 12 miles outside Buenos Aires.

The natural question that arises in the public's imagination is, why South America? Why Argentina? How was it that escaping Germans felt they were certain to be welcomed by like-minded *volk*? When the *Windrush* left port in the 1930s bound for Buenos Aires with a manifest of Germans escaping the depression in their home country for a new life in South America, how did she become implicated in creating one of the most fascist regimes outside of Europe – one which after the war would welcome as many Nazi-leaning Germans as could make it to her borders?

However, the *Windrush*'s first major disembarkation point in South America was not Argentina but Brazil, and the outcome there for German migrants was markedly different. In part, this arose from the countries' disparate roles in the First World War. Argentina had stayed determinedly neutral, but Brazil found itself drawn into conflict as the major South American exporter when its shipping lanes came under threat from German U-boats. In October 1917, Brazil had declared war against Germany. After it was over, it had three seats at the table when the post-war settlement was being discussed, and was one of the signatories to the Treaty of Versailles.

Versailles has divided historians ever since its signing, but the great economist John Maynard Keynes wrote in 1919 in his bestselling book *The Economic Consequences of Peace* that the treaty was marked by 'imbecile greed ... and hypocrisy [imposing] demands on a helpless enemy inconsistent with solemn engagements on our part on the faith of which this enemy had laid down his arms ... reducing Germany to servitude for a generation ... her children starved and crippled'.[3]

Versailles undoubtedly drove economic migration to South America, but Brazil's approach to German migrants was unique; it did not want to encourage an enemy within. For example, the agricultural settlement of Rolândia, in the middle of the jungle 250 miles south of São Paolo, became a haven for anti-fascist Catholics and Jews, and over time grew into a model community for the successful economic and social integration of refugees.[4]

A number of Brazilian anti-Nazi newspapers were set up in São Paolo, the most successful of which was produced by the Liga für Menschenrechte (League for Civil Rights). Political organisations created space for ethnic German refugees who despised the Nazi dictatorship, sending support to German Jews still struggling along back home. Such groups were widespread, with the Notgemeinschaft Deutscher Antifaschisten (NDA, Emergency Organisation of German Anti-Fascists) active in Rio de Janeiro, São Paolo, Curitiba, Rio Negro and Pelotas. After the Second World War, the NDA became a major fundraiser for starving Germans in Europe.

But when the *Windrush* sailed further south down the coast of Brazil the picture darkened. Her next stop was Montevideo, where Elisabeth Nietzsche had left ship to go upriver to Paraguay. The seeds she had sown had struggled at first, but then they'd flourished. Her Neue Germania had been joined by large German-speaking colonies in San Bernardino and Hohenau. Altogether, there were 26,000 Germans in Paraguay by the end of the 1930s. However, unlike Brazil, Paraguay's sympathies were towards the Nazis.

In 1931, the Nazis opened their first Latin American branch in Paraguay, disseminating German newspapers and propaganda pamphlets. This branch determinedly penetrated all forms of local German life – its schools, hospitals, youth clubs and churches. When war came, Paraguayan police trainees wore swastikas. If it had not been for President Alfredo Stroessner's fierce anti-Soviet rhetoric after the war, Paraguay would have remained a pariah state for many years.[5]

It was in Argentina, however, where hard-core Nazism took deepest root, and it was the *Windrush* as much as any other ship that enabled this. The Nazis in Hamburg had deliberately targeted the merchant seamen of the Hamburg Süd Line ships with two purposes in mind: to spread the Nazi movement among German-speaking communities worldwide and to procure funds for the party.

Hitler's early ally, Gregor Strasser, later murdered in the Night of the Long Knives, spent the early 1930s fighting to improve conditions for shipboard workers, and set up well-funded networks of help in foreign ports. The seamen loved him for this, feeling disdained by old-school German diplomats abroad. Strasser controlled Nazi overseas affairs through the Auslandorganisation and, by 1938, 25,000 of its 55,000 total membership were merchant seamen. No ordinary *Windrush* crew member would have been in a position to resist joining. In one respect she was a migrant ship, in another a vessel promulgating the Nazi movement at sea.

In Argentina, whenever the *Windrush* was in port, the German community of Buenos Aires was invited to attend Nazi rallies on board. In 1933, the arriving German ambassador, Baron Edmund von

Thermann, disembarked wearing his full SS uniform. He announced to the crowd that he came bearing personal salutations from Adolf Hitler, and then led them in singing '*Deutschland über Alles*' and the '*Horst-Wessel-Lied*'.[6]

Thermann's proselytising for the Nazi cause knew no bounds. At the Goethe School in Buenos Aires, where most of the students were Argentine, he insisted that for his visit it be decorated with Nazi banners and pictures of Hitler, and that he should again lead a sing-along. He also appeared in his SS uniform at a Nazi solstice festival in December 1933. His wife, meanwhile, told German women's associations in the Buenos Aires area that they were to be 'bearers of the National Socialist worldview'. Those who seemed either likely recruits or potential naysayers were invited to the embassy for tea and some more indoctrination.

Ambassador Thermann had an economic motive too. By the 1930s, the United Kingdom controlled the majority of Argentina's railways and meat-packing plants: the export of both corned and frozen beef was the keystone of the country's economy, yet a foreign power owned its infrastructure. Thermann helped initiate a German mission, eventually resulting in Germany taking 25,000 tons of beef per year. This trade deal helped Argentina loosen its dependence on Britain and gave both parties methods to barter produce, reducing their exposure to high-risk foreign currency fluctuation controlled by larger powers.

Meanwhile, Heinrich Volberg, the enthusiastic anti-Semite and embassy economic head, sought to persuade Argentine companies that they should favour Aryan German importers and goods. Volberg also tried to force these companies to sack Jewish employees, and then blacklisted German firms in Argentina who were thought to be insufficiently pro-Nazi.

A common coercive technique in small communities is to force local people to endorse and support a particular charity. In Argentina this was the Winterhof, which was in theory set up to help the unemployed but actually was a way of squeezing contributions from businesses who, if they refused, would be reported to Berlin and denied future contracts. It was in effect a protection racket, and Volberg demanded full access to company books to ensure he was not being denied his share. In this way, he and the Nazis had complete control of German business in Argentina.

There was a lunacy in so much of this. When the non-Nazi German language newspaper, the *Argentinisches Tageblatt* (*Argentine Daily*), wrote a negative editorial about Hitler, local Nazi Rudolf Seyd challenged the paper's editor, Ernst Alemann, to a duel. Another pro-Nazi paper, the *Ortsgruppe* (*Local Group*) marked its foundation by hanging the first swastika flag ever seen in the country.

However, the gravest outcome for Argentina of the German influence washing ashore on the *Windrush* in the 1930s was a combination of the military and eventually the political. Arms contracts had first been entered into between the two countries long before, in the 1890s, when German munitions firms began to supply the Argentine army. As a result, German officers were invited to organise the country's War Academy.

Thousands of Argentine officers travelled to Germany for training, but with diverging outcomes, reflecting the split in the Germans' own points of view. Some were fully committed to the idea of an army in awe of government; others had nothing but contempt for the infirmity of any power hampered by democracy. Only one idea would prevail.

It is clear that the expansion of professional ties between the Argentine army and the Wehrmacht during the 1930s played a part in shaping Argentine officers' philosophy and their political allies' approach. Hitler's anti-Semitism was widely accepted, as was the idea that Nazism was the sole alternative to the feared communism. Worse, this led to an awakening of racist, imperialist urges in the army, which fed the idea that it would be noble to seek to establish the superiority of the 'master Latin race' – Argentines – over the mixed races of Brazil, their historic rival for Latin American leadership.

Added to this toxic mix was an adherence to unquestioning nationalist Catholicism, and an admiration for Franco's fascist Spain. By the end of the 1930s, Argentina was no longer a country of gaucho folklore, but a prototype fascist state. By 1943 it was under full military control, and soon after the war the divisive figure of General Juan Domingo Perón had grasped the levers of power.

On 14 July 1950, almost two decades after the *Windrush* had first set sail for South America, a man going by the name of Ricardo Klement disembarked from a weary Italian steamer called the *Giovanni C* in Buenos Aires. He'd just travelled 7,000 miles across the Atlantic from the northeast Italian port of Genoa.

This man later wrote that his heart was filled with joy as 'the fear that someone could denounce me vanished. I was there, and in safety!'[7] He felt secure that many Germans had come before him, especially in the 1930s.

However, Klement was not the man's real name, and he did not, as his papers claimed, come from the Austrian village of Bolzano in the South Tyrol. Rather, Herr Klement had spent five years since the end of the Second World War hiding in the little hamlet of Altensalzkoth outside Celle, a few miles south of Hamburg. Under a number of pseudonyms, the last of which was Otto Heninger, Klement had hidden deep in the forest of the Lüneberg Heath after the Germans surrendered, first working as a woodsman before eventually emerging to become a moderately successful chicken farmer.

By 1950, Klement had saved enough from selling his eggs to afford his dream move to Argentina. There were no prospects for him in Germany. He'd hidden for half a decade within a day's walk of the former death camp at Bergen-Belsen, but now with the establishment of the new Federal Republic of West Germany he gave up all hopes of being gratefully welcomed back into the bosom of German governance. During five turbulent years in post-war Germany, he'd expected that his past deeds would be forgotten and his evident organisational skills then sought by a recovering country. 'Klement' was wrong – Adolf Eichmann was not going to be welcomed back into the Reichstag.

Despite the Nazis' best efforts, reams of evidence was extant against Eichmann. As a result of the notorious Wannsee Conference of 20 January 1942, Eichmann had become Himmler's chief administrator of the Holocaust across Europe, rising to become an SS-Obersturmbannführer. Captured in Austria after the war, he'd then escaped and became a fugitive.

Until 1948, a man like Eichmann could have depended upon the ODESSA[8] network to smuggle him to South America via the northern route. This ran out of Hamburg on a private vessel, and then away from Europe on an anonymous steamer from one of the ports of Sweden. That route was busted in 1948, so in 1950 the only way open to him was the southern route.

On a spring day that May, an old comrade drove all day to bring Eichmann the 600 miles from Celle to Bad Reichenhall on the Austrian border. There, he slept at a guesthouse run by a Nazi contact, before meeting his next helpers at Innsbruck, well known as a stopping point for fleeing war criminals. Eichmann was then smuggled across the border into Italy, south to Verona and east to the port of Genoa. Next, with the help of his new identity as 'Ricardo Klement' vouched for by the Catholic Church, he obtained a visa to enter Argentina.

When Adolf Eichmann arrived in Buenos Aires, he was not alone. A dozen other Nazis were on the same ship. In his hubristic account, *Meine Flucht*, which emerged after his arrest by the Israeli Secret Service on 11 May 1960, he recorded, 'I knew that in this "promised land" of South America I had a few good friends to whom I could say openly, freely and proudly that I am Adolf Eichmann.' For a while he was able to dream of a Fourth Reich, enjoying the friendship of the likes of Josef Mengele, the Auschwitz doctor who experimented on Jews as if they were no more than laboratory animals.

In Argentina, both these infamous Nazis found a highly sympathetic environment, supported by the press. The media baron Eberhard Fritsch had taken over the Dürer publishing empire, whose output included *Der Weg – El Sendero*. This was the most right wing of all the post-war Nazi magazines, as openly anti-Semitic, racist and National Socialist as if the Third Reich had never collapsed.[9]

Eichmann's wish was that in crossing the Atlantic he would be able to restore both his freedom and his name. For eleven years, his plan worked. However, his hubris met nemesis in the Mossad agents who abducted him to Israel in 1960. After a lengthy trial, he was hanged after a lengthy trial just after midnight on 1 June 1962 at the Ayalon prison in Ramla.

This aspect of the *Windrush*'s history has a long tail, and the story of Eichmann and the Argentine Nazis lived on. It started to twitch in the 1960s, blossomed through the deregulation of banking in the 1980s and reached its current seemingly unvanquishable climax with the present-day state kleptocrats and their money laundering increasingly understood today.

The seeds of all this were sown in the month Eichmann dropped though the trap door, when simultaneously in London the Warburg bank was issuing a new financial instrument, the Eurobond. The Eurobond was a cunning way of owning money but keeping it from being taxed in any jurisdiction. It fell into the category of 'bearer bonds' – little pieces of paper that bore no name: anonymous international money chips.

At last, all that Nazi wealth sleeping uselessly in Swiss banks could be turned into these pieces of paper, redeemable anywhere in the world. In essence, they were akin to travellers' cheques, able to 'defang the taxes and controls designed to prevent hot money flowing across borders'.[10] Listed on the London Stock Exchange, these soon became the most effective international tax-evasion devices in history.

So who was buying them? In the 1960s there were plenty of people still alive who'd looted Europe in the Second World War. They'd stolen Jewish money everywhere from Oslo to Auschwitz and banked the proceeds in Switzerland. But these thieves were unhappy: they couldn't spend the money outside Switzerland easily, and without it being put to work they felt it was a diminishing asset.

But at last, with the Eurobond, these Nazi war criminals had a risk-free, tax-free method to make their secret stash earn a living. In Argentina, certain German families who had only been in the country for a couple of decades suddenly joined the international jet set, acquired polo teams and did what Eichmann was never able to do: start again with a blank sheet of extraordinarily valuable paper.

The persistence of the Perónist regime after the Second World War, with the explicit help of both former Nazis and Nazi-trained armed forces who'd arrived on the *Windrush* and other ships, gave the United Kingdom a historically little-considered problem which came back to bite her in much more recent years. Because of this, nearly 1,000 men who would only be in their late fifties today have instead been dead for three and a half decades.

After the war, the United States feared world instability. Despite some analyses that an American hegemony began almost immediately, the USA was in fact fearful of going alone in a new world order in which British pink was entirely wiped from the geo-political map. The UK was allowed to wind down its imperialist interests at its own pace and keep as much diplomatic sway as it could negotiate.

Argentina, however, was a different case. The USA believed that on her own doorstep, where British influence was already weakest, it needed to seek a new stability, and so joined with eighteen Latin American countries in 1948 to sign the International American Treaty of Reciprocal Assistance – the Rio Pact. Much like the entente cordiale between Britain and France of 1904 or the Triple Alliance of Germany, Austro-Hungary and Italy of 1882, it was an 'if one is attacked, we've all been attacked' pact.

Almost immediately, Perón took the opportunity of the Rio Pact signing ceremony in 1948 to reassert his country's claims to the Falkland Islands, or Las Malvinas, which the United Kingdom had pronounced part of the British Empire in 1833. In the House of Commons, Prime Minister Clement Attlee reacted by saying that Her Majesty's government would not be 'checked or chivvied out of British territory anywhere in the world', and sent gunboats to make sure this was understood.[11]

To British anger, the USA, which had a massive fleet nearby and could have ended the dispute with one telegram, declared itself neutral. Perón was satisfied with this humiliation for his adversaries, being also aware that the British navy would overwhelm his if it eventually arrived off the coast of Patagonia. This incident festered in the imagination of the Argentine right.

In April 1982, the Argentine government was under the right-wing leadership of 'the Generals', specifically General Galtieri, who invaded and occupied the Falklands. A short but terrible two-month war followed when the British government, led by Margaret Thatcher, despatched the Royal Navy to the South Atlantic.

The islands were won back by the British, at the cost of 255 British and 649 Argentine lives, with 2,500 more wounded on both sides. In 1948, one of the British ships sent to the Americas to wave the British flag had been HMS *Sheffield*. Her namesake, newly operational in 1980, was sunk by Exocet missiles on 4 May 1982. The British public watched in horror as pictures of her ablaze were transmitted home. Many survived but twenty men did not, and a further twenty-four suffered terrible injuries, some involving burns leaving them scarred for life.

Beyond these dark immediate occurrences, the Falklands War, fought about islands few British had even heard of, had two historic consequences. Firstly, at a time when the Conservative government of Margaret Thatcher genuinely looked as if it would only govern for a single term, the war released a wave of patriotic 'Make Britain Great Again' feeling. Rather than succumbing to defeat in the following year's election, she won again. Her 1983 victory was the most clear-cut election win since Attlee's in 1945, creating a momentum that would keep the Tories in power until 1997, with all that implied for the advancement of the smaller state, and privatisation of national assets. The second consequence was to recognise the genuine suffering of the people of the Falklands, and to make amends for the British government seeming to have forgotten about their existence. This led to the resignation of Foreign Secretary Lord Peter Carrington when the war broke out, and all Falkland Islanders became fully fledged United Kingdom citizens. This was rushed through Parliament under the British Nationality (Falklands) Act 1983 passed in March of that year, three months before Thatcher's triumph that June.

The willingness to pass this Act so fast will be noted by the Windrush generation today.

5

STRENGTH THROUGH JOY

The *Windrush* was complicit in Germany's meddling with South American affairs throughout the 1930s, but she was not confined to these transatlantic crossings. During the European summers, she was cruising off the Scandinavian coast and in the Mediterranean. Evidence of what she was up to may be found in the stacks at the British Library, which are world renowned for containing a comprehensive collection of just about any book published in the English language. Many other documents in English have been collected too. Inevitably some of this material will be repulsive. One such item is a 1934 pamphlet which, like all the best propaganda in history, appears on the surface to be harmless, perhaps even a benevolent prospectus to the unwary.

In perfect English, translated from the German, this pamphlet introduces the 1930s British reader to a wonderful-sounding scheme known as 'Strength Through Joy'. On the surface, this might be the kind of slogan given to a school of yogic meditation, or perhaps a self-pleasuring Californian cult. In design, it looks like a pamphlet one might receive from a local council boasting of its recycling rate this year.

If you read its title in the original German, the scheme's name begins to sound a little harsher. It's all about Kraft durch Freude, commonly abbreviated to KdF. Then as the pages turn, a peculiar – alienating, even, to the liberal mind – idea is promoted. This KdF concept is that fun must be good for you: desirable, necessary, compulsory. By the end, 'Strength

Through Joy' seems like an oxymoron – a desperate and mad prospectus for burnishing the master race by the means of treating it to a well-drilled holiday.

The credited author is one Horst Dressler-Andress. He is described as holding not one but two key roles in the Third Reich: Reichsleiter of the National Socialist Community and President of the National Chamber of Broadcasting. In straddling these two roles, as political leader and dominant broadcaster, he foreshadowed the media figures who followed his example in the twentieth century such as Silvio Berlusconi.

Dressler-Andress was a powerful man, a Reichsleiter being just one rung down from the Führer. But even he knew where the most gushing praise had to be given, and it is when he reaches the page where the great benefactor of the Strength Through Joy scheme is thanked that the blood chills: 'KdF has become a conception, the programme of the cultural mobilisation of a working people! … It plays no small part in the realisation of the National-Socialist People's State, the cultural policy of the Third Reich under the leadership of Dr Goebbels.'[1]

Paul Joseph Goebbels had been by Hitler's side since the latter had prevailed over Gregor Strasser back in 1926. Initially, Hitler brought Goebbels to Berlin where he took over the riven Nazi party organisation. Once loyal to Strasser, he exceeded himself in denouncing him to prove that Hitler should have no doubts. When Hitler achieved power in 1933, Goebbels was brought into the Cabinet as head of a new Ministry of Public Enlightenment and Propaganda. Twelve years later, on the evening of 1 May 1945, he poisoned his six children in the Führerbunker then shot his wife and himself in the Chancellery Garden. Their bodies were supposed to be burned by his adjutant, but substantial charred remains were found by the Russians the next day.[2] It had been a self-immolating career.

The groundwork for Strength Through Joy was laid by another long-time Hitler loyalist, Robert Ley, whom Hitler had relied on to run the German Labour Front. This was supposedly to protect the interest of the German workers but in practice was a means to smash the unions. In the post-war Nuremberg Trials, one of Ley's assuring proclamations to these people came to light. In May 1933, he had said:

> Workers! Your institutions are sacred to us National Socialists. I myself am a poor peasant's son and understand poverty. I myself was seven years in one of the biggest industries in Germany and I know the exploitation of anonymous capitalism. Workers! I swear to you we will not only keep everything which exists, we will build up the protection and rights of the workers even further.[3]

On 2 May 1933, storm troopers occupied all trade union headquarters across Germany, and union leaders were arrested and put in prison or concentration camps. Many were beaten and tortured. All of the unions' funds were confiscated. Former union officials were put on blacklists, preventing them from finding work. Now the workers could only look to Ley's German Labour Front.

Ley, Goebbels and Hitler realised that every promise they were making to German workers would inevitably be broken. Wages were suppressed and working hours lengthened. Dreading insurrection, they continued with persecution. Their other method was to go the 'bread and circuses' route: Robert Ley would send them all on holiday on the *Windrush*.

Like Goebbels, Ley would live to 1945, but no longer. On 24 October, three days after being indicted at Nuremberg with an inevitable hanging to look forward to, he made a noose from torn strips of towel in his prison cell and hanged himself from a toilet pipe.

Scrutiny of Robert Ley's KdF shows it was a government-controlled leisure organisation funded and promoted by the Third Reich which in another time or place might be described as a travel agency backed by the state. Officially it was a division of the Deutsche Arbeitsfront (German Labour Front). But KdF was much more than a mere travel bureau. It was not really about pleasure or escape like a normal holiday firm; it had avowed aims, of which there were three.

The first was to gain more support for the philosophy of National Socialism, promoting it both within and without the country. The second was to reduce discontent amongst the German working and lower middle class, many of whom had yet to reap the benefits of the supposed economic boom under the Nazis. The third, which is how the *Windrush* became entangled, was to boost tourism as a driver of the faltering economy.

Like so many Nazi projects, the true financial cost or benefits gained are impossible to know. Nobody was publishing audited accounts. We do know that KdF's tentacles reached deeply into every German's leisure time. The KdF organisation sponsored concerts, day trips, art and fitness programmes, plays, domestic resort stays and, most desirable of all, cruises.

For many ship-owning lines, this sudden government investment in their business came at just the right time. Although Hamburg Süd were not losing money on their South American journeys, these were high-risk voyages for relatively little net profit. They'd always run tours of the Mediterranean and the Nordic countries, which used less fuel, but on the other hand they docked more often, incurring hefty mooring fees in the resorts.

The *Windrush* and her sister Monte ships were just about wiping their faces, and this KdF windfall backed by the Nazis' bottomless coffers was very welcome. From the Nazi perspective, the huge capital cost of building these ships had already been incurred, and KdF gladly chartered or purchased ten ocean-going ships. *Windrush* remained under Hamburg Süd ownership.

Much of what took place on the KdF cruises on the *Windrush* may be recognised as an awful dystopian version of what a twenty-first-century international cruise passenger might enjoy today. Unusually, this dystopian iteration came first.

A parallel today would be if one arrived at a Butlins or Center Parcs, perhaps took a P&O cruise or a railway trip on the Orient Express, and discovered that more than half of the bookings had been made by a government-endorsed cult – one which had in mind and would soon carry out the systematic annihilation of one of your country's races of people, all with the zealous support of one's fellow passengers. Then imagine that accompanying these merrymakers was a small cell of government spies who'd report back to one single, all-powerful government minister on the totality of both behaviour and misbehaviour on these holidays.

That is what Goebbels arranged, and we know so much about what went on aboard the *Windrush* and other ships during their KdF cruises not principally from the travellers but from the records compiled by Gestapo spies. There were at least two of these on every journey, who reported back to their masters with their impressions of each cruise. It was felt crucial to understand them as they stood at the pinnacle of the Strength Through Joy programme. Compared to playing supervised volleyball in a factory gymnasium or hiking in lines through the Black Forest, taking in the sights of Europe with everything included on board marked out a returning Nazi traveller as one of the chosen few. Except, as it turned out, not everything was included on board. These egalitarian KdF cruises were often riven with division over who had the most disposable income, as the Gestapo noted.

Goebbels, therefore, accidentally drove the development of the entire business of cruises as we know them today, but although he was happy to fund this, he was not a man prepared to cede control. In his entirely covert surveillance of the *Windrush* trips he anticipated the present-day desire of large commercial companies to harvest opinions and data without consumers' explicit understanding that this is happening. Now we disclose ourselves with the click of a mouse, but on the *Windrush*, as she cruised around the Mediterranean or up into the Norwegian fjords, data was mined by these agents mingling in the guise of genuine tourists. For the Gestapo agents themselves, this was a considerable perk, regarded as a reward for a good working year, and was particularly favoured as a bonus by their accompanying wives, whose presence on the ship was necessary to maintain their husbands' cover.

Not all of what the Gestapo had to report back was in accord with the Nazis' intention for the KdF cruises – to promote a sense of equality and instil a conviction in little-travelled Germans that they were superior to the people of the countries where they docked, particularly in the Mediterranean. It was hoped that on their return to the *Heimat* they would glow with renewed loyalty, a sense of superiority and purposefulness within the Third Reich. However, the way these passengers were perceived to behave was not considered by the Gestapo to be always in keeping with these ambitions.

The first problem was the most senior Nazis on board themselves. They were already widely believed back in Germany to have a pronounced gift for obtaining perks. On the ship, they had not lost this sense of entitlement. Informants had a wide range of criticisms, including ostentatious showing off, pushing in and taking any privileges for themselves. They also demonstrated a boundless appetite for affairs and adultery, and a complete lack of self-control with alcohol, even as far as wrecking passenger lounges like modern-day football hooligans.

The *Windrush's* KdF cruises travelled both north and south. The route to the north carried her into Norwegian waters with the KdF passengers offered a selection of routes, all of which would be recognisable today to anyone browsing the travel pages of a British newspaper. Hamburg Süd devised four different itineraries, including Norway, all of which departed from Hamburg and took between eight and twenty days.

The simplest eight-day package left Hamburg for Hellesylt, Merok, Loen, Gudvangen, Eidfjord and finally Bergen en route home. The first stop was Hellesylt, reached by entering the Storfjorden south of Ålesund and penetrating inland. Then the ship sailed down the fjord's western finger, the Sunnylvsfjorden, at the head of which stood the little town of Hellesylt.

Hellysylt lingered then, as it does now, under the shadow of a particularly gloomy prognosis. One day the fissure passing through nearby Mount Åkerneset will crack and millions of tons of rock will slide into the Sunnylvsfjorden, precipitating a tsunami capable of wiping out Hellesylt in a few minutes. Improbable as this may seem, there had been the very recent example in Norway of the Tafjord disaster of April 1934, when a massive rockslide from Mount Langhamaren tumbled into the fjord causing an immediate 62m wave ripping towards the town of Sylte, which it hit at a height of 7m high, instantly killing forty people living along the shore.

In 2015 the Norwegian director Roar Uthaug made a disaster movie called *The Wave* depicting a fictional tsunami at Hellesylt. This was a smash at Norway's box office, although presumably not good for property prices in the Sunnylvsfjorden area. One of the publicity stills shows a super-sized cruise ship, like a bloated grandchild of the *Windrush*, anchored at the fjord's head as a giant wave accelerates towards it. The Norwegians enjoyed this so much that the producers followed it up with *The Quake*, in which the same weary geologist protagonist – now perhaps understandably suffering from PTSD after his fjord adventure – predicts then endures an earthquake in Oslo. This new genre may be light relief from gloomily lit Scandi-noir dramas about hyper-intelligent serial murderers.

Once the KdF-ers had their fun in Hellesylt, the *Windrush* retraced her route along the fjord and took the eastern finger now to Merok. By the 1930s, the local Norwegians were primed for the arrival of more than a thousand tourists at a time. Those passengers disembarking, rather than staying aboard drinking beer and looking up at the fjord's summits, were able to see traditionally dressed farmers moving their reindeer from one pasture to another. Then they could wander through the town where similarly costumed local women sat outside their houses with spinning wheels while their children played in the street, their blond hair bleaching and skin tanning in the northern sun. If what the KdF crowd wanted was Nordic stereotypes, the people of Merok – as in so many other places the *Windrush* pulled in – were not about to disappoint.

The greatest treat was to climb on board a pony and trap, which then laboured its way up a series of very steep roads to the top of the nearest peak plateau, where a café had been built with a large open terrace, catering to any Norwegian or indeed German food or drink requirement. From there, the happy KdF-ers looked back down at the *Windrush* berthed hundreds of feet below as she dominated the small harbour – the kind of vision of the immense made small that is of a piece with the human foible for model villages: tiny perfections, sterile yet pleasing.

The next stop was the village of Loen, which gave the opportunity for the passengers to approach the Kendjal glacier at the head of the Innvikfjorden. For all those who have ever visited a glacier, the anticipation is not always matched by the spectacle of what is, in essence, a vast block of ice very slowly grinding its way through rock. If this wasn't enough, after that was Gudvangen, where they hiked for an hour inland to reach the Kjelfossen waterfall, identified as the '18th tallest in the world', being some 2,477ft high, with a single spectacular drop of 489ft.

Then on to Eidfjord. It is perhaps anachronistic to seem facetious about how much the passengers may have been enjoying all this, but the highlight of Eidfjord was a hike to yet another waterfall, the Vøringsfossen, on the way back visiting a stone church dating from 1309, and then a Viking burial ground from 400 AD with 356 Viking graves. Many may have been thrilled by it all, while others may have looked forward to getting back to the *Windrush*'s dining room for a hearty meal and as much alcohol as they could manage before closing time.

On the way back to Hamburg the final stop was in Bergen. It is possible that some of the Nazis on board the *Windrush* appreciated Bergen as the place that gave Henrik Ibsen six crucial years of development as a struggling dramatist at Det Norske Theatre. This may have been in the minds especially of those, which would have mortified the author, who considered his *Peer Gynt* their favourite play, both because of its Nordic mythical inspiration and because, extraordinarily, Edvard Grieg composed *In the Hall of the Mountain King* as incidental music for one of its five acts.

Favoured Nazi director Dietrich Eckart had produced a version of *Peer Gynt* mobilising nationalist and anti-Semitic ideas, in which Gynt represents the superior Germanic hero, struggling against implicitly Jewish 'trolls'. Eckart's rendering was meant as a racial allegory in which the trolls and Great Boyg represented the Jewish spirit.[4] The passengers may have known about all that, or equally they may have just enjoyed visiting the immense fish market.

A lot was packed into the seven nights at sea. But for the better-off Nazi, there were twenty-day cruises available too, which did not stop halfway up the Norwegian coast but continued onwards to the far north, to the Nordkap and the great whaling station at Hammerfest. It had been a Norwegian, Svend Foyn, who'd invented the explosive harpoon gun responsible for destroying much of the world's whale population from the mid-nineteenth to the mid-twentieth centuries. The *Windrush* passengers would have seen the landing stages where once the whales shot in northern waters were dragged ashore and flensed, their blubber rendered down to whale oil.

As the ship sailed even further north to Svalbard and its main town, Spitzbergen, they would have seen the already dying plants that once processed millions of tons of whale brought all the way over to Iceland, Greenland and Canada. Now these plants were quiet. The great Norwegian companies such as Christensen, which already owned much of the British whaling fleet operating out of Dundee and Aberdeen, were having to whale off the south coast of America. The day of the immense Norwegian-owned factory processing shops in the South Atlantic was at hand.

For any veterans of the First World War on board, that five-year conflict would have been greatly shortened without the glycerol derived from Norwegian whale oil, which was a key component in the nitro-glycerine in the explosive weaponry that killed millions. Now, German companies like IG Farben had replaced this component with new chemicals that would soon power another war, whilst elsewhere in their laboratories they were inventing Zyklon B gas.

On board the *Windrush*, however, whale by-products were essential. They greased the pistons, polished the saloon floors, bolstered the ice cream and provided the wax for passengers' lipstick. It is probable, however, that the tour guides chose to mention none of this.

6

A WARNING FOR THE WORLD

These trips to the north were Nordic, cold and bracing. The ones to the south were for the lotus-eaters. The Madeira cruise in particular was referred to as the 'bosses' trip'. On these, the Gestapo spies noted, more puffed-up passengers enjoyed striding around arrogantly on the promenade decks showing off their expensive Leica cameras, their wives adorned with fine furs and jewellery. Unbeknownst to them, the Gestapo were snooping into their sexual misconduct too, observing how many unaccompanied Nazi party officials tirelessly attempted to hook up with any unaccompanied women on board, no matter if either or both were married to someone back in Bad Homburg.

Ironically, one of the greatest miscreants was the very man who had invented these cruises, enjoying the personal patronage of both Hitler and Goebbels: Robert Ley. It is not known if the Gestapo made a report on him to their boss, but they didn't have to. Unguardedly, Ley invited the *Time Life* journalist William Bayles on a cruise so he could convey to an American audience the beneficence of Nazi social policy.

What Bayles reported must be one of the great PR fiascos in history.[1] He was first introduced to Ley in his cabin, where he found a dishevelled man completely drunk, with a bloody hand caused by breaking a bottle. Ley immediately tried to pour Bayles some wine, which flowed not into his glass but into his lap. Ley hollered for the immediate attention of the *Windrush* captain, who – evidently embarrassed – ensured that, on his boss's perambulation on deck with the astonished journalist, two minders stood either side to make sure he did not topple overboard.

Bayles also observed Ley's scruffy demeanour, and that he reeked of drink, cigarettes and German sausage. None of this seemed to hold him back from insisting on being attended by a retinue of blonde and blue-eyed 'Nordic' women, whose day job would have been in a factory or office back in Germany, but who had been commandeered by Ley to tend to his needs. As he told Bayles, he did not interpret the Nazi *Weltanschauung* as to mean abstinence: 'We don't regard a bit of love as unhealthy.'

Perhaps the fish rotted from the head down.

The Gestapo agents were also concerned that the longer and more expensive cruises were packed out with the party elite, who made up to two-thirds of the manifest. The most senior members appropriated the best cabins on the promenade deck, while older people with fewer connections but greater need were relegated to less desirable cabins below.

Hitler's own personal physician, Karl Brandt, took a cruise to Italy, Greece and Yugoslavia in late 1938 and insisted on dining at the captain's table every night at the expense of others. Indeed, a Gestapo agent reported: 'Likewise, one saw the captain and the officers only with this group of people, so that one cannot spare the captain from reproach that he hardly bothered to attend to the well-being of other vacationers.'[2]

Inequality was financial too. When the genuine working classes were lucky enough to get on to the cruise, they were offered less desirable accommodation, and soon realised their inability to afford the extras that other tourists had at their disposal. They also found themselves berthed in the bowels of the ship, crammed in with eighteen others without a locker for their belongings. Their iron bunks resembled military cots. When they left the below-decks accommodation it was reported that they were so unaccustomed to the furnishings in the ship's numerous common rooms that they dared not enter. By the time they got to port they were often suffering from a restless cabin fever.

Once ashore, the working-class passengers' troubles multiplied, for this 'all-in' cruise proved very expensive as soon as they descended the gangplank. In places like Naples they realised that to take a coach to Vesuvius or to Pompeii and then pay for entrance was beyond their means, and that the souvenirs and knick-knacks that the middle-class passengers could afford were simply too expensive for them. There were no such things as credit cards and, if they didn't have hard cash, that was all there was to it. This resulted in the extraordinary phenomenon on one cruise when hundreds of workers chose not to disembark in Venice, Dubrovnik or Corfu, with all their attendant splendours, and instead stayed on board playing the card game skat.[3]

The Gestapo kept a particularly close and sinister watch on the women on board. The advertising and imagery for these cruises on the *Windrush* seemed to promise great freedoms, especially outdoor and sporting, for female passengers. The reality was that this imagery was aimed at enticing bookings from men, and promoting an idealised image of German womanhood. In the opinion of the Gestapo, the women taking these cruises simply did not understand the true Nazi's ambivalence towards materialism. Could they not grasp that the conspicuous consumption of middle-class women was not consistent with the requisite austerity?

This showed particularly on the cruises where evening dances, costume parties and other kinds of entertainment offered opportunities for self-display for those who could afford it. 'A group of female passengers showed a taste for the sort of jewellery and attire,' reported an agent, 'which cannot be considered appropriate for a KdF vacation trip.'[4] The Gestapo could not square the circle that, back in Germany, the success of a family was often made manifest by the richness of what a woman wore in public – a habit the Nazis wished to somehow vanish away in the cause of phoney egalitarianism just because these women were now at sea.

They were also disturbed by behaviour described as 'shameless'. One report noted that a woman got drunk in the company of a Greek officer ashore, wobbling unsteadily as she returned to her ship loaded down with the money and gifts that her short-term companion bestowed upon her. Another report complained that 'again and again, women and girls were observed making contact with Italian soldiers, sailors and also civilians in the port cities, exchanging addresses and having their pictures taken with them arm in arm. The urgent and repeated appeals of the tour directors to show more discretion were hardly observed.' Finally, the report harrumphed that 'one is forced to assume that most of the women joined the Italian trip for erotic purposes'.[5]

The Gestapo even covertly ducked behind stalls to follow women visiting the souks in places such as Port Said. They came away with the conviction that these supposedly vulnerable female travellers were soft touches for souvenir sellers who eagerly accepted their Reichsmarks for shoddy goods aimed squarely at tourists. The Gestapo were irritated that the flower of German womanhood was sacrificing her nation's pride by swapping cigarettes for goods with Arabs. Ignoring warnings that their deportment flouted that demanded of a master race, the women also cheerfully posed for snapshots with Arabs and Africans, who were very happy to join them in the photo frame in return for more cigarettes.

A KdF tour director criticised the actions of two German women who on a visit to the ruins at Pompeii were observed in intimate conversation with two Italian policemen. Despite the women's arguments that they had lost their tour group, and anyway the policeman who came to their rescue knew much more about the antiquities than the German guide, the tour director warned that their conduct was liable to damage the reputation of German women abroad. These black marks were easy to ignore, as very few people on board had much time for the tour directors. Many passengers had much experience at their hands and hoped to explore new sites and wonders under their own steam, only to find themselves marched around from one site to the next at a brisk pace in Mediterranean heat receiving tedious rehashed information.

Goebbels, meanwhile, was able to use the Gestapo reports to assess the success of the KdF project as manifested on the *Windrush* and her sister ships. Despite the reported problems, there was much to please him. In pure propaganda terms, the photographic imagery produced showed smiling Germans thriving in far-flung parts of the world, presaging how well they might succeed when the Third Reich conquered the globe. The racial inferiority of these countries' populations, destined to fall under the German heel, was proven to him too.

Economically, most passengers, even the less well-off ones, visited ports where the local inhabitants were mainly markedly poorer, and on their return home they were able to comment on the great disparity in living standards between the average German and the average Egyptian, or even Italian. These cruises encouraged the perception of a causal relationship between their own well-being and the Nazi regime's attempts to remake Germans into the master race.

Politically, however, the outcome was less pleasing. The Gestapo agents, albeit perhaps themselves programmed to be overzealous in these matters, were disappointed by apathy and worse. An Italian cruise in 1938 coincided with *Kristallnacht* (Night of Broken Glass), a terrible pogrom against Jews that attracted much criticism from a large number of workers on board. In the harbour of Palermo, the following year, a passenger refused to remove his hat when the ship's orchestra played the 'Horst-Wessel-Lied' and was reprimanded by a tour leader. Rather than backing down, the passenger answered back, and the Gestapo observer covertly approached the tour leader to take the man's name so that a formal complaint could be considered against him later.

So concerned did the Nazis become about insubordination that when it came to the cruises to the Norwegian fjords passengers were discouraged from disembarking in certain ports for fear of leftist infiltration. In theory, Norway was felt to be like-minded, at least according to the nonsense of being cousins in Nordic racial identification. It might be imagined that these would be the very destinations where the Germans would be encouraged to disembark and mingle. But the Gestapo knew that, aside from the port town of Haugesund, where locals sympathised with Nazis, other coastal or fjord towns offered unfriendly environments for German tourists. In Bergen and Odda, with their sizeable communist or social democratic enclaves, hostile Norwegians tossed bottles and other objects at KdF ships, while crews of fishing boats refused to wave merrily at the arriving or departing ships in the customary manner.

However, overall, as far as Goebbels was concerned, the whole cruise ship venture had been a triumph. The KdF cruises, which peaked at 140,000 passengers per year in 1939, were a very small part of the programme, which 42 million people had taken advantage of in total.[6] But the glamour of these tours was quietly disseminated through personal travel accounts in factory newspapers, and in the organisation's widely distributed literature, like the pamphlet written by Herr Horst Dressler-Andress.

In what anywhere else might be regarded as endearing, the passengers on the *Windrush* cruises qualified for specially made lapel pins and luggage labels. Hundreds of official photographs were produced and given away, carefully showing well-dressed and lightly tanned Germans surrounded by palm trees observed enviously by the 'racially inferior' locals. In these photographs, the Germans were always shown to have agency, while the local people merely looked on idly. Many of these images were created in Tripoli, which had the double advantage of showing a North African country now in the hands of fascists: the Italians. 'If they can do it, so can we', was the idea.

Typical of the response of the average German was the Pooterish voyage diary of an Otto Kuhn, a civil servant from Stettin who had cruised from Portugal to Madeira. He said that he did not much care for the Portuguese in Lisbon or their scruffily attired children begging from the tourists. Neither did he like the look of the local dockers. Yes, most were white, 'but mixed in were half breeds and a few Negroes'. Neither did he like the better-dressed Portuguese either, feeling they were flawed by 'southern nonchalance'.

Kuhn kept many photos and stuck them in his diary but, like every dull-minded traveller in human history, he decided that there was no place like home, confiding that the voyage had done nothing more than deepen his patriotism. Yes, Portugal and Madeira had their attraction, 'but our great Northern Heimat with its mountains and valleys, planes, lakes, and sea coasts is on the other hand far more beautiful'.

For the *Windrush*, these years sailing contentedly at sea would soon seem as idealised as the Germany of Herr Kuhn.

A question which arises as one generation after another comes to study the rise of Nazism is, why did nobody stop it? Didn't anybody know?

In Germany, people did try to stop it, and the most cautionary aspect of Hitler's seizing power is that he attained it by means of the ballot box. The old nationalist right thought they could control him, while those for whom his populist message appealed to a sense of not being valued were blind to the apocalyptic implications and carried on voting him in. Of course, with power he continued to deal murderously with any opponents or rivals even within the Nazis, such as Ernst Röhm, at his side for the failed Munich putsch in 1923 and eleven years later murdered in custody as a consequence of the Night of the Long Knives in June 1934.

So people did know. An outstanding account by *Daily Telegraph* foreign correspondent Robert Dell published in his book in 1934 makes this explicit, and indeed argues that the propagandising trips of the *Windrush* around the ports of Europe were a growing part of the crisis.

Robert Dell's *Germany Unmasked* was a clarion call if ever there was one. What tipped him over the edge was the:

> guileless visitor ... who goes for his information to Nazi propagandists ... and meets agreeable young men who assure him that all the stories of ill-treatment of Jews and political opponents are false, and fill him up with accounts of the marvellous achievements of the regime in the economic sphere ... uniting all Germans in a common peace. The visitor goes home to bear witness to the absolute sincerity of Hitler's pacific declarations and the noble ideals of the Nazi movement.[7]

Dell is keen to stress that the credulous British visitors were not what might be perceived as upper-class twits from the right – the likes of the Mitford sister Diana, married to Oswald Mosley, who was obsessed with 'Herr Hitler' and was joined later even by the abdicating king, Edward VIII. Dell was more worried about Goebbels' success in duping the British left. He names a number, particularly a Professor Moore of Oxford, who in his letters to the *Manchester Guardian* after he had travelled to Germany, where he'd met 'leaders of opinion', was reassured that checks and balances were in place.

Dell mentions the 'Oxford Groups' too, who in October 1933 came back singing the Nazis' praises:

> One is struck in Germany, by the many points of resemblance between the Nazi movement and religious revivalism, and after all the 'Oxford Groups' are a Salvation Army for the middle classes. It would be worth looking up the letters apologising for the Nazi regime published in important newspapers and ascertain how many have been written by members of the 'Oxford' group.

For Dell this complacency – this allowing oneself to be used – was itself insane. At the time he wrote, Jews were already driven out of education, journalism and the arts, and were the object of world conspiracy theories of hollowing out the *volk* from within, even though only nine in every thousand Germans were Jewish. Dell was convinced that Goebbels had, through actions taken in June 1933, taken control of propaganda abroad from the Ministry of Foreign Affairs into his own German Ministry of Propaganda. Goebbels denied these 'Secret Instructions', but the reality was that German embassies and diplomats of every grade abroad were no longer conduits; they were to be aggressive propagandists. Nazism was going worldwide.

Dell was particularly worried by the soft propaganda efforts made with the KdF cruises on the *Windrush* and her sisters. He wrote:

> Tourism would seem to be a method of propaganda in a sense other than that mentioned in the Secret Instructions. Dr Schacht pleads

poverty of Germany as a ground for not paying German debts, and the condition of the German working class is undoubtedly miserable. Yet the German middle classes seem to have plenty of money for holidays abroad.

On the Italian Riviera east of Genoa there was a positive German invasion in the Easter holidays of 1934. At Rapallo on Easter Day one heard more German spoken than Italian, and about 90 per cent of the foreign visitors were Germans. They came from every part of Germany, and the majority of them looked like people in quite modest circumstances.

Can it be that Dr Goebbels is subsidising foreign travel? In any case, the policy of making it difficult for Germans to go abroad by severe restrictions on the amount of money that they could take or get out of Germany would seem to have been relaxed. One day in March 1934 a German woman went into a shop in Nervi to buy a German paper. The shop was full of Nazi publications and portraits of Hitler and other Nazi leaders were conspicuously displayed. To her surprise the customer was served by a German girl, who explained that the shop belonged to her brother, and that she had been there for a couple of months. The customer, not quite sincerely, admired the portraits of Hitler and asked whether business was good. The shop-girl said that it was quite satisfactory, and then the customer asked whether they were doing good work for Hitler. 'Oh, yes,' replied the shop girl, proudly but incautiously, 'that is what we are here for.'

That is what a great many people are starting shops for, and restaurants in Paris and other places. London is probably no exception, and in any case the number of Germans there to do good work for Hitler is very large. Every German newspaper correspondent abroad, for example, is now by German law an official agent of the German government.[8]

Dell's key question above is: 'Can it be that Dr Goebbels is subsidising foreign travel?' We know now that he was.

And was the *Windrush* the ship that so offended him docking in the area of Rapallo at Easter 1934? According to her voyage cards, she was, and would have set down a couple of thousand passengers and crew in the nearby Genoa harbour to venture out by coach along the Italian Riviera to Rapallo and Nervi via the coastal road to Portofino.

So it seems that not only were Goebbels' Strength Through Joy holidays for compliant low-to-middle-income Nazis reinforcing their loyalty to his dogma, but some of them were using these trips around the Mediterranean to nakedly propagandise. It might seem laughable: young women selling pictures of Hitler to tourists, like something from a 1930s detective novel where a German character is usually a spy. However, thriller writers were getting their idea from reality.

Perhaps a more shocking implication for the *Windrush*'s time in Genoa, which she visited many times, is that Britain was intimately connected with the rise of European fascism in a way that we overlook today. Dell, in what was really a few hundred pages of despairing wake-up call, wrote about something else happening in Genoa at the exact same time as the *Windrush* tourists were looking for swastika-embellished merchandise in Italian newsagents:

We have also to deal with our own Fascists … It may not be generally known, by the way, that there is a British Fascist organisation in Italy presided over by an English resident in Milan, according to *Secolo* [a newspaper published in Genoa]. The British Fascists from various places in Italy assembled in Genoa on a Sunday in March 1934. They attended morning service at the Anglican church where a wreath, afterwards put on the monument of an Italian Fascist 'martyr' was blessed by the Bishop of Gibraltar, who, according to information given to me by a British resident in Genoa, had not been told beforehand what was expected of him. At the end of the day's proceedings, the British Fascists who, from the names given in the *Secolo* appeared to be mostly retired military or naval officers, sent telegrams expressing their loyalty to Signor Mussolini and his subaltern ambassador to England, Sir Oswald Mosley. All this is merely ridiculous, but the Fascist movement in England is not merely ridiculous. It may not be dangerous yet, but there is all the more reason to stop it before it becomes dangerous.[9]

Ten years later, the sons of those retired British military fascists were back; in the Allied air attacks of 1944 they destroyed Genoa's Teatro Carlo Felice, the historic 1828 theatre and opera house. Those 1930s Italian fascists who had treated their British equivalents to a night of Mussolini-approved opera met with scant reward.[10]

7

ON THE MERIDIAN LINE

The most potent image of the *Windrush* in British waters, during her quarter of a century of life, will always be of her arrival at Tilbury in Essex in June 1948. However, this was not her first arrival in south-east England. During 1936, German travel agencies displayed Hamburg Süd posters for a six-day trip on the renowned cruise ship from Hamburg to London, all inclusive, for a cost of 65 Reichsmarks. The voyage cards show that throughout August and September that year the *Windrush* sailed to and from London on more than twenty occasions.

Meanwhile, in *The Times* and other publications, travel agencies such as Dean and Dawson of 81 Piccadilly and 163 Fenchurch Street were advertising 'Short Cruises to Hamburg'. Both ways, passengers had two days at sea, two days in either London or Hamburg, and two days' return voyage.

1936 was a strange and uncomfortable year. A short contemporary vignette by the writer Henry Williamson, famous worldwide for *Tarka the Otter*, gives a sense of this. In his non-fiction book, *Goodbye West Country*, he wrote of July 1936 when the Nazi airship *Hindenberg* flew along the coast of south Devon on the way out to New York, and then back along the coast of north Devon on its way home to Germany:

It was a wonderful sight! I could see the red emblem, with black swastika. It seems part of the summer sky, a cloud phantom. 'Look!!'

I said, to a man sitting near, blue reefer jacket and white flannels, Panama hat. 'The Hindenberg! Isn't she lovely?' They all stared into the sky above Morte Point. 'Humph!' said the man. 'Shouldn't be allowed to come over England like that in my opinion. They're only spying, taking photographs for the next war. 'But don't you think they might be feeling rather proud of showing their new airship to the English? They so earnestly want to be friends with us – just for the sake of old times.' 'Well I'm damned if I'd trust them.'[1]

A paragraph from the back-cover blurb for *Goodbye West Country* written by its publisher casts a little more light on to Henry Williamson's personal perspective:

He [Williamson] gives us his opinions on politics and literature, on scribes and on Pharisees. And then, having wandered far afield – to the Nurnberg rally of the Nazis and King George V's funeral in London – he will come back to the Devon countryside and give us one of those unsurpassable sketches of otter or salmon, red deer or badger, birds, fishes, plants or insects, which have so gained the love of his readers.[2]

For, as the Nazi flag glided gracefully past Morte Point near Woolacombe, around which people today may walk and cycle along the Tarka trail, the man in the panama hat questioning its right to do so was the true voice of the British people. He is disdained here by Williamson who by then was a convinced fascist – exactly the kind of apologist with a national broadcasting profile that Robert Dell had warned about.

Williamson had spent much of the previous year hosted by a friend working at a film studio in Berlin, with a minder called Chmitzer feeding him the official line on cleanliness, Autobahns and the wonders of the German Youth Movement. Williamson was even provided with tickets to see that year's Nürnburg rally. He swallowed the lot.

❖

This then was the divided kingdom the *Windrush* came into as she rounded the north Kent coast by the Isle of Thanet, passed the Dickensian marshes to her port side, sailed way beyond Tilbury to the north and on into the lower reaches of the Thames. As she pushed on past Woolwich, she entered the vast docklands of the old West India and Canary wharfs, until finally she came to a stop in Greenwich.

With the Royal Naval College buildings white in the sunshine, she lowered her gangplank in the heart of Greenwich, near to where the *Cutty Sark* is in dry dock now. The passengers walked just half a mile to Greenwich railway station, where they caught a train taking less than fifteen minutes, stopping only at Deptford and New Cross, to London Bridge and the heart of the City. Any German engineering enthusiasts might have been excited that this was the oldest passenger line in the world: 4 miles of entirely elevated brickwork mounted on 878 arches, genuinely famous at the time.

On their arrival at London Bridge station, their luggage was taken on for them by truck to hotels in the west end of London, and they were then guided towards a bus stop where they could travel just a few stops northwards over the river to what most had come to see. The Hamburg Süd posters that had caught their eye in Germany had marketed one image most strongly: a traditional beefeater guard with a fine white moustache standing sentinel at the Tower of London. Then as now, this was one of the greatest tourist attractions in the world.

After a morning there, it was on to the Underground at Tower Hill and west to get off at St James's Park, where they took lunch in a café and went to see the guards changing at Buckingham Palace. A short walk along the Mall brought them to Trafalgar Square, then up into theatreland and through Soho to the shopping attractions of Oxford Street. In short, what a German tourist arriving on the *Windrush* did in London in only two days was little different from what they would do today.

Yet these were confusing times to walk the streets with a German accent. For many Londoners, the previous war was nearly twenty years before, and as Williamson wrote, these Germans might only want to be friends. But there was a treacherous darkness in Britain too.

A woman who appeared to be an unremarkable Scot called Jessie Jordan living in Perth was a fully signed-up German agent. Her handler, Joanna Hoffmann, had cover as a hairdresser on another ship, SS *Europa*, and this gave her many opportunities to brief agents on voyages to both Britain and the United States. Once, Jessie Jordan even sailed out to Hamburg herself, where on the dockside she was given her first mission – to make a sketch of the Royal Naval Armament Depot at Crombie on the Firth of Forth. These drawings would be used to guide German bombers in the event of war to munitions stores and oil tanks.[3]

But MI5 was ahead of the game. Its agents had spotted that an address in Hamburg, PO Box 629, was receiving a disproportionate amount of post from Britain, and in early 1936 they obtained a warrant that all post bound for that destination be opened. The next year, when Jessie Jordan had opened a hairdressing salon in Dundee, MI5 discovered that, rather than providing shampoo and sets for the women of Angus, it was being used as an address for New York Nazis to send their various plots and intrigues to then be posted on to PO Box 629, Hamburg.

In London, the Fifth Column was in operation years before the war. A Rudolph Rosel was operating out of an office in Parliament Street, under the guise of the Anglo-German Information Service. There he developed a network of pro-German contacts and sent them Nazi propaganda articles. A Special Branch report noted: 'The articles are forwarded to offices of the Conservative Party in London, Edinburgh and Glasgow and to influential members of the British Legion who are interested in affairs in Germany, and Members of Parliament.'[4]

Even more sinister, Rosel kept records of the conduct at meetings of Oswald Mosley's British Union of Fascists – who amongst them was also pro-Hitler or anti-Hitler, and any speeches they may have given. Any who were anti had their activities recorded, and this information was sent to Berlin. Special Branch was certain that all of Rosel's reports were read in full by Hitler himself.

In such a way, a British Fascist from south-west England, who might have joined them because of the very peculiar single issue of the Tithe Wars but was otherwise a genial farmer at his gate at Widecombe-in-the-

Moor, could have come to the personal attention of the Führer himself with his name on Rosel's records so that after the war – in the event of German triumph – he would be held to account. This would have been a harsh price to pay for being drawn into the Tithe Wars – a dispute between many British farmers and the Church of England over a tithe paid by farmers to the church on agricultural land. This had once been paid in produce, before a financial formula had been devised which in the 1930s was argued to be too onerous by many farmers. Oswald Mosley used this issue as a recruiting sergeant in rural areas: a prime example of good people being manipulated by a political opportunist over a single-issue cause to support other policies they did not understand.

The ports of Britain were now completely porous to German spy networks. A retired German sea captain arrived by sea to England, made his way for unknown reasons to settle in Stroud in Gloucestershire, and drove from there at his leisure making notes and sketches of Portsmouth Harbour. Needing cash to sustain him, the Nazis arranged for him to be paid through a Mrs Dunscombe, a sub-agent in Hampstead. More money came via the German cook of a Lady Eleveden who lived at Gloucester Lodge on the edge of Regent's Park. The cook, Josephine Eriksson, held a passport with transit stamps showing she had travelled no fewer than six times between England and Germany between 1934 and 1938, each time coming back with cash. Throughout, her job was to pay expenses to Nazi agents in London and courier their intelligence reports back to Hamburg.

None of this is to say that this is what the majority of passengers on the *Windrush* were up to in 1936. The majority were in all probability there for the Tower of London. But if it were not also a ship of spies, that would seem extraordinary.

Domestically, two particularly unpleasant home-grown fascist organisations grew as the 1930s progressed, and were in full operation in 1936: the Nordic League and the Right Club. The Nordic League met at the

HQ of its sister organisation, the White Knights of Britain, also known as 'The Hooded Men'. Inspired by the Ku Klux Klan, their aim was to rid the world of 'the merciless Jewish reign of terror'.[5] They met above a pub in Lamb's Conduit Street in Holborn, and, in honour of Hitler, had a chancellor rather than a chairman.

The Board of Deputies of British Jews was very effective in sending in undercover spies. The Nordic League's membership was mainly upper middle class, unlike Mosley's Fascists, and from a military background. The member seen as the most dangerous by the British Secret Service was both an absolute fanatic and the Conservative MP for South Midlothian and Peebles, the Right Honourable Captain Archibald Henry Maule Ramsay, formerly of the Coldstream Guards, known as 'Jock' to his friends. Amongst his recorded idiocies was that the 'common enemy' is not 'the Germans or the Italians or the Japanese, but World Jewry ... It may be a revelation to some of you, but it is a proven fact that the Irish Republican Army is a Moscow controlled body financed by Jewish gold.'[6]

Ramsay's stupidity did not deter him; using as his postal address the House of Commons, he then tried to enlist members into an organisation even more determined than the Nordic League, which he called the 'Right Club'. Lucky applicants received a badge of an eagle killing a snake with the initials P.J., standing for 'Perish Judah'. He then made ready for a full-scale fascist *coup d'état* in Britain, while happily claiming his salary and expenses as an MP.

In Parliament, Ramsay was not alone. The House of Lords in particular was rank with Nazi sympathisers and anti-Semites. There were some big aristocratic brand names: Hugh Grosvenor, 2nd Duke of Westminster and one of Europe's richest men; Lionel Erskine-Young, 29th Earl of Mar; Arthur Wellesley, 5th Duke of Wellington; Randolph Stewart, 12th Earl of Galloway. With a lesser title but an extraordinary genetic contribution came David Freeman-Mitford, 2nd Baron Redesdale. His daughter Diana married Oswald Mosley at a ceremony at Joseph Goebbels' house, and her sister Unity became a devoted friend of Hitler.

All these men conspired later along with the Duke of Buccleuch for a 'negotiated peace' with Hitler. In 1936, not long before the first *Windrush* tourists of the year arrived, Edward VIII had abdicated. It seems beyond all doubt that in the event of the German defeat of the United Kingdom he wished to return as king within the Third Reich, and it's likely all the above men would have supported him and profited greatly.[7]

Not many of them were actively treacherous during the later war, although Lord Tavistock (a courtesy title while he waited to become 12th Duke of Bedford) would travel in February 1940 to Dublin to meet at the German embassy with a draft agreement suing for peace. He was named and shamed in the Commons for this, but had too much protection to come to any harm. His ranting anti-Semitic justification shows he accepted no wrongdoing. Of course, he should have spent the entire war in an internment camp. He did not.

Yet, the London the *Windrush* travellers saw was not all about the infestations of traitors and spies. In Soho they would have been tempted to visit the first milk bar in London, soon to be joined by a hundred more. These teetotal premises, with their monochrome interiors and chrome and mirrored decor, were an American art deco alternative to smoky pubs, with milkshakes and sandwiches on sale, stools to sit on and a youthful ambience.[8]

The street scene they walked around was looking new too. Whole streets of poorly maintained Georgian houses and alleyways had just been swept away to allow space for the Senate House, University of London, building in Bloomsbury, or the Adelphi Hotel on the Embankment, with its six lifts and underground parking for 450 cars. In the suburbs, commuters who had entered the Underground down two sets of escalators emerged in the light in modernist concourses at places like Cockfosters, then went to see films at newly built cinemas such as the magnificent Odeon in Woolwich.

Berthold Lubetkin's concrete Penguin Pool at Regent's Park Zoo was symbolic of much ambitious architectural design, and for humans outdoors the lido movement was in its heyday, with hundreds opening across Britain. These were particularly numerous in London, where the newly built Brockwell Park Lido between Herne Hill and Brixton remains a place of memorable summers for the Windrush generation of today.

What those German passengers would have been able to see and sense in London in 1936 was a place that was just getting its confidence back twenty years after the last war – an urban and suburban conurbation that might have grown into something truly magnificent. There was a plan for the people, if only within a few years other Germans had not flown back over the city dropping thousands of pounds of bombs.

The 1936 *Windrush* manifest had been privileged to see the beginnings of a London that never was. When they travelled back to Greenwich to rejoin the *Windrush*, perhaps they felt reassured by the mix of progress and stability they had seen. All year the news had been challenging. The League of Nations was almost paralysed. It had been unable to prevent Hitler remilitarising the Rhineland, Mussolini proclaiming the Berlin–Rome Axis or the outbreak of the Spanish Civil War.[9] Yet in London life seemed to go on.

As the *Windrush* had headed up the Thames to collect her passengers from Greenwich on 19 September 1936 – a Saturday afternoon – a huge commotion would have been heard as more than 70,000 football fans filled the Valley, home ground of Charlton Athletic in shouting distance of the Thames. In this small suburb of south-east London, a potential giant was beginning to arise, cheered on by the tens of thousands of soldiers garrisoned at Woolwich barracks and sailors from the Royal Naval College in Greenwich and all along the Thames. Charlton drew 2-2 with Birmingham City that afternoon and were slugging it out for that season's First Division title with Liverpool. But like the new London, the war would throw Charlton into reverse, blighted by historical events from which it only began to re-emerge in the 1980s.

The atmosphere back in Hamburg was already febrile. On 13 June 1936 one of the most astonishing images of the Hitler period was created in the same Blohm & Voss shipyard where the *Windrush* had been built six years earlier. A figure later identified as August Landmesser stands in a sea of his fellow shipyard workers for the launching of another ship, the *Horst Wessel*. Every one of them is making the Nazi salute, except Landmesser, who just looks on. He was in a relationship with a Jewish woman, Irma Eckler. In 1942, she was murdered by the Nazis. Landmesser, with whom she had two children, was killed in action in 1944. Their marriage was recognised by the Hamburg Senate in 1951, and their children were raised by foster parents.

As autumn came, the *Windrush* was bound for her season of sailing to South America again. Then, with the spring of the next year, she was filled once more with increasingly fervent Nazis on Strength Thorough Joy trips, to the Norwegian fjords. She would not return to London again for twelve years, but soon those fjords would loom ever larger.

8

NORWAY FALLS

For the earliest years of the war, the *Windrush* fades from view in the voyage cards maintained by Lloyd's of London. But not entirely. Whereas before her every mooring and departure was recorded to the nearest day and often hour through information cabled into Lloyd's from agents around the world, now Lloyd's depended upon agents in neutral countries like Sweden, who still had a view over the Baltic Sea and the Skagerrak linking it to the high seas. With the world erupting into war, the voyage cards, which were later backed up by British decryption of the German Ultra transmissions cracked by the Enigma project, reveal that the *Windrush* was destined to spend the greater part of her own war back in Norwegian waters playing a number of greatly different roles.

Beyond the Scandinavian nations, the involvement of Norway in the Second World War is a relatively little-known part of the familiar wartime tapestry stretching from Dunkirk to Pearl Harbor. In the United Kingdom, there are a mere three points of popular reference. Firstly, there is the 60ft Norwegian spruce despatched by the people of Oslo to be mounted every Christmas in London's Trafalgar Square – a present from the city's people to Britain for its support in the war. Generations of Britons have taken this tree as well-deserved tribute, even though initial British war policy in Norway amounted to abandonment when her troops mounted a humiliating evacuation from Narvik without even giving their Norwegian allies notice.[1]

These blunders by then First Sea Lord Churchill led to the demise of his Prime Minister Neville Chamberlain – a notable example, perhaps resonant in the present day, of one man's mistakes leading to his elevation rather than his downfall. With reference to Churchill's his own decision to cancel Operation Hammer, intended to relieve Trondheim, Churchill later wrote in *The Gathering Storm* that he'd had no option. General Percy Groves, however, observed that 'there are few paradoxes more striking than to be found between Mr Churchill's deeds as Minister and his words as a historian'.[2]

Curiously, the second and third points of reference to Norway's war are also associated with the British Christmas. Two films, *The Heroes of Telemark* and *633 Squadron*, involve key roles for Norwegian resistance fighters against German evils, and are broadcast on one channel or another every year. The Telemark story concerns the destruction of the German capacity to produce heavy water as a precursor to a potential atomic bomb. *633 Squadron* depicts the destruction by British bombers of a V-2 rocket-fuel plant at the head of a Norwegian fjord. In both films, cosily shown around teatime in the festive season, awful tortures are visited on captured Norwegians by the Gestapo in Oslo as the British eat their mince pies. The repetition of these broadcasts is mocked annually in *Private Eye*.[3]

Both put Norway's resistance to occupation to the fore, and much of the country's own war narrative features this. Indeed, Norway's wartime experience can make the even greater horrors elsewhere comprehensible for those who find the sheer breadth of world conflict hard to process; it had all the horrific elements but on a smaller scale. Yet sadly, whatever the worthy efforts of Norway's civic and paramilitary resistance to German occupation may have been, there were three groups of people it could not protect from terrible harm, and for all of these the *Windrush* would play a terrible part.

The women impregnated by German troops, the resultant offspring and Norway's Jews all would be doomed ultimately to be stolen from their homeland to Germany across the Baltic Sea on the *Windrush*, as the ship came to play her darkest role.

The first of these groups to suffer was the Norwegian Jews.

❖

Before that, however, the *Windrush* was to play a crucial part in creating the circumstances for these awful events to happen. By early 1940 she was based at the Polish port of Stettin on the west of the Oder estuary, from where she was ideally positioned to be loaded with German troops and equipment to go east to Scandinavia. From there she assisted in the German conquests of both Norway and Denmark, known as Operation Weserübung.[4]

Denmark fell first. On 9 April 1940, the Germans met only token resistance when they invaded, costing sixteen Danish lives. Many Danes, realising that topography left them with no means of defence across their flat peninsular, purchased swastika flags to flutter at crossroads and watched as land troops swept in towards Copenhagen.

From the sea, the *Windrush* and other merchant ships helped convey thousands of soldiers to the strategic island of Fyn, where assault forces landed without opposition on both the west coast at Middelfart and on the east coast at Nyborg. Danish forces on the island laid down their arms without a struggle, enabling a single motorcycle patrol to complete its occupation, taking over Hans Christian Anderson's birth town of Odense at its heart. Now that they held Fyn, the Germans controlled marine access from the Baltic into the Kattegat and beyond, with Denmark straddling the wide channel. Now they could sail unimpeded past southern Sweden and on towards Norway.[5]

Norway came next – a much tougher prospect. The Germans realised that they would need to take the whole country in one fell swoop, and not just begin at Oslo in the south. Potentially they would be facing a land battle grinding northwards over thousands of miles of challenging and still-frozen terrain where they could expect – as came later – well-organised guerrilla resistance.

The Nazi invasion of Norway became the first in history to be simultaneously executed through both seaborne and airborne operations, with the coastal towns of Narvik, Trondheim, Bergen and Kristians being softened up through aerial and naval bombardment. This was followed by parachuting fighters behind the lines, and a pincer movement as further troops were landed on the beaches and quaysides from the *Windrush* and other ships. The Norwegians showed much fighting spirit but, having been neutral in the First World War, their military machine was rusty and poorly organised, with a government calibrated only for peacetime and a passive deference towards its king. They reacted too slowly.

This most modern of invasions was then followed by an attempt to take Oslo which, by contrast, had a Ruritanian beginning when one of the prides of the German navy, the *Blücher*, entered the Oslo fjord through the Drobak Narrows only to be destroyed by a massive 1905-vintage gun from the Crimean War fort of Oscarsborg. This initial seaborne raid on Oslo was a fiasco and the simultaneous air invasion, depending on swiftly taking the airfield at Fornebu, faltered too.

However, the Norwegians could see where this was heading, and the order was given for King Haakon, his government and twenty-three trucks containing Norway's gold to flee 70 miles inland to Hamar. Soon, the anti-aircraft fire from Fornebu ceased, and heavily loaded German transport planes landed and disgorged the invaders.

With Oslo secured, the troops, supplies and arms ferried on the *Windrush* and the other merchantmen sailed all the way; the Germans simply disembarked without a shot fired and walked into the city. Nils Orvik, a 21-year-old veterinary student, ran into German soldiers marching down Karl Johans Gate, the street running through the heart of the city. He asked what they were doing there. A German replied, 'We were sent here to help you against the English.'[6]

Norway would not be free of the Nazis until May 1945, more than four years hence. And the most tragic group of human beings ever to travel on the *Windrush* were about to discover what occupation by racist, fascist, psychopathic murderers really meant.

On 27 January 2012, then Norwegian Prime Minister Jens Stoltenberg spoke at a ceremony in Oslo to mark International Holocaust Remembrance Day. The event was attended by the last surviving Jew

from a group of 532 deported in October 1942 on two ships. One of them was the *Windrush*, the other the *Donau*.

'Today,' said Stoltenberg, 'I feel it is fitting for me to express our deepest apologies that this could happen on Norwegian soil. It is time for us to acknowledge that Norwegian policemen, civil servants and other Norwegians took part in the arrest and deportation of Jews.'

It was a fulsome and sincere apology, making amends to an extent for a 1998 'acknowledgment' of some wrong, and an ex-gratia payment of £38 million to compensate Jews for property seized half a century earlier. This had been perceived to have fallen grievously short both of true recompense and of sufficient remorse.

In October 1942, when the Jews of Oslo, Stavanger, Kristiansand and Trondheim were bundled on to the *Windrush* bound for Hamburg, it was implicitly understood by most Norwegian officials that on arrival in Germany they would be put in filthy cattle wagons and taken directly to Auschwitz. Perhaps it could not be fully comprehended that most would be murdered on the day of their arrival, but clearly they were not being exiled from their homeland for their own well-being. The Norwegian officials seemed not to care.

As so often when looking at the deeds of the Nazis, the devil is in the detail, and some of the most telling in Norway can be found in the sheer greed for property and commercial gain implicit in so much that the Germans did, in Norway as elsewhere. Their methods were psychopathic but they were mercenary too.

Their first seizure of a major Jewish asset was the synagogue in Trondheim.[7] German troops vandalised it by scraping off all Hebrew inscriptions, and then turned it into a barracks. This was April 1941. Throughout that year they seized all Jewish stores in the city, putting them in the hands of a Norwegian agent of the Gestapo, Reidar Johan Dunker Landgraff, who hired 'Aryan' managers before reopening for business in time for Christmas.

Seeing this happen, the Abrahamsen shopkeeper family of Trondheim wasted no time in leaving the country for neutral Sweden, which offered sanctuary for Jews throughout the war. Unfortunately most other Jews were slow to follow. Their persecution was followed only in small steps at first, and for a while the treacherous puppet Prime Minister, Vidkun Quisling, had others in his sights. The Jews were not yet his priority.

Faced with quiet civil disobedience on taking power, Quisling first tried to break the unions, the press and the Church. These efforts met with passive and stubborn resistance and were an embarrassing failure. Nevertheless, Quisling was determined to beat the teachers, and tried to force them to reject their existing union for one of his own making: the Teachers' Front, which would then enforce his favoured pro-Nazi curriculum. However, utilising a covert network of communications, the teachers voted, in a ballot Quisling had expected to unanimously endorse his educational programme, to reject it by more than 90 per cent.

Like all natural bullies, Quisling, inspired by Nazi methodology, tried to divide and rule. He arrested 300 'ringleaders' of the teachers and interned them at Grini concentration camp near Oslo, from where they were deported to Kirkenes, close to the Finnish border in the Arctic Circle. A Norwegian doctor, one of his own Nazi members, was so appalled by the conditions on the ship carrying them there that he leaked a critical report. Quisling responded: 'The Measures which are being taken against Norway's teachers are a direct consequence of their treasonable activities.'

Yet still the teachers would not come to heel. The Church then spoke out in condemnation and he was cornered. Without his backing down, schools would have been unable to open for the autumn term of 1942. Quisling had to agree to the return of the 'troublemakers' from Kirkenes, who arrived back as heroes.

But in their triumph lay doom for the Norwegian Jews. Quisling now needed a quick victory, and he had a defenceless community right under his nose.

For centuries there had been no Jews in Norway, and their immigration was discouraged by law and custom. The first Norwegian constitution drafted in 1814 barred the entry of Jews (as well as Jesuits) to the country.

This ban was lifted in 1851 after a long campaign for reform by the poet Henrik Wergeland, and the first Jews arrived from Lithuania the next year.

Thereafter, the Jewish population grew very slowly and by the German invasion in April 1940 was little more than 3,000 strong; they were primarily engaged in the small-scale manufacture of shoes and tobacco products and in retail. An extra 300 were political refugees from Hitler's Germany. Initially, even the hotheads of Quisling's Nasjonal Samling party had not expressed open anti-Semitism as a priority.

For the first year after the invasion Quisling's anti-Jewish programme was all about confiscation, or larceny. This grand theft was eventually formalised by a decree in October 1942 which stated simply that assets of any kind belonging to Jews with Norwegian citizenship would be confiscated for the benefit of the state. A second paragraph assigned responsibility for implementation to the Ministry of Internal Affairs of the Quisling government and mandated that the names of the persons affected be published in *Fritt Folk*, the official newspaper of the Norwegian Nazi party.

The weasel words of the ensuing paragraphs guaranteed the rights of third parties owed money as a consequence of confiscation, and threatened severe punishment for those concealing Jewish property. According to an instruction of 12 November 1942 from Quisling to Reichskommissar Terboven, the German governor, exceptions were to be made for confiscated gold, silver and jewellery which, unsurprisingly, had to be handed over to German security police as a contribution to the war effort. Wristwatches were also to be appropriated by the German army 'for military use'. In accordance with a separate agreement, the property of any German Jews in Norway was to be retained by the German authorities.[8]

In November 1942, the Norwegian government established a liquidation board under the Minister of Finance to manage the confiscation, administration and liquidation of Jewish assets. As in Germany, separate files were kept for each Jewish household, managed by an official receiver, to facilitate the settlement of outstanding debts. The proceeds were all siphoned into a 'Communal Fund', and there was plenty to be liquidated.

Life-insurance policies were cashed in, bank accounts dissolved and securities sold. Proceeds from the securities either went to the Communal Fund or were deposited in the Christiana Bank in Oslo to accrue interest.

Furniture and any other goods that could be moved were sold at auction or through special distribution centres, which favoured specific groups within the population and marketed the items at knockdown prices. One beneficiary of low-value items was the Norwegian Nazi party's own welfare organisation. Most of the unsold merchandise from liquidated stores was sold to other Norwegian businesses, in large batches, well below market value.

On 18 December 1942, the Norwegian government-in-exile in London issued a provisional decree guaranteeing Jews the restitution of their homes, stores, apartments, personal belongings and communal property. This was intended to dampen the Nazi appetite for Jewish property. Nevertheless, many Norwegian individuals benefited from the confiscations, especially those directly involved in the process; they paid themselves high salaries and in some cases engaged in embezzlement. Businesses bought up stock or whole companies cheaply, while party members similarly acquired furniture and apartments. It was an entirely corrupt enterprise.

Therefore, although the Jews of Norway were of not the least real interest to Quisling, he found them useful for two prosaic purposes. The first had been simply this matter of theft, on a grand scale. Profiteering from the ruination of others, the Communal Fund totalled 11,361,507 Norwegian crowns from a total of 1,053 separate estates.[9] This was calculated in 1952 from government records, when restitution was arranged for some and a third of the value was retained, taken in salaries and liquidation costs.

The second prosaic purpose after losing his battle with the teachers was that Quisling needed a public win. The tragedy of the Jews who had remained in Norway was that, because their persecution had moved so slowly, many of them were caught off-guard and would be trapped with Sweden no longer a possibility. On 25 November 1942, two ships, the *Windrush* and the *Donau*, pulled into Oslo harbour. They had been specifically commissioned to remove Norwegian Jews to Germany.

9

MOSES AND AARON

Historians are fortunate that three extraordinary tales from the persecution of Norway's Jews survive. The first two are remarkable and awful tales of 'out of the frying pan and into the fire'. The third is one of a no less remarkable escape.

Moritz Rabinowitz was a 55-year-old businessman and philanthropist. His removal from Norway on the *Windrush* was a genuine tragedy: Moritz had spent the previous ten years warning international leaders in correspondence of just such an outcome for the Jews. As a 19-year-old he had escaped persecution once already, from Białystok in Poland in 1909, and wrote later of the brutal murders he had personally witnessed in the pogroms there.

Little more than a decade after his arrival in Norway, the Rabinowitz clothing retail outlets were a mainstay of six of the largest cities and towns in the country. He had also founded his own clothes manufacturers, Condor, and with his profits built a superb concert hall in Haugesund in the Karmsundet Sound on the south-west coast, where Thor was said to wade through the waters for a morning walk.

A renowned social activist, Moritz was a prominent figure in Haugesund who had successfully sued the *Nationalt Tidsskrift* newspaper for anti-Semitic defamation. As far back as 1933 he was known in Germany as the de facto leader of Norway's Jews, and in 1938 had written a telegram to Neville Chamberlain begging him to encourage world leaders to intercede on behalf of German Jews.

One journalist wrote, 'Rabinowitz is the kind of Jew who shouts from the rooftops that he is a Jew ... some may find this irritating but in truth Rabinowitz is more Norwegian than most of us.' He was a marked man.[1]

When the Nazis invaded in April 1940, they soon reached Haugesund and made Moritz's capture their highest priority. He hid in Skånevik, 30 miles east across the waters of Karmsundet Sound, but Norwegian Nazis monitored his employees conveying messages to him, and he was caught and imprisoned in Oslo's Mollergate jail in February 1941. He remained there until his deportation on the *Windrush* on 22 May, six months before the mass round-ups began. Later that year the Jews would be taken to Auschwitz from Hamburg, but in Moritz's case the *Windrush* sailed back on her familiar route to Stettin. From there, he was taken by train to Sachsenhausen, where he was placed in the barracks for Jews, though he was officially categorised as a 'political prisoner'.

This distinction would not save him. Moritz died on 27 February 1942, his death certificate listing 'pneumonia' as the cause. However, according to a fellow prisoner, Moritz was kicked to death outside Sachsenhausen's Barrack 38. Later, Moritz's brother, daughter, grandson and son-in-law (he had been a widower) were all deported on the *Windrush* and sub-sequently murdered in Auschwitz. Moritz conveyed a final message via a German inmate, and on through another non-Jewish inmate from Haugesund, to the local people, which was reproduced in his obituary published on 20 June 1945.

Moritz also dictated and signed his last will and testament to a fellow prisoner, Christian Wilhelm Rynning-Tønnesen, leaving all his worldly goods to his daughter Edith, expressing a wish that she continue his businesses as going concerns. But as Edith and her entire family were also murdered, what was left of his estate went into probate after the war.

After the Nazis had confiscated his businesses, and with at least 300,000 Norwegian crowns in cash and securities, his estate was valued at 986,000 crowns in 1945. The Norwegian government managed to justify imposing fees and taxes of 450,000 crowns on that sum in the course of the next ten years. The devil was in the detail for post-war Norwegians too.

In central Haugesund today the Karmsund Folkemuseum has the expected range of exhibits, with herring fisheries and the shipping trade to the fore. In a corner of the ground floor, an authentic reconstructed 1930s office is on display. Its former occupant was an extraordinary Norwegian philanthropist and activist for human rights, who happened also to be a Jew: Moritz Rabinowitz.

Nearby in 1986 the people erected a granite standing stone, with Moritz's profile in bronze and beneath that a few simple words marking his resistance to the '*Nazismen*'. The inscription ends with: 'He understood that freedom and tolerance are the making of mankind.'

Another victim of the *Windrush* and *Donau* forced transportations was Ruth Maier, whose little-known story remained one of the great untold tales of the war until fifty years after the event. Unlike the well-established Rabinowitz, Ruth Maier had only been in the country since 1939.

Ruth's family was from Vienna, and had had the means and the vision to make an escape after the Austrian Anschluss, when the Nazis seized their country on 12 March 1938. Ruth's younger sister, Judith, was sent on the Kindertransport programme to England, but Ruth was already an adult, so it was decided that she should make her own way to Norway.

In Lillestrøm she became very close friends, and possibly lovers, with a young female poet called Gunvor Hofmo. Their relationship was intense, self-examining and troubled; both of them had issues with their mental health. We know about this, and about Ruth's tragic end, because Ruth kept a brilliant diary, on the cusp of adolescence and adulthood, from before she left Vienna to the time of her transportation.[2] Gunvor was so traumatised on learning that Ruth would never return from Auschwitz at the end of the war that she was admitted to an asylum, where she wrote volumes of published poetry.

Ten years after Ruth's death, Gunvor tried to have Ruth's diaries published – but no Norwegian publishing house would agree to do so. Was it 'too soon' for them? And so, Ruth's thick single volume lay buried in Gunvor's belongings until it was discovered by Gunvor's literary executor, the poet Jan Erik Vold, after her death in 1995. Eventually Ruth's diary was published in 2007, an astonishing record of displacement at the very outset of adulthood but, perhaps as valuably, also containing her own beady-eyed observations of the occupation.

She recalled that one day in May 1940, she was walking by the water-side in Oslo where the *Windrush* was berthed, having ferried another regiment of troops from the Fatherland. Some soldiers were sunbathing on the deck:

> They wink at people gawping at the ship. A loudspeaker is playing
> '*We're Flying Against England*'. The soldiers look well-fed. Later they
> march by and I think of Rausching's comment: 'A people has found
> its melody; the German people are on the march'[3] ... I actually do
> not hate them when they are standing there in front of me. But if I
> could, I would, I'd shoot them without thinking twice about it ... A
> small group of Norwegians stare at the Germans as if they were exotic
> animals. The girls have red lips. They're waiting, they're ready.[4]

Ruth Maier's legacy from her few years in Norway was remarkable for someone still just 22 years of age when she was murdered. She was a notable diarist, of course, as became apparent later, and the inspiration for Gunvor's poetry. But she was also an artist's model, inspiring Gustav Vigeland and Asmund Esval. Vigeland's sculpture of her cast in bronze still stands in Oslo's Frogner Park today.

As time passed, the environment became more hostile, and she had become required to 'register' as a Jew wherever she lived, bullied and estranged by erstwhile friends. A year and a half after she had stood in relative freedom on the Oslo dockside scrutinising young Nazi troops, and having slowly learned of the grave threat under which Jews lived in Norway, she was brought back to that waterfront.

Jens Stoltenberg's account and testimony stands good here, in his same 2012 Holocaust Memorial speech:

> The Holocaust came to Norway on Thursday 26 November 1942. Ruth Maier was one of the many who were arrested that day. On 26 November, just as the sky was beginning to lighten, the sound of heavy boots could be heard on the stairs of the boarding house *'Englehjemmet'* in Oslo.
>
> A few minutes later, the slight Jewish girl was seen by her friends being led out the door of Dalsbergstien 3. Ruth Maier was last seen being forced into a black truck by two big Norwegian policemen. Five days later the 22-year-old was dead. Murdered in the gas chamber at Auschwitz.
>
> Fortunately, it is part of being human that we learn from our mistakes. And it is never too late. More than fifty years after the war ended, the Storting decided to make a settlement, collectively and individually, for the economic liquidation of Jewish assets.[5] By so doing the state accepted moral responsibility for the crimes committed against Norwegian Jews during the Second World War.
>
> What about the crimes against Ruth Maier and the other Jews? The murders were unquestionably carried out by the Nazis. But it was Norwegians who carried out the arrests. It was Norwegians who drove the trucks. And it happened in Norway.

As Jens Stoltenberg said in his speech, Ruth's final place of residence in Norway was called 'Englehjemmet'. In English this means 'Home of an Angel'.

Irene Berman is a Norwegian Jew who has lived in America for three-quarters of a century, first in Minneapolis and latterly in New York, where she worked as a translator, including of six Ibsen plays. She has a large family, including many grandchildren, and lives as full a life as any of us can hope for.

However, Irene Berman and her family only escaped being sent to Auschwitz on the *Windrush* at the eleventh hour. In the autumn of 1942 many of Norway's Jewish men had already fled for Sweden as the sense of peril had begun to grow, but it was thought that women and children would surely be safe. Irene Berman's father, who was already in Stockholm, was unconvinced.

On the night of 26 November 1942, 4-year-old Irene was led to the Swedish border with her nanny, her mother, Rosa, and Lief, her 7-year-old brother, by a 'scout' named Haakon. All these courageous scouts, or people smugglers, were called Haakon after the king-in-exile who was still regarded as a hero. King Haakon himself had fled for London from Tromsø in June 1940 and, despite Reichskommissar Terboven's urgings, the Storting refused to depose him in his absence or force him to abdicate. After the war Haakon returned to common jubilation and reigned until his death, aged 85, in 1957.

Irene's perilous adventure first took her party as discreetly as possible by train from Oslo to Lake Magnor. Once there, they stole a rowing boat. In her fine memoir she recalls:

The full moon illuminated the water. Halfway across the lake a pilot pointed to a house located on the shore and said: 'be very quiet now, there are Nazis over there' … Around 4.30 in the morning we finally reached the area in the forest that the Haakon felt was the Swedish border and reached a small house. The sheriff and the customs people were called and came to greet us. These officials were from the border station at a place called Toecksfors and were now accustomed to receiving Norwegian refugees.

We learned later that the Norwegian state police in Oslo, under orders from the Gestapo, had requisitioned one hundred taxis at round 5 o'clock in the morning for the purpose of mass arrests. The first phase of the arrest of Jewish women and children in Norway started at the same time that we reached Sweden.[6]

Irene Berman's life had been narrowly spared, but on that same night her aunt's husband, Israel, became one of a number of relations and friends who were forced on to the *Windrush*.[7] Irene has spent many years piecing back together what happened to them all on her subsequent visits back to Norway: all her relations died and just two of the Jews on the ship with her uncle Israel lived to see Oslo again.

532 Jews are known to have been forced to leave Oslo on the *Windrush* and the *Donau*. On their way down the Oslo fjord for the open sea, they passed the same elderly guns that had blown the *Blücher* out of the water. These two guns were named Moses and Aaron.

For this vile purpose the *Windrush* was transformed from troop carrier to prison ship. The below decks areas had been cleared of tables and chairs and become a series of huge cages, where the prisoners would be divided by sex and age. The food on board was little more than thin soup and oatmeal.

On arrival in Hamburg, the transportees were made to board wagons at gunpoint. These were hitched to a steam engine destined for Auschwitz. Their plight was compounded by the fact that in the history of Auschwitz and the Nazis' 'Final Solution', 1942 and 1943 were years of hideous acceleration of the genocide. In April 1943 the Jews of the Warsaw ghetto had begun to fight back, and the Nazis were terrified that that they were not murdering Jews with sufficient speed. By horrific chance, in late 1942 the SS architect Walter Dejaco repurposed the basement mortuaries at Auschwitz into four crematoria, which were commissioned in early 1943. Now, murder of the Jews would take place in factory conditions with a capacity of 150,000 victims a month.

This pre-mediated 'efficiency' was made even more repulsive with the fruition of the twin aims of Heinrich Himmler and Reinhard Heydrich at Wannsee, in January 1942, that Auschwitz must focus on work, and then murder. Himmler saw a balance in this. If there were too many 'workers' for the work required, the definition of 'fitness for work' could be reset upwards and 'surplus' labour could be exterminated.

With victims arriving now in their hundreds of thousands, the piles of loot to be stolen by the SS grew higher. Even the camp commandant, Rudolf Höss, admitted that 'the treasures brought in by the Jews gave rise to unavoidable difficulties for the camp itself'. The SS 'were not always strong enough to resist the temptation provided by these valuables which lay within such easy reach'.[8]

Just as in Norway, the Jews were faced with theft and corruption. But now they were confronted by a genocidal regime too. They didn't stand a chance. Less than 1 per cent of them survived the war. On arrival at Auschwitz women, children and any men too old to work were murdered in the gas chambers within hours. Able-bodied men were put to hard labour but nearly all had died of hunger or disease before the end of 1943.

Back in Norway, those standing on the waterfront, where Ruth Maier had stood two years before, were outraged. A group of Norwegian bishops and professors sent a personal petition to Vidkun Quisling begging him to intervene, denouncing anti-Semitism as unethical and contrary to the tenets of Christianity. Quisling answered thus:

> There are many who say that a Jew cannot be expelled simply because he is a Jew. In my opinion, no such reasoning could be more superficial. A Jew is not Norwegian, not European, he is an Oriental. Jews have no place in Europe. They are an internationally destructive element. The Jews create the Jewish problem and create anti-Semitism.[9]

A vivid testimony survives of the consequence of Quisling's banal cruelty, written by a man called Odd Nansen, the gentile architect son of the polar explorer Fridtjof Nansen. He was imprisoned in Sachsenhausen for resistance work, and heard the plight of the Norwegian Jews at Auschwitz from a fellow inmate. He described what he learned in a diary of his years in imprisonment:

> Yesterday I was talking to a Jew. There actually are a few of them alive in the camp. This one is named Keil, a watchmaker, and has been in Norway. He came here from Auschwitz in Poland. An extermination camp of the worst type. What he told me about that camp was so horrible, so incomprehensible in ghastliness, that it defied all description. He told me that of the Norwegian Jews who were sent there … Only a very few were still alive: about 25 was his estimate. Most of them were gassed. Whole transports went straight into the gas chamber and thence into the crematorium. Men, women, and children of all ages.
>
> I asked about Dr Becker and his brothers. They had all died in the gas chamber. The Kaplan family? Only one, the youngest boy, was still alive. He had been spared for some reason, probably because he was in the squad where they needed him. The whole Sherman family had been killed. And all, all the others!
>
> Keil himself had been spared because he was a watchmaker. They needed watchmakers to repair all the hundreds of thousands of watches they were stealing from the dead. I asked him about Rabbi Samuel. Oh, he died on the steps of the hut. He was returning from work, was done for, just collapsed and was dead. Klein, the Klein family? Oh, they all died in the gas chamber. Muller, Bernstein and all, all the rest of them, dead all dead. Starved to death, beaten to death, worked to death, or sent to the gas chamber.[10]

Today Norwegians and others wishing to reflect on this aspect of their history may visit the Holocaust Centre at Villa Grande in Oslo. It is in the Museum Quarter, on the Bygdøy fjord peninsula, some way inland from the more famous Kon-Tiki and Viking museums. But the prosaic walk into the suburbs is salutary; it reminds visitors of the banality of the evil which once passed this way.

The museum does its best to pay homage to the murdered Jews of Norway. There is all that one might expect – copies of the Nasjonal Samling party manifesto, and of the Nuremberg Laws which codified anti-Semitism. But there is the unbearably personal too: a tiny pair of child's shoes on loan from Auschwitz, an account of the post-war trial of forked-tongued Norwegian collaborators and a final remembrance hall with nothing but the names of Norwegian victims of the Holocaust written in plain black on white walls.

The building itself, the Villa Grande, is indeed grand in a restrained Nordic way. Begun in 1917, it was originally intended for Sam Eyde, founder of the Norsk Hydro Company, but works were much delayed and it was only finished in 1941. It was then appropriated as headquarters and personal living space by the very man who would seal the fate of Norway's Jews, Vidkun Quisling. Today the house stands as Norway's main memorial to the victims despatched on the *Windrush* to the cruellest place on earth.

When Ruth Maier, Moritz Rabinowitz, Israel Steinfeld and the hundreds of other Jews were forced out of Oslo, the last edifice they would have been able to see on the port side as their ship sailed into the Oslofjord was the fourteenth-century Akershus Fortress, looming over the waterfront as it had for 600 years, the symbolic point of control repelling any invaders to Norway. It had fallen without resistance back in 1940, but five years later it hosted the execution by firing squad of Vidkun Quisling – having previously been the location where many Norwegian resistance leaders had been shot.

In 1994, Kristian Ottosen, a former Norwegian resistance leader, who had spent three years in German captivity mostly in concentration camps, published *In Such a Night: The Story of the Deportation of the Jews*.[11] Ottosen had extensively researched, complemented by the persistent efforts of Jewish organisations, the identities of expelled Norwegian Jews, their backgrounds and ages at the time of their murder. From this, a number of names, though not all, can be identified of those who were forced on to the *Windrush*. Many women had fled for Sweden before, and this list is mainly male, with nearly all dying at Auschwitz.

These people's names deserve full recognition here:

Name	From	Profession	Date of murder	Age
David Becker	Telemark	Merchant	1 December 1942	44
Wulff Becker	Oslo	Physician	17 February 1943	35
Annie Louise Benkow	Akershus	Entrepreneur	1 December 1942	47
Ruben Berg	Oslo	Mechanic	Not known	22
David Bermann	Oslo	Businessman	22 January 1943	43
Herman Bernstein	Oslo	Watchmaker	20 November 1942	68
Paul Bernstein	Oslo	Physician	7 January 1943	39
Richard Bernstein	Oslo	Office clerk	21 January 1943	60
Otto Leo Bing	Oslo	Sales agent	14 January 1943	59
Selig Blomberg	Oslo	Merchant	1 December 1942	59
Abraham Borochstein	Romsdal	Merchant	1 April 1943	50
Conrad Caplan	Tromso	Warehouseman	10 January 1945	22[12]

Name	From	Profession	Date of murder	Age
Herze Caplan	Tromso	Merchant	3 March 1945	72
Jacob Caplan	Norland	Merchant	19 March 1945	39
Solly Caplan	Tromso	Manager	16 December 1942	34
Meyer Dvoretsky	Oslo	Merchant	Not known	48
Nathan Fein	Oslo	Retail clerk	15 March 1945	57[13]
Herman Fischer	Kristiansund	Factory Owner	24 March 1943	49
Idor Fischer	Kristiansund	Pupil	2 January 1943	11
Martin Fischer	Nordland	Merchant	5 January 1943	47
Alexander Goldberg	Oslo	Businessman	15 January 1943	37
David Goldberg	Oslo	Merchant	1 December 1942	63
David Gorvitz	Oslo	Roofer	8 February 1943	23
Isidor Isaksen	Oslo	Tailor	9 April 1943	46
Moritz Jaffe	Ostfold	Merchant	Not known	53
Moritz Klein	Tromso	Merchant	17 February 1943	32
Leonard Levin	Oslo	Physician	19 January 1943	37

Name	From	Profession	Date of murder	Age
Sigurd Levin	Oslo	Merchant	January 1943	44
Aron Levinsohn	Hedmark	Merchant	4 January 1943	42
Bernhard Levinson	Oslo	Merchant	January 1943	53
Isak Lieb Marianson	Hordaland	Transient	17 February 1942	53
Leif Sigurd Markus	Hedmark	Bookkeeper	May 1943	23
Selik Markus	Hedmark	Merchant	January 1943	60
Einar Nathan	Oslo	Attorney	January 1943	56
Isak Pickelner	Nordland	Executive	January 1943	55
Zemack Resnick	Tromso	Merchant	14 January 1943	49
Selik Sakolsky	Tromso	Merchant	1 December 1943	55
Julius Samuel	Oslo	Rabbi	10 December 1942	39
Ernst Savosnick	Trondheim	Watchmaker	13 June 1943	63
John Scelowsky	Oslo	Textile Agent	1 December 1942	55
Rudolf Seelig	Oslo	Tailor	17 February 1943	21
Saloman Shotland	Tromso	Bookkeeper	11 February 1943	40

Name	From	Profession	Date of murder	Age
Hermann Smith	Tromso	Merchant	13 February 1943	36
Israel Steinfeld	Alesund	Merchant	15 May 1943	53
Herman Valner	Oslo	Merchant	20 December 1942	54
Josef Weinberg	Oslo	Merchant	22 January 1943	57

Also in respectful memory of those unknown.

THE BEAST

The *Windrush's* next mission would keep her in Norwegian waters, where she became the peripatetic servant of the Nazi pocket battleship *Tirpitz*. For some this name will mean little; for others it is infamous, along with the *Scharnhorst* and the *Bismarck* – ships dreaded by naval and merchant seamen alike.

For a generation of British children raised after the war on comics such as *The Victor* and *Commando*, *Tirpitz* was a name to be hissed and booed. The very sound of the word fulfilled the linguistic stereotypes the British comics kept alive through the yelled utterances of caricature square-helmeted Germans: '*Achtung*', '*Gott in Himmel*' and, above all, '*Schweinhund*'. Arguably, exposure to this discourse may have infected the British perception of Germany in the past, and may well continue to do so until the 1960s and 1970s generation of war-comic readers passes away some time in the mid-twenty-first century.

In early 2019, Tom Enders, the German-born CEO of aeronautical giant Airbus, warned in an open letter of the dire economic consequences of a no-deal British crash out of the European Union. For his pains he was attacked by Conservative MP Mark Francois on 25 January 2019 live on BBC News. Francois began by describing Enders as 'a German paratrooper in his youth' – a youth that would, of course, have been spent decades after the end of the Second World War.

The member for Rayleigh & Wickford in Essex continued:

I'm a patriotic Englishman, but I'd never dream of telling a German MP how to vote in the Bundestag and I think Mr Enders should pay us the same courtesy. Mr Enders' intervention is a classic example of the sort of Teutonic arrogance, which is one of the reasons why many people voted to leave the European Union. If he thinks because he runs a big company he can bully British MPs how to vote, he is going to be sorely mistaken. My father Reginald Francois was a D-Day veteran, he never submitted to bullying by any German, neither will his son. So if Mr Enders is watching, that's what he can do with his letter.

And with that Francois ripped a copy of the letter into shreds. Some may wonder what his Conservative predecessor and enthusiast for a European project, Winston Churchill, would have made of that. Indeed, was letter-ripping by his Right Honourable son one of the freedoms Reg Francois had in mind in May 1945? *Gott in Himmel!*

By the standards of the world's navies in the 1940s, the *Tirpitz* was a 'beast', as Churchill always referred to her. Designed for speed, resistance to attack and devastating destruction, she cost 191.6 million Reichsmarks to manufacture, and could achieve a top speed of 29 knots – a knot faster even than her short-lived sister, the *Bismarck*. At a speed of 19 knots her range was 8,870 nautical miles and her gross registered tonnage was 28,160 tons.

The *Tirpitz* bristled with weaponry. Her main battery was eight massive guns, set in four turrets each with twin 15-inchers. The turrets facing forward were named 'Anton' and 'Bruno', and the turrets aft of the superstructure were 'Caesar' and 'Dora'. These turrets were electrically directed, and the guns themselves were elevated hydraulically. Their range was a terrifying 22 miles.

Her secondary weaponry was twelve 5.9in guns paired in six turrets. These could fire a 100lb shell 14 miles. Also on deck were sixteen 4.1in anti-aircraft guns, and sixteen 1.5in light anti-aircraft guns.

Whereas 'Anton' *et al.* had to be manually reloaded and at best could fire three shells a minute, these smaller guns could fire eighty. The ship also had twelve 20mm anti-aircraft machine guns, able to fire 120 rounds per minute.[1]

Every spare foot of deck was weaponised, and this power was matched by her armour. She was armour plated with Krupp cemented steel, containing 0.34 per cent carbon, 3.78 per cent nickel, 2.06 per cent chrome and 0.31 per cent manganese. This plating ranged from 8.7 to 12.6in thick, around the armoured deck, and 2.6 to 4.7in below. However, the forward conning tower was even more protected, with 14in of thickness and 7.9in on its roof.

To add to her self-protection, she carried four Arado Ar 196 seaplanes for reconnaissance and patrol. These low-wing monoplanes also carried heavy weaponry and had the potential to carry two 110lb bombs. Without the dedicated airplane deck of a carrier, the Arados had to be catapulted on launch, before landing back in the sea on their return, winched aboard and stored in hangers.

The *Tirpitz* was a ship no British sailor would wish to meet on a dark night in the middle of the sea.

Of course, by building such a ship Hitler was knowingly breaking multiple agreements under the Treaty of Versailles of 1919 – in particular article 190. But the Germans had being playing tricks with this for a decade. Under article 191, for example, they had been specifically prohibited from building submarines, so instead three German companies combined to back a Dutch submarine company, and thus had access to all its intelligence on construction as the Dutch happily built submarines for the Turkish, Finnish and Spanish governments. As each submarine was completed the Nazis possessed every blueprint and specification they would ever need.

The most blatant breach of all was the building of the so-called pocket battleships like the *Tirpitz*. These ships, the Bismarck class, just about qualified under the 10,000-ton net weight limit agreed at Versailles. However, with their extraordinary armoury and weaponry they were brutal battleships in all but scale. Indeed, being designed smaller meant they were even faster and more lethal at sea, although the *Tirpitz* was still a sixth of a mile long.

Tirpitz's twin sister, *Bismarck*, was knocked off the blocks on 14 February 1939, at the very same Hamburg shipyard at Blohm & Voss from which the *Windrush* had been launched eight years earlier. Where once Blohm & Voss had made oceangoing pleasure cruisers, now it was creating the most aggressive vessels ever to have been put to sea.

Back in London on 31 March 1939, Neville Chamberlain told the House of Commons that Britain would automatically defend Poland in the event of any invasion to a chorus of 'hear, hear!' Perhaps under the law of unintended consequences, this spurred Hitler the very next day to make an even more bull-headed speech than usual when he launched the *Tirpitz*.

Arriving in Wilhelmshaven on the morning of 1 April 1939 in an open-topped Mercedes, and seeming to relish the thousands of stooges lined up to wave swastika flags, he made use of the occasion to declare that 'he who declares himself ready to pull the chestnuts out of the fire for these powers [i.e. Poland] must realise he burns his fingers'. There would be no backing down for either side – four months later they were at war.

Finding someone to accept the honour of naming the ship by smashing a bottle on her side proved troublesome for the Third Reich. Germans of the old guard, more at ease in the Weimar days, were still processing the fact that their head of state now held the powers of both president and prime minister; they took subtle care not to overtly endorse the Nazis unless forced to. The ship was named after the late Alfred Peter Ferdinand von Tirpitz, once a great favourite of Kaiser Wilhelm III, who promoted him rapidly to the rank of Secretary of State of the German Imperial Navy.

Von Tirpitz's career was initially meteoric and was then shattered by disappointment. Becoming a Grand Admiral in 1911, he had devised a seventeen-year plan for the German navy to rule the waves. He did not expect the First World War to break out just three years later, interrupting his schedule and leaving his ambitions in shreds. Blamed for the dreadful stalemate at the Battle of Jutland – a stand-off costing 6,000 British lives and 2,500 German – he left his post in 1916. Finished as a sailor, he turned to politics. He was never reconciled to Versailles and so became a senior member of the German National People's Party, and the first to beat the nationalist and expansionist drum. He died in 1930, with his party propping up the Nazis in coalitions in many German states. Von Tirpitz was Hitler's type of German.

Predictably, the brand-obsessed Nazis wanted one of von Tirpitz's own family to launch the ship, but his widow refused, as at first did her two daughters. Eventually, the Nazis prevailed and one of the daughters, Frau von Hassell, took the role. Just over three years later, Hitler thanked her for this by executing her husband, Ulrich (by then German ambassador to Rome) for his role in the 20 July plot to assassinate Hitler.

From the start, Hitler feared for his new ship. This dread was combined with a paranoia that his Achilles heel in the theatre of war would prove to be a possible Allied invasion of Norway, even after the British debacle of 1940. The Norwegian coast was hundreds of miles long and, although landing armies in the fjords was not straightforward, Hitler was convinced that it was impossible to defend every potential invasion point. 'Every ship that does not lie in Norway is in the wrong place,' he said.

At first, Hitler's fear for the ship prevailed over his worries about Norway. He wasn't willing to allow the *Tirpitz* to leave the safe waters of the Baltic for anywhere, and for nearly two years the battleship did little more than pootle about out of harm's way, her movements reported back by British reconnaissance planes to a relieved British government.

Captain Karl Topp took command in January 1941, and for most of the rest of that year he tested her to the limits. Following the *Tirpitz* around like a loyal hound was the *Windrush*. She bobbed nearby, offering further supplies and transportation while her master tested her big guns, fired her anti-aircraft weapons at a drogue pulled by aircraft, released torpedoes and launched then recovered the Avro seaplanes.

For months on end, to replicate conditions at sea the *Tirpitz* was not allowed to come into port and the *Windrush* travelled back and forth from Kiel to wherever her master was manoeuvring, topping up her provisions, bringing out fresh engineering personnel when required and helping bring the gallons of oil devoured during this odd latent period. But on 7 January 1942, according to Enigma decrypts, the captain advised his naval command that on 10 January he would have completed every possible test and trial and would be ready to go into full service on the high seas. *Tirpitz* returned to Wilhelmshaven on 15 January accompanied by the *Windrush*, then on 17 January, with an escort of four destroyers, made her way to Trondheim, about one-third of the way up the Norwegian coast, for the place that would become her regular berth in the coming years, Fættenfjorden.

At last she was going to play a role in Norway, even if her Führer was too afraid to send her into battle. It now became apparent that, despite the huge cost of her construction and the thousands of man hours making her ready for battle, the *Tirpitz*'s destiny was to become what had been referred to for hundreds of years as a 'fleet-in-being'. Under this strange idea, an enemy's awareness that their opponent possesses such an enormous ship will prevent them from taking aggressive action themselves. In other words, by staying put in harbour, just the knowledge that the *Tirpitz* was there would alter Allied behaviour – a passive-aggressive deterrent.

To a great extent this worked. Churchill was obsessed with making sure the *Tirpitz* did not escape out into the Atlantic to attack the convoys to and from the USA and Canada. Therefore, he retained dozens of his own powerful ships in the North Sea, which were in fact always desperately needed in both the Mediterranean and Far East theatres. Meanwhile, even in this passive role, the *Tirpitz* was able to keep safe the vital supplies of iron ore and nickel being ferried down the coast from northern Norway, providing a healthy disincentive to any British ships thinking of sinking these German merchantmen. Set back in the jagged fjords just a few minutes' fast sail from the open sea, she lurked like a spider on a skirting board.

It is certain, though, that Captain Topp hoped he would not be spending the war moored in a Norwegian fjord in what any proud naval captain would consider as a less-than-distinguished role. His great hope, expressed to Hitler in person on the day he had taken command, was to be allowed to join the fray in the Battle of the Atlantic. His hopes were greatly diminished when the British sank the *Bismarck* on 27 May 1941 – a loss that made Hitler cleave to the *Tirpitz* even tighter. Topp meanwhile clung to the idea that his Führer might change his mind. How could Hitler resist the idea of this stunning ship breaking out either north of Scotland or even straight down the English Channel, leaving all Allied pursuers in her wake, ready to pick off Atlantic convoys at will?

On 28 March 1942, Topp's hopes were finally dashed. The British had pulled off the destruction of the only port in occupied western France big enough for her to berth, St-Nazaire, which had been expanded to allow for the great peacetime French cruiser *Normandie*. The British loaded 3 tons of explosive on to HMS *Campbeltown* and, in a commando mission much celebrated in later years, left Falmouth, crossed the Channel and sailed her all the way up the mouth of the Loire until she was challenged by the enemy and identified herself by using German Morse code.

The Germans only became aware of her mission eight minutes before, at which point awesome firepower was directed at her. Of the 611 men on the *Campbeltown* and the commando craft in support, 169 were killed, 215 were captured and 228 managed to escape back to England on the motor launches. There were five awards of the Victoria Cross, two posthumous. But as in so many stories of war, although it was a great military success that indeed stranded the *Tirpitz* in Norway, unexpected suffering was caused. The ensuing reconstruction efforts of the St-Nazaire basin (not completed before the end of the war) were undertaken by slave labour dragooned under Operation Todt from concentration camps and the captive fit males of conquered countries.[2]

But as far as the *Tirpitz* was concerned, that was that. She never would reach the Atlantic. For the next two years the *Windrush* served her, at first like a loyal butler, but increasingly as a triage nurse as the battleship moved from fjord to fjord attempting to repel Allied attacks, a sitting duck.

On board the *Tirpitz* herself a dangerous torpor began to take hold amongst the sailors tired of the fjord views. Finally, one morning the ship's muster was taken and a young anti-aircraft gunner called Turowski was found to be AWOL. Captured ashore the next day, he was asked by Captain Topp at his court martial to explain himself. Turowski simply said that he had deserted because he was bored – that nothing ever happened. Topp wrote to his admiral for permission to perform the necessary punishment on the *Tirpitz* to set an example to the other men.

The next day, 18-year-old Turowski was blindfolded and shot dead by a team of his former comrades.[3]

11

FIRE IN THE CHIMNEY

Though the tragic Turowski found himself bored as a sailor in a ship which hardly ever took to the open seas, the *Tirpitz* remained a constant preoccupation for the British. Shivering under hundreds of yards of camouflage netting, she wouldn't be easy even to locate. But if she was and waves of Halifax and Lancaster bombers were sent to try to sink her, the ship's primary and primitive defensive tactic of throwing up a smokescreen caused complete confusion. Captain Topp made it his last mission on the *Tirpitz* to raise the defensive proficiency of her crew. He was then promoted to a role alongside Albert Speer under the rank of Konteradmiral as the Commissioner for Shipbuilding, and early in 1943 was replaced by the one-armed Captain Hans Mayer.

On the slopes of whichever fjord she was hiding in, dozens of crew stood ready with massive artificial smoke generators, calculating the prevailing winds and ready to initiate at a few minutes' notice. If one of the Avro biplanes patrolling above the fjord saw a Lancaster or Halifax approaching, a signal was sent and within moments the fjord disappeared into a smoke cloud. It was effective, but deeply neurotic. The British might come from the west from an east coast airbase, or from the northeast out of a Russian airbase near the Arctic Circle. It was gruelling, boring, but effective.

From the British perspective, this failure to sink a stationary target continued to cause consternation to Churchill and his War Cabinet.

Ultimately, for the PQ.17 convoy, it led to great disaster. The merchant convoy had gathered in Hvalfjörður north of Reykjavik in Iceland. It comprised thirty-four merchant vessels and four support ships, intending to resupply the Russians as they fought to defend Stalingrad.

The PQ.17 convoy was to be protected on its voyage to Archangel, going to the north of Bear Island, by six destroyers, four corvettes, three mine-sweepers, four trawlers, two anti-aircraft ships and two submarines.[1] It was attacked from the outset and, worse, the British intercepted Kriegsmarine messages seeming to suggest that the *Tirpitz* would join in too. One confirmatory message followed by an apparent countermand followed by the other – this confusing picture was unwisely communicated to the commanders of PQ.17. Finally, the Admiralty decided that the ships of the convoy were too big a target for the *Tirpitz* to miss if she was on her way. Tragically, the order was given that PQ.17 should scatter – the worst possible order for any convoy. Scattering was always a desperate last resort; it diluted all defensive solidarity, leaving individual ships isolated, easy prey.

However, throughout all this time, the *Tirpitz* remained at anchor at Altenfjord (now Altafjord). Not knowing this, PQ.17 had panicked and dispersed over 25 nautical miles ready to be picked off. At this moment an exhilarated Captain Topp believed he had received an order to join in the fight and claim as many scalps as he could, but almost immediately intelligence was received suggesting a British aeroplane had seen his ship. Hitler's absolute rule was that she was not to set sail if there was any chance a nearby aircraft carrier might carry out an attack in open sea. The *Tirpitz* was told to retreat back under her humiliating netting.

For the Allies, however, terrible damage was done. PQ.17 was attacked by U-boats and by the Luftwaffe on 5 July 1942. Twenty-four merchant ships were lost and 153 sailors died. Of the vital military supplies bound for the Soviet Union, 3,358 vehicles, 430 tanks and 210 aircraft that had been loaded in Iceland were now at the bottom of the sea. And without firing a shell, the *Tirpitz* had caused the chaos that led to this. Now the British were determined to sink her, and once again the *Windrush* would be brought into history in the aftermath of what was called Operation Source.

The pressure from Churchill was unceasing. Ultra intercepts disclosed that by January 1943 the *Tirpitz*, with the *Windrush* in her usual supply mode, had been refitted and was performing gunnery trials in Trondheim fjord. The Prime Minister wrote to the Chief of Combined Operations, to the First Sea Lord, to the chiefs of the Air Staff and to Bomber Command, pleading:

> Have you given up on all plans of doing anything to the *Tirpitz*? We heard a lot of talk about it five months ago which all petered out. I should be much obliged if you would take stock of the position, if possible together, and thereafter to give me a report. It is a terrible thing that this prize should be waiting, and no one able to think of a way of winning it.[2]

By March 1943, the German navy was becoming concerned too that it was never seriously deploying its most dangerous weapon. *Tirpitz* was ordered to sail north to Kåfjord, east of Tromsø, and from there in September she fired her only ever salvos when she was engaged in a 'sledgehammer to crack a nut' operation attacking a meteorological outpost at Spitsbergen.

As the Strength Through Joy passengers coming ashore in Spitsbergen from the *Windrush* had discovered six or seven years earlier, it was little more than a collection of old whalers' huts. From these, Norwegian and British scientists had been sending weather reports crucial to the convoys heading from Britain below the Arctic Circle to supply the Russians at Archangel and Murmansk. Six weathermen were captured and thousands of gallons of precious fuel were expended but at least the bully boat was allowed to flex her muscles.

The British, though, took serious note, and urged on by their leader, came up with a plan to send miniature submarines into whichever Norwegian fjord *Tirpitz* was lurking in. The concept was to affix magnetic explosive charges to her hull on a time delay, make an escape and look on as the 'Beast' was blown sky high. This was Operation Source, and in the early summer of 1943, these small two-man craft were towed from their place of origin in Portsmouth to the Kyle of Bute and finally on to Loch Cairnbawn near Drumbeg. At 4 p.m. on 11 September 1943, six submarines each with a midget sub, or X-craft, in tow, made for Kåfjord – a finger of the Altenfjord.

In a manoeuvre worthy of the *Commando* comic, one of the two successful X-craft broke into the fjord by following in the wake of a coaster passing into the entrance gate as a ferryboat passed out. X6 and X7 simply improvised and followed into the fjord in the coaster's wake. Both craft managed to successfully lay charges on a one-hour fuse, but were unable to break back out through the torpedo nets on the way to the sea; they were tangled up just 100 yards from the *Tirpitz* with their predicament spotted by the Germans, who accepted their surrender. The British submariners waited anxiously on board knowing that in minutes the explosive charges they had just attached to the *Tirpitz*'s hull were set to blow up under their feet.

The unaware German naval officers did their best to interrogate the submariners, but the phlegmatic British refused to help. Edmund Goddard, one of the captured X-craft men, later recalled:

> They lined us up before a group of guards with Tommy guns … then an interpreter asked how many boats there were and so on, but we just gave them our numbers. He got very annoyed and said that if we didn't play he'd have to shoot us. He pointed at Lorimer and said to me, if you don't give the information, I shall have to shoot your comrade too. Oh well, I said, you go ahead and shoot him.[3]

The captain realised these men wouldn't talk and gave them coffee and schnapps. A little later the explosives blew up, killing one man and wounding fifty. The damage to the ship was not fatal, but it was crippling. None of the three propeller shafts would now function, control instruments had been destroyed and two of the mighty turrets containing Anton, Bertha, Caesar and Dora were destroyed.

The captives were sent off to POW camps in Germany, while the Germans were left to deal with the havoc the X-craft had caused. Meanwhile, the *Tirpitz* needed to be repaired. The usual practice would have been to limp south back to dry dock at Wilhelmshaven under tow. But this would have meant that for a thousand miles she would be a slow-moving target for every British plane, ship and submarine in the area, and it could be certain that Churchill would not have failed to seize this opportunity to be rid of the ship for good.

Therefore, the *Windrush* was enlisted yet again to assist in what was still a relatively new engineering technique: full-scale restoration while still at sea. This was to be carried out under the supervision of a Herr Krux, director of German shipping repairs. He convinced Grand Admiral Dönitz that repairs could be conducted in situ, with the added advantage that by not moving her the British would not discover the true extent of the damage.

So, in early October 1943, the *Windrush* carried hundreds of engineers, welders, electricians and fitters from Kiel to Altenfjord, and continued to ply a route to and fro until the following February. Some of the *Tirpitz* crew slept on the *Windrush*, whilst others were allowed to stay ashore.

The engineers she had brought mended the three propeller shafts by creating a void area via a coffer dam, draining out all the water around them so that work could go ahead in safety. The damaged rudder was fixed in this way too. This also allowed access to mend holes in the ship's hull, which were sealed with water-resistant cement. Conditions were deeply hostile all winter while the men laboured, with just a few hours of available daylight, mainly under electric lamps feeding off the ship's generators.

The British didn't know it, but the X-craft had dealt such a blow to the *Tirpitz* that the Germans realised she could never sail out on the high seas again. She would become a battery ship – little more than a floating gun emplacement.

For the *Windrush*, however, there was no option to remain as deep as possible into a fjord under the cover of smoke and netting. Repeatedly, she had to make her way up and down hundreds of miles of Norwegian coast before turning east into Oslo to replenish the *Tirpitz's* crew and supplies, or heading further to Kiel for engineering parts and technicians. The danger of her acquiring the status of a serious target was very real.

On 1 April 1944, the British press reported that, under her then identity as the *Monte Rosa*, the *Windrush* had just come under Allied attack the day before:[4]

PLANES TORPEDO NAZI LINER

Two torpedo hits were obtained by Coastal Command Beaufighters during an attack on Thursday night on a heavily-escorted German liner off the Norwegian coast.

Two escort vessels are also believed to have been damaged and at least one Me 110 shot down, says the Air Ministry News Service. Two Beaufighters are missing.

First attack on the ship, the former 14,000-ton liner Monte Rosa, was made when the liner, bound for Germany, was hugging the coast with an escort of three flak ships and 15 fighters.

Second attack was made after midnight. At that time the liner was proceeding at reduced speed.

There are no German merchant navy records available which record whether anyone was killed or injured on the *Windrush* as a consequence of this attack, but it is hard to conceive that if she was hit as claimed there were not significant casualties. It had been a serious and premeditated attack. British Intelligence, through the Ultra signals monitoring programme, had become aware of the work the *Windrush* was engaged in. She may have just been a merchant ship, but by sustaining the *Tirpitz*, which was still regarded as a great threat, she had become a legitimate target herself.

The press did not report details at the time, but later it was established just how concerted an attack it had been.[5] The *Windrush* had been sailing near the Norwegian island of Utsira, famous then and now as the best spot for ornithologists in Scandinavia. She was on her way back to Kiel as part of a convoy with three flak ships and a destroyer, all overseen by fifteen German Messerschmitt Me 110 fighter planes.

The attack came from eighteen aircraft, nine from RAF 144 Squadron, of which five were loaded with torpedoes, and another nine from the Royal Canadian Air Force (RCAF) 404 Squadron, which bore armour-piercing RP-3 rockets. The planes were all Bristol Beaufighters, which were one of the main weapons of RAF Coastal Command, itself a separate section of the RAF with a brief to defend Allied convoys. They also used their offensive torpedo-carrying capacity to sink Axis supply ships just like the *Windrush*.

The RAF Beaufighters took off from Wick in Caithness in the far north-east of Scotland. The RCAF planes flew from Thorney Island in Chichester Harbour. One plane from each was lost in the attack, with a claim that one of the Messerschmitts was destroyed too.

The *Windrush* took heavy hits: two torpedoes were claimed to have struck her, with eight rockets on target as well as much strafing with cannon fire. Her accompanying flak ships fired back, but for her own part she was defenceless. Despite this, she managed to limp on to Aarhus in occupied Denmark.

No sooner had she reached port than news came through that even if she had stayed by the *Tirpitz*'s side she would have been just as likely to have been damaged there. On 3 April 1944, the Allies launched Operation Tungsten. It arose from a significant development in the British capacity to launch planes carrying sufficiently damaging heavy bombs from an aircraft carrier. Now, nine Barracuda attack planes could carry a new 1,600lb bomb, while another twenty-two would carry 500-pounders.

The Fleet Air Arm trained for two months until they launched the attack from the carriers HMS *Victorious* and HMS *Furious*. The *Tirpitz* was hit fifteen times, killing 122 and wounding 316. This was 15 per cent of the crew, including the wounded Captain Mayer, who never served again, and was replaced by the apparently unpopular Captain Junge.[6]

Once again, the patched-up *Windrush* was despatched north to Altenfjord with Werner Krux, the naval engineer, who assessed that she could be repaired but never be battleworthy again, not least because yet again the *Windrush* and other ships would need to spend the rest of April and May bringing more than 150 skilled workmen from Kiel. However, despite their efforts, the *Tirpitz* was now living on borrowed time.

The *Tirpitz* while isolated in Norway's fjords had been targeted by the British a total of eight times in less than three years. Like a whale struck over and over again by multiple harpoon shots, all that was left now was to finish her off. In whaling terminology it is called 'Fire in the Chimney', when the final lance is thrust into the blowhole causing a spurt of red blood to burst out over the creature's own head.

Nemesis would come in the form of Barnes Wallis, famous for creating the bouncing bombs of the Dambuster raids, who had just invented a 6-ton bomb, the Tallboy, which could be carried by reinforced Lancasters. So heavy were they that there was no way they could fly from Britain to Norway and then return, so it was agreed they would fly from Scotland to the Russian Yagodnik airfield near Archangel and then mount the operation to Kåfjord from there.

On 15 September 1944, under Operation Paravone, just one of these bombs dropped from twenty-seven Lancasters actually hit, but the damage left the *Tirpitz* crippled for life, holed above and below the waterline. A few days later the German naval command accepted that all she was good for now was as a floating battery – a hunk of metal studded with weaponry that would be hauled to a strategically useful place and take on her role as a gun replacement.

Sufficient repairs were made to allow her to meander her way out of Kåfjord to the island of Håkøya near Tromsø. Fatally, this move also brought her 200 miles closer to Britain, and into range of direct attacks by the Lancasters. Although it was perfectly well understood by the British that she no longer presented a threat, Churchill wrote on 26 October 1944 to the Admiralty, 'I think it will be regarded as a very serious misfortune if the *Tirpitz* succeeds in returning to Germany. I consider that every effort should be made to attack this ship. Even if losses have to be incurred.'

So finally, on 12 September 1944, twenty-nine Lancasters were ordered to fly east off from RAF Lossiemouth in Scotland in the direction of Tromsø.

In our age of information technology, with the heightened paranoia that malevolent forces own our data and wish to turn it against us, it may be salutary to remember that advanced spying technology is nothing new. Back in the 1940s, the British Admiralty had been able to maintain a day-by-day diary on the *Tirpitz* from her launch at Wilhelmshaven under Hitler's mad eye, via her single pathetic venture out to attack the meteorological huts in Spitsbergen, to her final destruction.

Reconnaissance planes, land-based spies across Scandinavia and a consistent flow of intelligence from Norwegian fishermen all meant that the ship had no real chance of discreetly hiding away in the fjords. Tightening the noose were the stunning intercepts by the Ultra programme. The *Tirpitz* hardly sent or received a radio signal without someone in Buckinghamshire deciphering it and couriering this on to the Admiralty. In a number of these intercepts, the time was taken to add the detail that the *Windrush* was alongside her too.[7]

When the British were not able to obtain intelligence that predicted every movement, they debriefed everyone concerned in rigorous postmortems. Ultimately, they were able to obtain the personal report from Kapitänleutnant (captain-lieutenant) Fassbender who constructed the dramatic moment-by-moment account of the hours between 8 a.m. on 12 November 1944 and 9.52 a.m. when the *Tirpitz* capsized.

At 8 a.m., Fassbender recorded that it was 'a clear, cloudless day with good visibility'.

A few minutes later, the ship began to receive reports of Lancaster bombers approaching the fjord.

At 9 a.m. they knew they must be the target, and requested air support from the Luftwaffe urgently. This never came.

At 9.27 a.m., the alarm sounded: 'Captain to All. We are expecting a heavy air attack, and the ship's company of the *Tirpitz* will again fulfil its duty and prepare a hot reception for the four-engined bombers.'

A minute later the command was given for all *Tirpitz's* many ferocious guns to fire at will. But at 9.42 a.m., the Tallboys struck. 'There is a marked decrease in defensive fire due to casualties in material and personnel,' recorded Fassbender. She was done for.

Then, at 9.52 a.m., Fassbender said:

> The ship capsizes to port and is lying at an angle of about 135 degrees. A small number of the crew were able to remain on the capsizing ship. The rest of the men on the upper deck tried to reach land by swimming it with the assistance of floats or objects drifting around. After about a quarter hour the first rescue vessels arrived.[8]

An officer remembered the rest. Oberfähnrich zur See Bernstein[9] was trapped in the hull of the ship as she capsized. With fellow survivors, Bernstein crawled his way in the dark to the near-empty oil tanks that the *Windrush* had once helped to repair and replenish. The survivors started to tap out in Morse code that there were sixteen of them trapped there. Eight hours later, they were rescued, being cut out through the hull.

Others were not so lucky. Of the 1,700 men who awoke that morning, 971 were dead by afternoon. The last great German battleship was no more.

❖

In Hitler's determination to create such a monster lay her tragedy. *Tirpitz* was doomed from conception by his neurotic hubris to idle impotently in the lee of fjords – protected seaward by torpedo nets and from the hills above by anti-aircraft batteries – even though her enemy knew precisely where she was for almost every second of her life. Her preservation was an obsession for Hitler, and metaphorically he locked her in the attic until the inevitable outcome.

Equally, the desire for her destruction burned in Churchill's mind just as fervently. From the hour he heard that she had first sailed through the Kiel canal in January 1942 and had successfully reached the Norwegian coast at Fættenfjorden he repeatedly expressed his anxiety: 'The destruction or even crippling of this ship is the greatest event at sea at the present time. No other target is comparable to it. I regard this matter as of the highest importance.'[10]

In just three and a half years of the *Tirpitz*'s fleet-in-being role in Norway, the *Windrush* and other merchant ships were obliged to clear up after no fewer than eight full-frontal assaults by the British. In these attacks hundreds of servicemen from both sides lost their young lives. As so often in the life of the *Windrush*, she had found herself close to one of the most dramatic events in world history, in which, perhaps not understood at first, there were also concealed the seeds of change.

In his memoir, Grand Admiral Dönitz wrote:

After the loss of the *Tirpitz* the surface ships of the German navy were unable to take any further part in the war at sea. Here, indeed, was a clear indication that the Air Arm was becoming an ever-increasing menace to heavy warships. This was a development which finally led to the paying off of the British and American battleships in 1958.[11]

The news of her loss travelled the world within twenty-four hours. The *Windrush* returned to her role as a transporter ship in Norway. In Oslo, she had become as hated as any German battleship.

The Norwegian resistance could stand this no longer.

12

MAX MANUS

Individual characters react to war in different ways. It is often wondered if the methods of war leaders derive from their psyches formed through particular experiences in their earlier years. Hitler's failure as an artist in Austria is often cited. If his watercolours had sold in Vienna, would he have been sitting down in Vienna's Café Central in 1938 chatting to Sigmund Freud over a *heisse schokolade*, rather than annexing Austria, exiling Freud and murdering 200,000 Viennese Jews?

Likewise, might Vidkun Quisling have followed a path other than the one which led to his name being ranked second after only Judas as a moniker for a man who would betray his own? What if he'd taken up cross-country skiing, rather than festering in his gloomy Protestant home developing a wholly deluded sense of both his own uniqueness and that of the Norwegian 'people'? Would he then have been able to avoid becoming the puppet of the equally deluded but also psycho-pathic Nazi Alfred Rosenberg?[1] It was Rosenberg who offered Quisling a Mephistolean pact. In return for power, he'd have to accept being in ultimate service of Adolf Hitler.

All three men were and remain villains to the Norwegian people. Their national hero, who most British people have never heard of, is Max Manus, the man who tried to destroy the *Windrush* so that it could not inflict cruelty on any more lives. He was the man who nearly succeeded in sending her into the deep, the man who might also have denied the Windrush generation their name. His character was not formed by bitter personal failure or delusions of grandeur as a child. His character had a much more modern origin.

Maximo Guillermo Manus was born on 9 December 1914, and he was raised in a family destined for an unamicable divorce, which was unusual in those days. In his early teens, he was sent to Cuba by his father to toughen up, and as a result became profoundly independent, resourceful and allergic to any such temptations as Norwegian fascism, which he regarded as obviously vile but also ludicrous. The school of hard knocks created a hero.

A man of both his and our times, Max realised that in occupied Norway, with newspapers censored and free-speech radio banned by Quisling's Nazis, there was a need for an underground press. He and his associates decided to write, edit and distribute an illegal free news-sheet. They moved fast but on the day he was back at his flat with the galleys for the first edition in his rucksack, it was raided by the Gestapo. As if in a dark cartoon, Max reacted by running across his sitting room and leaping out of a second-floor window. Unable to move, he was caught and incarcerated in a hospital, until a week later he escaped from that too, out of another window.

The next stage of Max's journey to freedom is one of the least known epics of the Second World War. Somehow he needed to escape Oslo and get to London, where both a government-in-exile and massive British support for future missions were awaiting him. These days, a flight from Oslo to London takes between two and two and a half hours. Then, no such flight was available, and all sea and land routes were choked with Germans.

So, first, like Irene Levin Berman, Max smuggled himself into neutral Sweden, where he made contact with London. From there he went to Helsinki, across to Leningrad and took trains south to Constanza on the Romanian Black Sea. He took a ferry across the sea to Istanbul, which he described as 'a nest of spies',[2] then a British steamer – twice strafed by German fighters – down the eastern Mediterranean to Port Said.

On he went through the canal, down the east coast of Africa to the Cape, then up to Trinidad, New York, Halifax in Nova Scotia and from there to Lunenburg on the Canadian coast. As if from an adventure story, many Norwegian compatriots were there too, having managed to escape the Germans in their whaling ships. One of these was a captain from Bergen, whose ship hooked up with an Allied convoy and ferried him all the way to London. The entire trip from Stockholm to London had taken Max seven months.

Now he was there, he was determined to get the training and resources to be able to go back to Oslo and sink the hated *Windrush*, which had become despised as a German troop transporter but now, after taking the Jews to Germany, was reviled. Every time it berthed in the harbour it was a reminder to Max that the country he loved had failed to protect its own people.

As soon as he arrived in Britain, Max was enlisted in the First Norwegian Independence Company. They received exhaustive training or, as Max put it, 'we were turned scientifically into criminals'.[3] Nothing was omitted, and they became proficient in knifecraft, strangulation, poisoning, shooting, parachuting and, particularly impressive to Max, lying. Their main aim was to be the destruction of ships back in Oslo.

In the midst of all this preparation, Max was driven down to meet the exiled Norwegian King Haakon, residing at that point in the Dorset seaside town of Bournemouth. This encounter imbued him with a notably patriotic fervour. Max recalled:

We left him with an overmastering feeling that we loved King Haakon more than anything else on earth, and that if he asked anything of us we would do it even at the cost of our lives. Ever since that meeting I have been better able to understand how it is that the Japanese suicide airmen dive down joyfully to certain death.[4]

The final part of Max's training was specific to what would become the attack on the *Windrush*: 'The plan was to lie on our backs in rubber suits and in the darkness of the night glide into harbour to sink ships with limpets.'[5]

In order to breathe they were given the Davis escape apparatus, which was a small bottle of oxygen worn on the chest with a mouth-piece and a clip for the nose. This allowed for up to three-quarters of an hour underwater.

The limpet mines were set up for delayed detonation: a spring was restrained by a steel arm held back by a firing pin encased in salt, which would take half an hour to dissolve under water; this would then release itself without the salt barrier and trigger an explosion. Max met other fighters also being trained in this limpet mine technology from Yugoslavia, Greece, France, Holland, Poland, Czechoslovakia and Denmark, as well as more of his fellow Norwegians.

Finally, the men were kitted out in tailored civilian garb and, as their faces were on wanted posters all over Norway, their appearances were changed by a make-up artist. Max became convinced that he must have had Jewish ancestry because, using expressions of the time, 'I looked like the very worst Jewish jitterbug dancer who ever appeared in a show … It was quite incredible. And here I was going to Oslo at the height of Jewish persecution!'[6]

The next day, Max and his best friend Gregers were parachuted into a wilderness area outside of Norway. The attack on the *Windrush* was on.

Max Manus and his resistance friends hated all Nazis operations, but they had grown impatient in particular to see the destruction of two ships more than any others: the *Donau* and the *Windrush*. They were fully aware of the history of the vessels both in the invasion of Norway and more recently in the transportation of Norway's Jews. With his pro-nounced loathing of injustice of any kind, Max had been determined to act. He wrote later that he was never prepared to risk his own or anyone else's life without good reason, but the prospect of sinking the *Windrush* was in a different category.

Max's cause was helped by the existence of another counter-Nazi cell, the Oslo Marines, who kept records of every ship movement from the port, including the cargo and the number of troops on board. Max had a particular contact called 'Ivar', who was very familiar with an area known in peacetime as the America Line's jetty. Ivar advised that the jetty was mounted on a large concrete sub-structure, along which, if Max could get down there, he could move freely from one side to the other. He and his collaborator, Gregers, could even hide down there for days on end until the *Windrush* arrived in harbour.

But first they needed to sneak their equipment and explosives into the dockyards close to the America Line's jetty. Max planned to pull this plot off as a duo with Gregers, and yet again their methods resemble those of a far-fetched plot from a war comic.

Their first task was to procure a tradesmen's van, for which Ivar provided two workmen's passes to allow them on to the jetty. They then borrowed a second lorry, which would hoot impatiently behind them if German guards took too long examining these passes or seemed to want to look inside the van. Their contingency plan, their only backup if it all went wrong, was simply to screech away in the van with Gregers firing off every round available in the direction of the receding German guards.

Fortunately, it did not come to that. The Germans did decide to open the back of the van, and if they had looked properly they would have found twelve limpet mines, a rubber suit, Sten guns and hundreds of rounds of ammunition. Seeing the Germans start to rummage, the lorry driver in the vehicle behind – not part of the gang but prevailed upon to do them this one favour – parped impatiently on his horn. This irked the Germans so much that they immediately dismounted, waved Max and Gregers through, and became very irate with the lorry driver. They searched his vehicle from top to bottom, which of course contained nothing but legitimate goods. Apparently he even took the opportunity to complain about this colossal waste of his time.

Meanwhile, Max and Gregers drove to the side door of a warehouse giving access to the jetty, and hid their gear at the end of a blind alley under a tarpaulin, along which Ivar had said nobody ever ventured. They then got back in the van and calmly drove back out of the docks, Gregers singing their favourite battle song, *Beethoven's Ninth*.

On the morning of Saturday 27 June 1944, Max and Gregers gathered four days' worth of provisions, and a book each, and made ready to return to the jetty. The provisions were mostly water, biscuits and brandy. The books they independently chose were both by, of all authors, P.G. Wodehouse: *Thank You, Jeeves* and *Piccadilly Jim*. At that time, Wodehouse – to some a traitor for his wartime broadcasts from Berlin (which any thinking ear will realise were lampooning the Germans) and to others a man caught behind enemy lines at the wrong moment, a naïf in a cruel world – was marooned in occupied Paris. It is possible to understand his appeal to Max and Gregers at that dark time in the perfectly plotted comedies of Bertie Wooster, a likeable idiot being rescued by an infinitely wiser butler, Jeeves.

But Wodehouse had a sharp satirical edge too. J. Washburn Stoker is a crass American millionaire in *Thank you, Jeeves*, knowing the price of everything and the value of nothing, and of more contemporary relevance to the two anti-Nazis there is no finer spoof of the British fascist Oswald Mosley than Sir Roderick Spode in 1938's *The Code of the Woosters*, with his depleted followers, the Black Shorts. Wodehouse twisted the knife by making Spode the 7th Earl of Sidcup, which as a south-east Londoner would have struck him as a particularly belittling nomenclature for a self-declared supreme being.

Max and Gregers had a cover story as they hauled their heavy canvas bag containing the limpet mines across the base; they were there to mend an electric cable. Gregers even managed to persuade a sentry to help him carry a heavy tool box. When nobody was looking, they went to the edge of the jetty and climbed down a ladder to the water's edge. However, the underside of the jetty was not as described by Ivar at all; there were no gangplanks allowing movement from one side to the other.

Realising they'd need an inflatable boat to transport their gear to where it would be needed when the *Windrush* docked, they left the docks yet again and took a tram back to their flat. There, they folded up the inflatable into a small tight bundle, wrapped it in brown paper, attached it to a bicycle, and the pair of them cycled back to the docks, where their friend the sentry waved them through.

Back down the ladder, they loaded the boat and pushed along to a shelf, where they unloaded the Sten guns and some hand grenades and took off their overalls to reveal their Norwegian army uniforms. Max wrote:

> We loved our uniforms and were at heart a little envious of the regular soldiers who could fight openly, face to face, with the enemy, and were not obliged to do all sorts of rotten things as we were … for example, going to spend several days under this jetty among smells of foul water and floating excrement.[7]

For three days, they were plagued by enormous rats, the excrement, the risk of spikes attached to the underside of the jetty and a smell of 'old decomposed bodies'. As the pair awaited the arrival of the *Windrush*:

> there followed the three strangest days I have ever experienced. It was like a nightmare, like the most grotesque scene in a film from the darkest underworld. By crawling and twisting ourselves forward we found a place where a strip of light entered, where we could at least read. We had only to hold our books at the right angle … We not only read the books, we chuckled and laughed all the time, and this must surely be the best advertisement Wodehouse ever had.[8]

The days and nights passed, until their reading was interrupted one day by a sudden great commotion from the jetty overhead. It was making ready for the incoming *Windrush*. Before long, tanks and cars could be heard ready to be winched on board, and horses too.

Quietly, Max and Gregers rehearsed their action for that night when they would lay cortex fuses between two charges connected to eight limpet mines. If all eight limpets exploded they were confident it would cause a chain reaction from the engine room, causing the *Windrush*'s holds to fill quickly with water. Their plan was to attach the limpets at such a moment that when the fuse dissolved the explosion would go off when the ship was well out to sea.

Both men were troubled by this. Max wrote:

> It is a queer feeling preparing devilish charges which take the lives of three thousand human beings. Many of these soldiers, I felt, were conscripted against their will … But the mere thought of the Gestapo made us as hard as flint … We were young men who were wasting the most important years of our lives because a mad man wanted more *Lebensraum*. We would do our best to put an end to the war and the madman, and that was exactly what were occupied with at the moment.[9]

It was a long day, and at 6 p.m., under cover of first darkness, Gregers took to the inflatable and began to pull himself along the hull of the *Windrush*, attaching the first four limpets. He paddled back to Max and said he was concerned that there was some electrical resistance from the ship's side interfering with the magnetic force of the mines, but he had managed to attach them.

Now it was Max's turn to attach his four limpets, but just as he approached the side of the ship she began to move. Max was fearful that in his small inflatable he would be dragged underneath, but was able to struggle away, hauling back under the jetty, where the two men's thoughts turned to escape.

First, they needed to defuse the four unused mines, which they then hid under a dark beam. Then they sliced through the side of the inflatable until it sank. Putting their overalls back on, they struggled their way to a ladder up from the water, then brazenly joined the throng of soldiers and workers and wandered back to the dockyard gate, where they wished goodnight to their friend the sentry and disappeared into central Oslo.

The timer on the mines had been set for twenty-four hours' delay. Max looked forward to news of their biggest military triumph yet. Two days later he received a coded telegram from London: 'To N.12 from F.O. Hard luck. Try again.'

Max was, in his own words, deeply depressed by this. It would only be after the war that he learned that the mines must have exploded because the *Windrush* was forced to pull in for unscheduled repairs to Aarhus for two weeks.

Max's gang had greater success with the *Windrush*'s fellow 'slave ship', as Max called them, the *Donau*. In January 1945, they repeated the endeavour, and she exploded in the Oslo fjord, destroying 200 ambulances, much war materiel and a number of horses. A few days later Max went down to Drøbak, where he had a clear view of the *Donau* listing in the water but not yet sunk. He was astonished to hear many rounds of gunfire and was told that this was because the Germans believed the 'English saboteurs' were still in the vicinity.

Max Manus became a hero. After liberation at the end of the war he was appointed personal bodyguard to the returning King Haakon, and can be seen in newsreel footage riding alongside him as the king's car processes through Oslo.

He was never far from the Norwegian imagination, even being granted his own 'This Is Your Life' on Norwegian television forty years after these events. A major feature film was made about him in Norwegian and English in 2008, called *Max Manus: Man of War*, directed by Espen Sandberg and Joachim Rønning.

But he was haunted by it all. For much of his life the heavy drinking he'd utilised to keep his emotion in check during the horrors of the war occasionally took him over. His dear friend Gregers had been killed by the Gestapo, betrayed by supposedly sympathetic Germans, in a café shoot-out in November 1944. Exactly fifty years later Max unveiled a bust of Gregers in Oslo. Less than two years later, on 20 September 1996, Max died.

However, his courageous failure to sink the *Windrush* affected the destiny of another group of unfortunate Norwegians. He wrote about them himself, again using the language of the times, referring to the day he first escaped the Gestapo by jumping through a glass window: 'There was a disgusting atmosphere in Oslo in the winter of 1940–41. Drunken Germans with their Norwegian girls, letting their natural instincts get the better of their discipline, were everywhere in the street after it began to grow dark.'[10]

He clearly disapproved of these women, their 'fraternisation' also seen by Ruth Maier that day down at the docks in 1942. These women ran many risks, and the *Windrush* would prove their downfall.

THE TYSKERPIGER

By August 1944, it was five years since the *Windrush* had sailed merrily across the Baltic carrying tourists and Strength Through Joy adherents from northern Germany to Oslo, and up to the dramatic fjords of the west coast. Back then she had been glossy black up to her plimsoll line, topped with a layer of pristine white paint, over which hung white life-boats. Her twin white funnels had been crested in red. Now she could not be mistaken for a jolly cruise ship; she was a Kriegsmarine troop carrier – battleship grey from top to toe, her previously highly polished wooden deck blackened with paint.

It was two months since the Allied D-Day invasion in northern France. In Amsterdam that August, the betrayed Anne Frank was taken from her attic hiding place to Bergen-Belsen concentration camp, where she died the following February. Meanwhile, Adolf Hitler called back every plane in the Luftwaffe to the Western Europe theatre.

The British government could see that Hitler was bringing thousands of troops back from Germany to eventually perish in the Battle of the Bulge and other rear-guard actions. On 10 August 1944, the *Daily Mail* ran a story about the *Windrush* (*Monte Rosa*):

'German Troops Leave Norway'
STOCKHOLM, Monday. Several large liners formerly used for cruises
to the Norwegian fjords and the West Indies are now ferrying German

troops between Oslo and the Danish port of Aarhus, according to Stockholm paper *Allehanda*.

One ship, the Monte Rosa, made three double trips last week, says the paper, being full sailing to Denmark and empty on her return voyages – *Reuter*

Every journey from Oslo to Aarhus was crammed with men, who in Norway had experienced one of the easiest wars in the world, occasionally having to deal with menaces like Max Manus, but mainly manning distant outposts in remote fjords watching for the invasion from the west that never came. During those nearly five years, many of them had developed relationships with local women. Some of these involved prostitution, but thousands involved genuine love affairs and even marriage.

On the upper passenger decks from Oslo that August, many of those women, some pregnant, many with children, were on their way to an uncertain future in Germany, because Adolf Hitler and his sidekick Himmler, despite their multiple woes as the Third Reich began to crumble in every quarter, were determined that these women now 'return' to the Fatherland. But they were not interested in the 300 women on board; they wanted the Norwegian *Lebensborn* – the children conceived by local women and the occupying German troops.

After the war, these women were stripped of their citizenship and not permitted to return to Norway. Those who stayed behind faced persecution. One of these was Synni Lingstad, an 18-year-old from near Narvik who'd had an affair with a 25-year-old German sergeant, Alfred Haase. Haase was evacuated from Oslo on the ship; Synni was left behind. They had a daughter, Anni-Frid.

So terrible was the persecution after the war that Synni's mother, Arntine, took Anni-Frid to Sweden, where they were joined by Synni a few years later, just before she died aged 21 of kidney failure. Anni-Frid Synni Lingstad was then raised by her grandmother in Sweden. On 6 April 1974, at the Dome in Brighton, Anni-Frid took to the stage and with the three other members of ABBA won the Eurovision Song Contest with 'Waterloo'.[1]

In the final short years of her life, Synni would have been known as a 'Tyskerpiger'.

❖

In May 1941, Toralv Øksnevad, the Norwegian voice of the BBC in London, had broadcast the following sarcastic message to his country-men: 'As we know, the German master race, ruler of nations and world conquerors, is comprised of quite irresistible individuals. However, ordinary Norwegian women can demobilise these men's conceitedness, and more than 999 per thousand do so.'

Øksnevad's effort to diminish the idea of Norwegian women falling for German men was aimed at keeping home morale high, but his claim that only one in a thousand women had affairs with Germans was not supported by the facts. It was later acknowledged that of a total popula-tion of 3 million, some 50,000 had sexual relations with Germans. The officially recorded number of children born with Norwegian–German parentage was 9,000.[2]

After the war, many of these Tyskerpiger were identified as a consequence of the banal Nazi efficiency of brothel records, which in 1944 began inventories of women known to have been infected with venereal diseases. As elsewhere in Europe, the Tyskerpiger became the victims of vigilante 'cropping' – a punishment exclusively meted out to women who had fraternised sexually.

Their hair was initially cut off with scissors, then a trimmer was used to shave their heads. Often a larger crowd gathered to witness their clothes being ripped away and swastikas drawn with black enamel paint on their backs and breasts. They were then forced out on to the streets without being allowed to cover themselves and made to file past hundreds more spectators who had gathered to jeer, shout and lunge at them.

From the comfort of his BBC microphone in London, Torlav Øksnevad had laid the ground for this persecution: 'Given the circumstances, severe reprisals from the Norwegian camp are impossible as long as the Germans rule in the country. But these women who do not spurn the Germans will pay a terrible price for the rest of their lives.'

Perhaps the provocative broadcaster could not really anticipate the appalling circumstances of the women boarding the *Windrush* in August 1944 bound for Germany via Denmark. Unlike the equivalent women of France, for example, the Norwegian women had the privilege initially of being considered 'Aryans' and part of the Germanic 'race'.

The children of such relationships had caught the eye of the Nazi leaders. On 28 July 1942 Hitler had issued 'a decree concerning the care of children fathered by members of the Wehrmacht in occupied countries'. This was only ever fully applied in Norway and Holland, where there were good possibilities 'of preserving and promoting racially valuable German stock'.

The dominant organisation overseeing this horrifying breeding programme in Norway was called the Lebensborn Eingetragener Verein, personally overseen from Germany by Heinrich Himmler. The Lebensborn project was launched in Norway with the SS catchphrase: 'After the victory on the battlefield follows the victory in the cradle.'

The organisation had 300 employees and a budget as large as that of the Norwegian police force. Expectant mothers were offered maintenance many months prior to birth, then given board and lodging at a maternity home. Orphanages could be arranged for their children if they wished not to raise them, or a maintenance allowance was given if they did.

Much of the Lebensborn work might almost resemble a genuine welfare policy, yet the overall objective was to boost the population of Nordic peoples in fulfilment of Nazi racial policy. The expectant mothers had to furnish information about their ancestors, while their own appearance and character was evaluated. They were photographed and questioned about their own political beliefs. Few were rejected, except the Sammi women from Finnmark in the far north of the country.

The unfortunate women boarding the *Windrush* did so at the command of Hitler himself. The Führer considered those who had married German soldiers German subjects in their own right. They were now under orders to look up the families of their German husbands, with whom they were then supposed to live.

Many of the women who travelled across the Skagerrak to Aarhus then endured a long train journey into war-torn Germany only to discover that the address given to them by their German lover was nothing more than a heap of rubble. By the beginning of 1945, conditions in Germany had become so chaotic that the 'repatriation' programme was called off.

Then their condition worsened. The *Windrush* Tyskerpiger who found themselves in defeated Germany at the end of the war were effectively rendered stateless. Just as Max Manus was driving King Haakon triumphantly through Oslo, the re-established Norwegian government wasted no time in amending the nationality laws retroactively so that any woman who had married a German soldier after 9 April 1940 was stripped of her citizenship if and when she left Norway. This applied even though Hitler had ordered them out of Norway.

In this way, the women became German subjects, and even those who had not left the country could yet be expelled. This was exacerbated for the women and their children in the zone that became East Germany. All hope of repatriation would be lost for another forty-five years as they disappeared behind the Iron Curtain.

These stringent regulations were only gradually relaxed. In 1950 a new law was passed allowing the women to return if they did so before 1955. They were able to reclaim their Norwegian citizenship but forced to leave their husbands – who would not be granted leave to join them – behind in Germany. It took thirty years for a public debate to come to fruition in Norway and an amendment was finally passed in 1989 which made it possible for women who had married 'citizens of the enemy state' to regain their lost citizenship.

Those Tyskerpiger who had managed to stay in Norway and resist Hitler's call in 1944 had to face the judgement of a Norwegian post-war commission called the Krigsbarnsutvalget (War Children Committee).

It decided that the remaining women and children were indeed Norway's responsibility, but placed them under an immense stigma. One of its commissioners wrote:

> As far as I know, there has been no official examination of the girls who fraternised with German soldiers, but based on general experience there certainly seems to be a disproportionate number among them who are backward or antisocial psychopaths – mentally deranged girls even. These are mental defects which are for the most part hereditary and there is a certain risk that this hereditary disposition will be reflected in their offspring.

This fear amongst the Norwegian population that half-German children were genetically conditioned to harbour Nazi sentiments was widespread and led to much bullying and humiliation of such children over many decades.

On Tuesday 19 October 2018, the Norwegian government finally gave an official and unreserved apology to the Tyskerpiger and their children, both those who had endured decades of abuse at home and those who'd been deported by Hitler. It seems significant that the apology was spoken by the female Prime Minister, Erna Solberg, at an event to celebrate the seventieth anniversary of the Universal Declaration of Human Rights. She said:

> Young Norwegian girls and women who had relations with German soldiers or were suspected of them were victims of undignified treatment. Norwegian authorities violated the fundamental principle that no citizen can be punished without trial or sentenced without law. Today in the name of the government, I want to offer my apologies.

It was a fulsome apology, but it had been a long time coming. In so much of the *Windrush* story, those wronged have often had to wait a very long time to reach such a point. In his 2000 millennial address, then Prime Minister Kjell Magne Bondevik offered an initial apology, especially to the Lebensborn children. Yet it took two more years for a Justice Committee to make a recommendation, backed by all parties, that compensation should be paid. It took until 2005 for this to begin to be distributed.

Anni-Frid Lingstad's own story was, in relative terms, a lucky escape. As more light was thrown on to this period, tales emerged of just how terribly the Lebensborn children had been treated by the Norwegians. After the war their mothers were interned, their children taken from them and either forcibly adopted or incarcerated in children's homes. At one notorious home in southern Norway, at Trysil, they were treated with all the cruelty of one of the industrial schools exposed in Ireland.

When they protested, the authorities ratcheted up the cruelty. Paul Hansen was born in a Lebensborn home in 1942, and said, 'I spent the first 20 years of my life in mental institutions just because my father was a German. We were war children and therefore must be "retarded".'[3]

One of the children, Tor Brandacher, said:

Nobody was older than four years old when hell began for them, People suffered abuse all their life. They were called German bastards, Hitler bastards, human garbage, mentally retarded and fifth columnists. It was pure racism. A nation which doesn't see clearly what it has done in the past is doomed to do the same again, Norway will always be a fairy tale country for the rest of the world, but it is not.[4]

Despite the apologies of 2000 and the beginnings of compensation in 2005, a group of Lebensborn took Norway to the European Court of Human Rights, but their case was ruled inadmissible as too much time had elapsed. The suspicion will always remain that when the ultimate apology was uttered by the Norwegian Prime Minister in 2018, it could be finally done mainly because nearly all the Tyskerpiger were now dead and only their children would cost the exchequer.

In the field of equal treatment of the sexes, Norway after the Second World War is a dismal case. Those who had profiteered deliberately from the theft of property stolen from Norwegian Jews murdered at Auschwitz walked away without a blot on their copybook. But, as the historian and director of the Centre for Holocaust and Minority Studies, Guri Hjeltnes, says: 'We cannot say women who had personal relations with German soldiers were helping the German war effort. Their crime was breaking unwritten rules and moral standards. They were punished even more harshly than the war profiteers.'[5]

The Jewish passengers who were forcibly transported on the *Windrush* had faced worse fates. But it is doubtful they left Norway with any more malicious and sustained contempt from their fellow Norwegians. If Henrik Ibsen had still been writing in Bergen, what a play he might have wrought from this.

arah O'Connor (third from right), with Labour MPs David Lammy (fourth from right) nd Dawn Butler (first from left). They are accompanied by Windrush campaigners (left right) Anthony Bryan, Paulette Wilson, Sylvester Marshall and Elwaldo Romeo. Sarah's terview shown on the BBC was an embarrassment for Prime Minister Theresa May. ʹui Mok/PA Archive/PA Images)

Above: The *Windrush* was built by Blohm & Voss, a Jewish company in Hamburg that started off as a humble ship repairers operating from these harbourside workshops in the 1870s.

Left: The *Windrush*'s famous journey from the Caribbean was not her first time in London. Throughout the 1930s she brought tourists under her former name, *Monte Rosa*, attracted by designs like this from German painter and graphic artist Ottomar Anton. (Shawshots/Alamy Stock Photo)

Above: In the 1930s membership of the Nazi party became obligatory for merchant seamen. On arrival in Buenos Aires, on *Windrush* the men were always willing to put on a display of loyalty for the benefit of Argentine onlookers. (INTERFOTO/Alamy Stock Photo)

Left: Tirpitz was one of the most feared vessels in the world, but spent her entire war skulking in Norwegian waters. Hitler dreaded losing her and Churchill was obsessed with her destruction. *Windrush* was her supply ship. (The Picture Art Collection/ Alamy Stock Photo)

Above: Some Norwegian Jews escaped to Sweden, but nearly 800 died in Auschwitz – many taken there on the *Windrush*. One 13-year-old victim, Cissi Klein, has this Trondheim park named in her honour. (Statue created by Tore Bjørn Skjølsvik and Tone Ek, 1997)

Lieutenant Colonel J.P. Carne, commanding officer of the 'Glorious
Glo'sters', embarking for Korea. He spent his two years and four months as
a captive in solitary confinement, where he carved a Celtic cross now to be
seen in Gloucester Cathedral. (Keystone Press/Alamy Stock Photo)

Opposite: The monument to those who came to Korea on the *Windrush*
and never returned at Gloster Hill Memorial Park in Paju. Pat Angier left
a fine collection of letters and diaries recalling the journey east; his name
is commemorated here. (Ryu Seung-Il/ZUMA Wire/Alamy Live News)

The 22 June 1948 arrival at Tilbury brought many talents, including the blues singer Mona Baptise. She became a music star in the UK and Germany with her songs 'Calypso Blues' and 'There's Something in the Air'. (Trinity Mirror/Mirrorpix/Alamy Stock Photo)

A difficult encounter for Prime Minister Theresa May with the Prime Minister of Jamaica Andrew Holness at 10 Downing Street in April 2018, just as the Windrush scandal was breaking. He urged her to act quickly to help the victims. (Peter Summers/ PA Archive/PA Images)

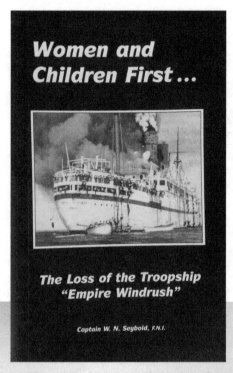

Women and Children First ...

The Loss of the Troopship "Empire Windrush"

Captain W. N. Seybold, F.N.I.

Captain Wally Seybold was a junior officer on the night the *Windrush* exploded and sank off Algeria. Unhappy with the official inquiry, he gathered accounts from crew and passengers to form a fuller picture, defending the reputation of Captain 'Tug' Wilson. (Captain W. Seybold)

The first survivors of the *Windrush* sinking arrive in Gibraltar. (Keystone Press/Alamy Stock Photo)

14

WAR PRIZE?

After Max Manus' attack in the summer of 1944, there were conflicting reports as to just how much damage he had inflicted on the *Windrush*. The British had communicated to him that it was negligible, but in 2008 a Norwegian man called Odd Claus wrote an autobiography called *Witness to War: A Norwegian Boy's Experience in Germany*,[1] which suggested a possibly different outcome.

In 1944, Odd Claus was 14 years old when Hitler summoned the Tyskerpiger and their children to Germany, but he and his sister were unusual cases. They were already teenagers, conceived by their mother from a German father some years before the war. Despite their ages, they were forced into the same Lebensborn category and required to go to the Fatherland on the *Windrush*. Odd Claus was appalled by the racism of the obsession with 'pure' Germanic and Nordic lines, but nevertheless had no alternative but to comply.

The evidence he has to offer is significant, but there is an element of confusion. He states that his voyage was in September 1944, whereas Max Manus' attack had been mounted in the August. It is hard at first to be certain, as throughout both months the *Windrush* was consistently spotted leaving the port of Oslo to destinations not recorded, and then waiting in the Oslofjord at Drøbak, before coming back into port to collect more passengers.

It is possible, therefore, that Odd Claus was on a different voyage to the majority of the Tyskerpiger, or it may have been the same. One detail which suggests it may have been a later sailing is that his account states the *Windrush* did not leave from Oslo port itself, as the one Max Manus sabotaged did, but from a place called Moss, further south on the eastern side of the fjord.

Yet according to the voyage cards, still maintained even at this late stage of the war by Lloyd's of London, the ship only left Moss on a single occasion, on 24 September 1944. It is likely therefore that this was the ship that Odd Claus and his 16-year-old sister, Erica, were aboard.

This is important. In his book, Odd Claus states that having been brought to the Akershus Fortress, they were then put on a train to Moss, where they embarked. At 5 a.m. the *Windrush*, packed with soldiers returning to Germany, struck what Odd believed was a mine.

The captain reacted by closing the bulkhead doors to prevent water flooding throughout the hull and sinking the ship, and in so doing, according to Odd's account, 200 trapped passengers were drowned. He believed that some of them would have been other Tyskerpiger women together with Lebensborn children like him. In this tragic event, it looks as if Max's hands were clean, but suggests the suffering of the Norwegian women and children was even greater than once thought.

The *Windrush* must have been seaworthy, because she was able to sail back up to the coast of Norway at Trondheim, making a number of return voyages to Copenhagen and Aarhus in the first five months of 1945. She was acting as both a troop carrier and a hospital ship. Month by month, the Soviet army had swept up through Finland to the Finnmark area, taking Kirkenes in northern Norway on the Barents Sea. The German army had to retreat south, deep into Norway, and Trondheim was one of the places chosen to treat the injured and return the fleeing troops, now needed in northern Germany, before they were potentially cut off in Norway.

When the war in Europe finally ended on 8 May 1945, her voyage cards record the *Windrush* as being in Copenhagen, which had just been liberated after five years of occupation. She was certainly there on 23 June 1945, but on 24 June she was back in Kiel on the north-east German coast, between the border with Denmark and the port of Hamburg, where she had been made.

Having been captured by the British, she was still called the *Monte Rosa*, but not for long. She was about to enter a period of stateless-ness and bureaucratic uncertainty. In British hands now, however, she at last begins to appear in the files of The National Archives as the story unfolds of how she was claimed by His Majesty's Government, and how she was finally given her famous name.[2]

At first it seemed so simple. The war was over, the British had taken Kiel, and the *Windrush* was in the harbour. It was an enemy ship that had prosecuted an illegal war against the British and the other Allies, and it was therefore plainly going to be a 'war prize', or 'war booty'. The process started smoothly, reflected in a National Archives folder containing immaculate paperwork recording the entire process.

On 26 July 1945, an affidavit was signed jointly between the captain of a ship he had been used to calling the *Monte Rosa*, Kapitän Willy Lüdecke, and Sub Lieutenant John McBeath Leech. The latter was described as 'in His Majesty's Navy and of His Majesty's Ship of War, ROYAL HAROLD, whereof Kenneth Robinson Esq is commander'.

The paperwork trail seems on the surface to be immaculate. The two co-signed documents cover a range of issues. The first was to do with money captured. It is recorded that there was a receipt extant dated 10 July 1945 stating that a Sub Lieutenant W. Saville had taken 207,853 Reichsmarks off the *Windrush* at the point of capture in Kiel. This is described as 'public money'. In addition he removed 12,416 Reichsmarks of 'ships' money'. There is a note added by McBeath: 'I do hereby declare that on the 26th day of July 1945 I delivered a Copy of the Certificate to the Master of the MONTE ROSA and that he made no complaint.'

Another document written in German dated 26 July and signed by McBeath and Lüdecke gives a perfect pen portrait of how the staffing area of the ship was configured at the end of the war:

Bridge–Deck				
1	Captains Living Quarters	furnished for	1	person/s
11	Cabins for Officer	" "	11	"
2	Cabins for Radio Officer	" "	2	"
A–Decks				
6	Cabins for Deck Personnel	" "	34	"
1	Cabin for Chief Steward	" "	1	"
Ship Operators				
9	Cabins for Cooking Personnel	" "	16	"
7	Cabins for Stewards	" "	82	"
12	Cabins for Engineers	" "	12	"
8	Cabins for Machinery Pers.	" "	18	"
1	Cabin for Mobile Hairdressers	" "	4	"
2	Cabins for Laundry Personnel	" "	14	"
1	Cabin for Stewardesses	" "	6	"
1	Cabin for Asst Chief Steward	" "	1	"
1	Cabin for Musicians	" "	4	"
1	Cabin for Luggage masters	" "	2	"
2	Cabins for Paymasters	" "	3	"

This made for a total of 211 crew and, from the perspective of someone back in Whitehall a few days later receiving all this paperwork, it makes her look just like any other innocent cruise liner. The details are beguiling. We can see that she was set up, for example, for four hairdressers, four musicians and no fewer than eighty-two stewards.

This is, of course, accurate enough, but something about omitting a description of the other decks at this point seems disingenuous: no mention of the troop decks for Nazis invading Norway or the improvised prison quarters for the Jews brought to Auschwitz. As if in the middle of one of Doctor Who's periodic regenerations, her original identity begins to fade from view.

The final item co-signed by the British sub lieutenant and the German captain is a vignette of the care with which paperwork is always kept by any functioning navy in the world. It was important to the British to have this all shipshape, handed over and logged. The logged paperwork was received by the Procurator General back in Whitehall, the person responsible for what would prove a surprisingly slow process of registering definitive British ownership.

This is an itemised of the paperwork that Lüdecke handed over to McBeath in July 1945 as recorded at The National Archives:

1. Engine Room Log
2. File of private correspondence
3. File of letters from captain
4. 2 medical certificates
5. Ship's medical category certificate
6. 2 ship's class certificates & 1 Engine Room Certificate
7. Certificate of Registry
8. 1 Security certificate & 5 shipping union certificates
9. 24 lamp test certificates
10. 15 Germanischer Lloyd anchor certificate[3]
11. Extract from ship's certificate & Lloyds list of Agents
12. Register of test certificate for loading tackle
13. 25 manilla & wire rope test certificates

14. 16 various test certificates, boats davits etc
15. 6 compass test certificates
16. 1 medical certificate
17. 3 certificates on exemption from deratting
18. 1 International freeboard certificate & 1 map
19. Flag certificate
20. 7 barometer test certificates
21. Certificate of seaworthiness & 3 chronometer certificates
22. Permit for use of W/T transmitter[4]
23. 2 permits for us of radio in lifeboats, permit for use of W/T transmitter & receiver, permit for use of D/F set[5]
24. Various documents for use in Spanish harbours[6]
25. Extract from ship's certificate
26. 3 International Sanitary Convention certificates
27. Engine Room Class Certificates
28. File of correspondence from the captain
29. Ship's log

Thus, with all the above paperwork and much more, the *Windrush*'s transformation from Nazi troop carrier to peacetime British cruiser should have no obstacles to overcome. However, there was a hitch. The problem came because at her point of capture, and as clearly insisted upon by her captain, she was not a fighting ship at all, but a hospital ship. The rules for seizure were different for such a category.

On 10 August 1945, a W. Hanna of the British Admiralty's Naval Law Branch wrote to a H. Hull of Her Majesty's Procurator General's Office:

Dear Hull

You will have seen from a signal that the hospital ship MONTE ROSA has been seized in Prize and Naval-Officer-in-Charge, Kiel, has been told that in future recognised hospital ships should not be seized as condemnation cannot be secured.

2. I am not clear to which Allied Government MONTE ROSA will ultimately be assigned, but it will be necessary to ensure a good

title to that Government. Would you be good enough to let me know whether we should merely seize this vessel as being part of the war equipment of the enemy without prize proceedings, or whether it would be advisable to arrange for a compulsory transfer by the appropriate German authorities to the Government to whom MONTE ROSA will be assigned.

3.   Presumably, the authority in whom the title is registered at present could be compelled by the Allied Military Government to execute a Bill of Sale for a nominal consideration.

Therefore, the British government was becoming nervous about simply seizing German assets without it being transparent to the four victorious occupying powers – itself, the French, the Americans and the Soviets – that it was being done legitimately. This was a time of extraordinary chaos, with the Allies trying hard to ensure the legitimacy of their occupation. Four months later, the Nuremberg Trials would begin, lasting from that November to October 1946. In the event, it took almost as long for the *Windrush's* fate to be definitively declared.

The initial legal opinion from the Procurator General on 25 August 1945 was couched in vagaries but seemed to give the thumbs-up, Whitehall-style: 'In my opinion, as this vessel was a public enemy vessel the title passed from the German Government when she was captured. Whether it passed to H.M.G absolutely or to H.M.G. on behalf of the four Governments to whom Germany surrendered is another matter.'

This was a positive signal, but one filled with the potential for later deniability. This issue seems to have hung in the air for a very long time, until the Procurator General had examined, slowly, all the paperwork supplied by Sub Lieutenant McBeath. Nearly a year later, on 5 July 1946, Hull wrote concerning a number of vessels. Some of these, he was happy to declare, could categorised as 'seized in prize'. The *Monte Rosa*, however, he opined did not need to be seized in prize 'as title passed on capture to H.M. Government'.

In reality, Hull was simply engaged in a tidying-up exercise. He had decided that, even though hospital ships could not technically be seized, this one could as it had been captured, and that was all there was to it. Perhaps the actuality influenced his finding, for possession had become nine-tenths of the law, and even while doubt hung in the air, the ship had been taken first to Tyneside for engineering work and then on to Glasgow where she is recorded as being refitted in June 1946.

On 27 March 1947, the nautical advisor to the Ministry of Transport wrote from his office in Berkeley Square, Mayfair, to His Majesty's Procurator General at Storey's Gate, St James's Park:

'Ex Enemy Vessels'		
'General San Martin'	now named	'EMPIRE DEBEN'
'Pretoria'	"	'EMPIRE DOON'
'Antonio'	"	'EMPIRE HALLADAL'
'Ubena'	"	'EMPIRE KEN'
'Cap Norte'	"	'EMPIRE TROOPER'
'Monte Rosa'	"	'EMPIRE WINDRUSH'

The above named vessels are now owned by the Ministry of Transport and are to be used as post war H.M Troop-ships.

2. The German plans and other documents relative to hull and machinery, which were surrendered with the ship, are required by the director of Sea Transport for the purpose of planning the new 'lay out' of the ships for trooping purposes and also in connection with repair work that will have to be done on main and auxiliary engines, boilers, refrigerating plant, overhaul of sanitary piping and plumbing, electric cables etc., and certain other modifications that may be required.

3. It would be appreciated if any of these plans and documents that may be available could be forwarded to this office at your earliest convenience.

This was the moment, just fourteen months before her most famous voyage, that the ship acquired her renowned name, and the identity with which she would sink into the deep off the coast of Algeria seven years later.

Enter SS *Empire Windrush*.

15

SORE SPOTS

Just how much misfortune can a ship destined to change her name sustain before Long John Silver's saying has a ring of diabolical truth? 'Now, what a ship is christened, so let her stay, I says.'

By the time she arrived in Glasgow to be refitted, we can be confident that in her life so far *Windrush* had suffered a number of misfortunes. Her first was in 1934 on an extended Nordic cruise to Iceland. The British United Press Agency reported:

> The German tourist ship Monte Rosa is reported to have gone aground soon after leaving Thorshavn today in heavy fog. The Monte Rosa is carrying 1,300 passengers and 300 of a crew. The owners received a message from Captain Carl Luebbe, master of the ship, stating: 'Everything in good order. Passengers calm, Rescue ships advised. Cabins are watertight.'[1]

Thereafter, it is established that she was torpedoed by British Beaufighters in April 1944, and that she then suffered an explosion at the hands of Max Manus in June 1944. It seems probable that she hit a mine in September 1944, as reported by Odd Claus.

However, her luck did not change with her new name. Her time on Clydeside in Glasgow seems to have been another series of mishaps. On 5 December 1946, when fire took hold, it was extinguished but left her, as her voyage cards record, with her 'insulation ruined'. On 18 February 1947 she was venturing out of the Clyde but had to return with 'engine trouble'. On 18 March 1947 she tried to leave Glasgow behind again, and again she had to return with engine failure.

Then at last she was ready to make her way to India to help evacuate troops in the late summer of 1947 as the country began to descend into a chaotic civil war at Partition. This trip too showed that she was in real trouble. Her steering motor failed, leaving her potentially rudderless and adrift on the oceans, and having limped her way back up the Suez Canal, she spent a week at Port Said having emergency repairs. This complete lack of reliability with patching-up operations carried out while out of port was unacceptable for any ship, let alone a troop carrier with 2,000 returning soldiers and airmen, many with families who had spent a decade or more in India and the Far East.

These problems with the *Windrush*, and the constant flurry of rumours about them, would persist for the next seven years. For now, though, they were no longer the concern of Hamburg Süd. It was a British government problem, and the government had decided to engage the private sector. *Windrush* had been transferred on a long lease to the New Zealand Shipping Company, a subsidiary of P&O. This shifted the financial burden of capital costs off the British books to an extent, but it introduced an at-one-step-removed relationship in the ultimate safety of the passengers.

The New Zealand Shipping Company was incorporated in 1873 in Christchurch, New Zealand, by a group of local farmers and merchants who were dissatisfied with the existing shipping facilities and their inability to cope with the country's rapidly expanding trade.[2] Initially it was administered from New Zealand with a London 'Board of Advice' in the City. It began by purchasing four second-hand iron-clad sailing ships and within four years was operating seventeen vessels under its own flag along with other ships it had chartered. In 1882, it became one of the first companies involved in the transport of refrigerated meat across the globe in ships fitted with Haslam's cold-air refrigerating machinery.

Through a series of acquisitions and mergers over the next twenty years, it moved into the Australian trade. Then in 1906, with a major presence in London, a controlling interest was taken by the Peninsular and Oriental Steam Navigation Company (P&O). This new security allowed it to expand into operations around the world, from Canada to South Africa, but it was always the relationship to the mother country that was the most important, and the most lucrative.

After the Second World War, the United Kingdom government was not in a financial position to replicate the merchant maritime bureaucracy already mastered by companies like the New Zealand Shipping Line. It was happy to sub-contract operations out and keep the costs off the balance sheet. On 11 February 1947, an M. Picknett of the Ministry of Transport wrote a letter to a Mr Tallents of the New Zealand Shipping Company seeking advice. It is indicative of austerity Britain that Picknett's notepaper was still headed 'Ministry of War Transport' with the word 'War' simply blanked out by four heavily typed capital Xs:

Dear Mr Tallents

Consideration is being given to the arrangements which will be necessary for meeting the Ministry's future responsibility for movement of Service personnel by sea.

As you know, The Ministry has acquired certain Passenger liners and ex German ships which are now in operation as troop ships, and there appears little doubt that we must continue to utilise these ships for so long as they can be considered economical, although their future service as troop ships entails a fairly large refitting of the troop decks etc. to meet peace-time needs. Some of these ships are also in need of a good 'beat-up' in respect of their hulls, machinery and equipments. All this, of course, entails a considerable expenditure of money, and I am anxious that we should not undertake such expenditure on any of the ships reconditioned unless we can reasonably expect 10 years trooping service with only minor repairs in each individual ship, during this period.

It occurs to me that your people must know the 'sore-spots' of the ships under your management, and it would help me very considerably if you could let me have the benefit of that knowledge and your own views as the reasonableness, or otherwise, of reckoning on the continued use of the 'EMPIRE WINDRUSH' as a long-term troop ship.

Yours faithfully

M. Picknett

Tallents' reply on 13 February stated only that he promised to let the Ministry know his opinion on the engines after she had run her sea trials. Picknett must have wondered why nothing further was heard as the early summer began, during which the *Windrush* had made her first major foray under a British flag, sailing from her anchorage in the Clyde to Malta, Port Said and back to London – a two-week journey.

He chased Tallents on 12 May: 'As she has made one voyage to the Middle East, I am wondering whether you are now in a position to let me have the desired information.'

Two days later, Tallents of the New Zealand Shipping Company replied:

Dear Mr Picknett,

'EMPIRE WINDRUSH'

In answer to your letter of 12th May 1947. I am sorry that I have been so idle in letting you know about the engines.

Our technical people's advice is that they are reasonably confident that the ship is good for a life of at least 10 years from the time of going into commission, provided that she has the usual repairs which one expects to be necessary for a vessel of her age, running in the trade in which she is employed.

Our Superintendent Engineer points out that although he has no reason to anticipate any trouble the machinery is not of a type to which any British owner is accustomed and that if anything went wrong with it, especially with a gearing, it might need a considerable time to remedy it.

Yours sincerely

One reading of this correspondence is that it is of two men being helpful to one another in a civil and informative manner. Another, if we bear in mind her history of damage, and what would befall her seven years later, is that it is the correspondence of the client – a desperate government over a barrel with an unanticipated post-war need to continue moving troops across the world – and the service provider, a for-profit shipping company keen to undertake this work in the interests of their bottom line.

The New Zealand Shipping Company's reply is reassuring in one respect; in another it is saying, 'we warn you, these engines will need serious scheduled maintenance, which will be up to you, and one thing we should flag up is that no British companies know how to maintain or repair these German engines. But, we're already at sea so let's just crack on.'

Strike one occurred just four months later as the returning service people from India had an unexpected layover in Port Said.

The Second World War was over, yet for the United Kingdom there seemed to be no peace dividend at all. Over the years, we have become accustomed to seeing Pathé newsreel footage of young men and women dancing around Eros on Piccadilly when peace was declared. On history syllabuses students then pass on to Attlee and Bevan, austerity and the setting up of the National Health Service. On the global stage they learn of the 'Iron Curtain' descending from 'Stettin in the Baltic to Trieste in the Adriatic' in Winston Churchill's remarkable speech given at Westminster College in Fulton, Missouri, on 5 March 1946.[3] Students are left thinking that the government's main concern now was to manage service personnel looking east in Cold War Europe. This was not the case.

In Europe, the British were still engaged in fighting with partisans in Italy who were claiming the Adriatic port of Trieste on behalf of the Yugoslav communist government. In Greece, British troops were fighting a resistance movement that had arisen during the German occupation and that now wanted a socialist state rather than a returning monarchy.

Britain was stuck in Greek conflicts until 1948, and the last peace-keeping troops out are recorded in *The Guardian* departing on the *Windrush* on 5 February 1950.[4] Some 550 troops from the 1st Battalion of the Bedfordshire and Herefordshire Regiment, who had been stationed in Salonika for eighteen months, boarded there. The *Windrush* stopped at Piraeus to embark a further 180 troops and their families.

The biggest problems, however, came from beyond Europe. With the elimination of Japanese domination in Indochina and the Dutch East Indies, British troops still remaining in Burma had swept in to reclaim Malaya, Singapore and Hong Kong. More fundamentally, Britain had to resolve major problems of its own that had been brewing long before the war. In India, the clashes between Hindus and Muslims were out of control. This was exacerbated by the understandable desire for India to see the back of the British after nearly 300 years, from the exploitative rabble of the East India Company to the full imperial charade of Queen Victoria becoming Empress of India.

Meanwhile, any troop ship travelling back via Port Said would have seen arrivals from the north bringing reinforcements to shore up the war in Palestine, in which Britain found itself as a third party fighting the Irgun, who were determined to consolidate a new state of Israel, and the Arabs, who could not understand why a new country was being founded from Tel Aviv on the Mediterranean to Eilat on the Gulf of Aqaba, on the eastern finger of the Red Sea.

It is worth considering the insolubility of this for a moment. The Jews had lived in the area for millennia, but by 1948 Arab Muslims and Christians were a clear majority and had been for a thousand years.[5] But with the introduction of the Mandate for Palestine in 1923 under the League of Nations, with Britain as the Mandate authority, the Jewish movement, made more desperate by pogroms and then the Holocaust, backed more settlement there. Tensions boiled over and a tired and depleted Britain abandoned the area to the United Nations in 1948.

The UN decided on a Partition, to which the Jews agreed but the Arabs refused. In the ensuing war, the first wave of fleeing Palestinian refugees filled the West Bank and Gaza, while Jewish refugees migrated inwards in ever greater numbers. The complexities are like three-dimensional chess. Formerly Ottoman Syria, for example, still quietly considered the whole area rightfully Syrian. Nothing is resolved many decades later, and does not seem likely in most readers' lifetimes. On all of the *Windrush's* first trips, therefore, men were sent to take part in this and other conflicts, and many would return wounded or traumatised.

The peace dividend seemed to elude Britain entirely. The world was still war-torn and the British were trapped by so much of it. In response, in July 1947, the Labour government proposed a National Service Act, which required 18-year-old males to take part in a year and a half of military service, which came into force in January 1949. For some this involved peeling potatoes in Catterick Barracks and kicking their heels in the confines of their own country. For others, they could be suddenly despatched on the *Windrush* and other troop ships to parts of the world they had never heard of to take part in policing operations they did not understand. It was a lottery when they received their call-up papers what their destiny would be.

Clement Attlee, the Prime Minister, as a volunteer in the First World War, had a long-standing antipathy to the idea of conscription,[6] but it was a necessary counterbalance to the sudden reduction of the military after the war, with hundreds of thousands of men and women demobbed within a few months. One of the main reasons for this shortage of personnel was the independence of India on

15 August 1947. In one sense the British had simply dropped a hot potato and relinquished any responsibility or financial liability for India. In another, Britain had lost the services, devotedly given in two world wars, of the Indian army. Britain was short of fighting men, with trouble still breaking out in many of her remaining colonies. It was because of this that troop ships such as the *Windrush* were desperately needed.

The scale of conscription under the National Service regime was considerable. Twice a month, 6,000 men (peaking at 10,000 in the later Korean War) reported on Thursdays for induction. The feeling among these men was that the War Office was either stupid or bloody-minded, as they were often sent hundreds of miles from home even when a major regiment existed in their own home towns.

Men of Irish extraction, for example, 'ordinarily resident' on the mainland (making them liable for National Service) were perhaps understandably ferried to Northern Ireland to join up. Yet an almost equal number of men identifying as born-and-bred Londoners were sent there too.[7] It made little sense, and increased a belief that, after bluffing its way through the war on the efforts and sacrifice of ordinary people, the British establishment neither cared nor knew what it was doing. If there is a disconnect between government and people today, it is nothing new.

The situation of former Indian army officers on the *Windrush* was especially complex and in a state of flux for a few years after the war. The officers of the Indian army had all been British. Their leadership was crucial in the war, and their abilities valued. Throughout the conflict nearly 300 cadets had been sent to India every month for training. At the end of the war, indigenous Indian troops returned home after serving in Malaya, while the Gurkhas of Nepal then divided between the Indian and British armies. In the period leading up to Partition on 15 August 1947, extraordinarily, any British soldiers in India were usually passive spectators to the savage inter-communal riots and massacres.[8]

The journalist and author Brigid Keenan is one of many who have written of the complex emotions, backgrounds and predicaments of

164

those returning from India on troop ships. She sailed 'home' at the age of 8 in 1948 to a country she had never been to and to a brother trapped by war at an English boarding school who she did not know. Her family had been in India for five generations, with French and Irish blood. She was struck by how 'colonised Irishmen became part of the colonisation of India'[9] and that Kipling's famous *Kim* was actually Kimball O'Hara, the orphan of an impoverished Irish soldier serving in India.

When she arrived at port in England she was overwhelmed by the cold grey sky in unfriendly post-war Britain. Arriving a year after Independence, with few job prospects and no contacts, her father became a cowman and his friend, an admiral in India, became a lavatory attendant at Waterloo station. Her father found it hard to forget the slaughter he saw in the Punjab after Partition, and when he died her family:

> discovered a packet of agonised letters he had written to our mother at this time, lamenting the horrors he was witnessing. He blamed the 'bloodbath' (as it became known) on Mountbatten's bungled planning: the British police had been sent back to the UK at independence, along with the majority of British soldiers serving in India, so there was no neutral power left in the subcontinent to keep the peace.

Ultimately, Keenan writes, those troop ship returnees were:

> faintly despised. The feeling seemed to be that they had lived high on the hog, they hadn't suffered the Blitz or rationing or cold winters and so what could they expect now? … The Indian writer Shrabani Basu (author of *Victoria & Abdul*)[10] is no friend of the Raj, but she read my recent memoir and said: 'It must have been particularly painful for the children, as India was the only home they knew.' Exactly.

To read the Indian press in the period of Partition, however, might cause an Indian subscriber to feel that *Windrush* had sailed in not on an ill wind but on a gust of goodwill. In the *Times of India* on 19 September 1947:

GOODWILL MISSION IN BOMBAY
Crowded Programme

An Indo-British Goodwill and Cultural Mission comprising five representatives of different cultural and social organisations of Great Britain arrived in Bombay from London on Thursday morning by 'Empire Windrush'.

Led by Swami Avyaktanand, founder and head of the Vedanta movement in England, the Mission intends to tour the country as extensively as possible, and will convey the 'Sincere and affectionate regards' of the Britishers to the Indian people. The Mission also hopes to carry back with it a similar message from India.

Of the five members two are women. They are Miss B. Jenkins, President of the Society for the Cultural Fellowship with India in England and Mrs. Margaret Flint, Assistant Secretary for the Federation of Mankind.

The Mission was particularly interested in cementing friendship with India on a sound basis and would meet prominent Indian officials and politicians and would visit many towns and villages. The Ramakrishna Ashram at Khar[11] is looking after the accommodation of the members.

This is in many ways a bizarre report. There is something of the ilk of King Canute about well-intentioned blue stockings arriving on the *Windrush* to build social and religious bonds with the very country whose sudden withdrawal would displace 14 million people and leave up to 2 million dead. As they were attending civic receptions in Bombay, thousands of displaced refugees were arriving at the docks every day.

Yet there is hope in the *Windrush*'s naïve mission too. The Vedanta movement in Britain continues to this day, operating from a centre in Bourne End in Buckinghamshire. Quietly, generations of British adherents have prayed and meditated according to the original Vedic teachings, doing nobody any harm. In one way it is reassuring to know that the *Windrush*, which was mainly transporting troops and guns around the world on retreat from or in pursuit of war, was capable even at such a time of planting the seeds of peace.

She was about to plant some more.

16

THE POLES

Over the last twenty years, as was discussed earlier, the *Windrush* name has become a brand. At first it was a positive, shorthand description for a generation of migrants of black origin arriving in the United Kingdom in the decades after the war.

Then, more recently, the Windrush generation became an identifier for the same group of people, but seventy years on. Now it signalled gross maladministration by the UK government in denying two generations of black British people their birthright and in many cases 'sending them back' to places to which they had no allegiance, even though under every legal definition – except that they had not got round to applying for passports – they were British subjects, as much a Londoner or Brummie as any white person born in the north-west European archipelago of the 'British Isles'.

Therefore, there is a risk that in trying to understand what happened on the *Windrush*'s only trip to the Caribbean in her lifetime it will be impossible to see beyond these fixed ideas, and the endless ensuing reruns of old newsreel of a man singing 'England is the Place for Me' on the ship after it had docked at Tilbury on 22 June 1948.

The 1948 voyage, then, comes loaded with preconceptions. Perhaps the best way to put these to one side is to approach at first from a completely different angle.

Between January and April 1948, the *Windrush* had made two more full round trips from London to Bombay and back. It is noteworthy that London was the port at the British end rather than Southampton, indicating just how many of those returning from India were not military personnel but rather their families for whom being offloaded in the Solent would have been geographically of little use when they would then need to catch onward trains to all parts of the country.

In May 1948, she began her most famous journey outward bound from Tilbury, on the north side of the Thames estuary. In the voyage cards it is recorded as carefully as ever by Lloyd's, with red writing for Sailings (Sd) and black writing for Arrivals (Ar). This was the completed itinerary:

Sd	London	May 6
Ar	Southampton	May 7
Sd	Southampton	May 7
Ar	Trinidad	May 20
Sd	Trinidad	May 20
Ar	Kingston (Ja)	May 24
Sd	Kingston (Ja)	May 27
Ar	Tampico	June 2
Sd	Tampico	June 2
Ar	Havana	June 3
Sd	Havana	June 4
Ar	Bermuda	June 8
Sd	Bermuda	June 11
Ar	London	June 21

By examining this schedule, we have the first opportunity to challenge the received stereotype of the *Windrush's* arrival in Tilbury; it was not just a journey from Jamaica carrying West Indians. It took sixty-six other migrants on at the port of Tampico in Mexico too, but none of them was Mexican; they were Poles. This group of Polish migrants, by the time they reached England, had made a journey across the globe that made Max Manus' eight-month voyage from Norway to London seem like a day trip.

As so often in the story of the *Windrush*, it is necessary to look below one familiar layer of history to a layer or two beneath. We know 1 September 1939 as the date that Britain declared war on Germany in response to the latter's invasion of Poland. We are less familiar with what happened little more than a fortnight later when Stalin's Soviet army invaded Poland from the east on 17 September. From that point on, Poland was divided in two.

Some will know from various novels and films that in April and May 1940 the Soviets murdered 22,000 Polish officers and members of the intelligentsia, and buried them in a forest at Katyn.[1] What is not widely understood is that the Soviets then forced a further million Polish citizens to work in slave-labour camps in Kazakhstan and Siberia, more than half of whom were women. Of this million, it is thought that half had died by the end of the war.

Meanwhile, Polish fighters who had managed to escape both invasions via France, or who were already overseas, had flocked to London in 1939, volunteering to fight on the Allied side. In the Battle of Britain in August and September 1940, when the outcome of the war was on a knife's edge, 148 Polish pilots were responsible for destroying 203 German planes, with thirty-five probables claimed and thirty-six damaged. On 24 August 1940, Sergeant Anton Glowacki claimed five enemy aircraft in one day.

The commander-in-chief of Fighter Command, Air Chief Marshal Sir Hugh Dowding, had mistrusted the Poles from the start, worried about language barriers; he had also fallen for the prejudice that Poland had 'allowed' itself to be easily conquered by the Germans, and thus had little appetite for a fight. But looking back on the events of the Battle of Britain he said, 'Had it not been for the magnificent work of the Polish squadrons and their unsurpassed gallantry, I hesitate to say that the outcome of battle would have been the same.'[2] In those two months, twenty-nine Polish pilots died.

Indeed, the Polish contribution to the war had begun even before it broke out, with the inter-war Polish deciphering unit operating from the Kabaty Woods at Pyry. It was they who, just a few months before the war, cracked the German Enigma codes – intelligence that they provided to Bletchley Park (and to other Allied countries) which allowed the British to read the Ultra signals used by the Germans throughout the war. As we have seen, amongst hundreds of other purposes, this permitted the British to have almost day-by-day knowledge of the plans and movements of the *Tirpitz* and, when she was serving her, the *Windrush*. The former Bletchley mathematician and cryptologist Gordon Welchman wrote, 'Ultra would never have gotten off the ground if we had not learned from the Poles, in the nick of time, the details both of the German military … Enigma machine, and of the operating procedures that were in use.'[3]

When the war ended, the Poles in Britain expected that, with the Nazis vanquished, they could reclaim their country as an independent state, but in negotiations at the Yalta Conference in February 1945 the British signed up to an awful betrayal. Because Stalin had taken eastern Poland – the Kresy area – at a time when this was still under his former agreement with Hitler, he was to be allowed to keep it. Then, at the end of the war, he installed a puppet communist government to rule the rest of the country too. The refrain from Polish fighters during the 1945 victory celebrations in London was 'What victory?!'

However, the British, and in particular Churchill himself, were deeply ashamed of what they had done, and in 1947 Parliament passed its first ever piece of legislation specifically aimed at encouraging a group of migrants to settle permanently in the United Kingdom. The Polish Resettlement Act allowed combatants to stay and their exiled relatives to join them.

❖

For the people who had been forced out of Kresy, the journey to their new home was extraordinary. Many of them had been on the move for years making their way through Iran and Uzbekistan to India. The *Windrush* group left Karachi (still in India then) on 13 May 1943 for Bombay, then transferred to an American cruiser, *The Old City of London*, for a six-week voyage to Los Angeles, escorted by the US navy. On landing in America, which to them was the epitome of liberty, they were first interned in a camp also holding innocent Japanese Americans. After four days, they were placed on trains with sealed windows and taken to the Mexican border, where they boarded another train and were allowed to open the windows.

Now they had reached their first truly safe space of the war, the Mexican refugee camp at Colony Santa Rosa. With the help of various Polish exile charities worldwide, they set up provision for education and healthcare. From New York, other Poles sent enough books to run a decent library. Before long, piano and violin recitals and choral concerts were being held too. In this little village near the city of Léon they spent nearly four years waiting to return to Poland.

So it came as a crushing blow with the end of the war in June 1945 for them to realise that Poland was never going to escape from under Stalin's heel, and they became reconciled to spending the rest of their lives as exiles. When the British passed the Polish Resettlement Act in 1947, they looked for a ship that would could take them there. It was time for them to make their way to Tampico where the *Windrush* awaited them on 2 June 1948.

However, when the newsreel cameras arrived at Tilbury on 22 June the journalists did not seem to be aware that they had not one scoop, the arrival of the Windrush generation, but another as well: the end of a four-year journey out of insecure exile of people from a country Britain had recently, although not without protest from some political quarters, betrayed.

Some of those arrivals decided to stay in Britain only for a while. Stefania Nowak's name was the thousandth of the 1,027 'Alien Passengers' listed on the manifest (as opposed to 'British Passengers').

Her proposed address was 'Shobdon Camp, near Kingsland, Hereford'. She was already 28 years old but after staying just a few months she immigrated finally to Canada, where she lived until her death in 2012 at the age of 92 in Hamilton, Ontario.

Others dispersed to one of forty-five 'Polish Resettlement Camps' across Britain. These were usually former army barracks or prisoner-of-war camps, initially surrounded by barbed wire and high fencing but soon domesticated. Jadwiga Dubicka, aged 43, and her sons Czeslaw, 15, and Jozef, 11, were bound for Camp Blackshaw between Leek and Buxton in Staffordshire. Anna Jucha, 39, and her daughter Janina, 18, were off to Lynn Park Camp in Aberdeen. Irene Procinska, 46, and her daughter Lucyna, 16, and son, Mieczyslaw, 17, were destined for Roughan Camp near Bury St Edmunds. What differentiated the disembarking Poles from their fellow West Indian passengers is that they all had somewhere decent to go, arranged for by the British government. Later that same day, many of the Caribbean migrants ended up underground in a disused air-raid shelter by Clapham South Tube station.

Janina Folta was just 12 years old when she arrived at Tilbury on the *Windrush*, and went to the Baron's Cross at Leominster in Herefordshire. She remembers Mexico fondly, where she was allowed to live in a hacienda for nearly five years and where her family dined on tortilla and stews. Once aboard the *Windrush*, she realised that she didn't know how to use a knife and fork. Her family's passage, paid for by the British government, was spent in the cabins beneath the waterline, causing much seasickness. She was only allowed to walk on the decks under strict supervision and never met any of the other passengers.

When she walked down the gangplank her father and brothers were waiting in their forces uniforms, but she remembers feeling a little down. She hardly knew her father, who had been fighting for the entire conflict and was awarded the Italy Star, the 1939–1945 Star and the 1939–1945 War Medal. Extraordinarily, she was not even aware that she had travelled on the now famous *Windrush* until the writer Jane Raca, her daughter-in-law, performed some family research and found Janina's name in the passenger manifest seventy years later.[4]

For many of these Polish arrivals, the next fifteen years would be spent living in Nissen huts, whole families separated only by a curtain or a plywood partition. One of these Nissen encampments was Northwick Park, near Chipping Campden in Gloucestershire, just a stout walk for a tourist today to the River Windrush flowing through the equally touristy village of Burford. The cemetery of St Catherine's church in Chipping Campden holds more than sixty graves of Polish people who died of natural causes at Northwick Park, most of whom were born in the nineteenth century. In the nearest cemetery to the camp, at Station Road, Blockley, there are a further 120 graves.

By 1968 nearly all the camp residents had moved on to lives in other towns and cities, and the few remaining moved to another one, Ilford Park in Newton Abbot, Devon. To this day this remains the last Polish resettlement camp, but now it is called the Ilford Park Polish Home. The site was constructed to provide for the expected injured from D-Day, but two years later it became a home for the displaced Poles. Now, its population has an average age of 92, half of whom have dementia. A Polish priest lives on site holding a daily Mass.

In the years since the Second World War, the role the Polish played in the conflict has been widely recognised, and their positive cultural and economic contribution well appreciated. Sadly, this good feeling was contaminated by the nature of the public discourse towards 'immigrants' in the lead-up to the UK's referendum about leaving the European Union on 23 June 2016. After months of anti-immigrant rhetoric in the run-up to the referendum the number of racially aggravated offences recorded by the police that month was 41 per cent higher than in July 2015.[5]

Laminated cards were left outside primary schools and posted through letterboxes of Polish people in Huntingdon, Cambridgeshire, with 'Leave the EU/No more Polish vermin' written in English and Polish.[6] Bartosz Milewski, a 21-year-old student, was stabbed in the neck with a broken bottle because his perpetrators heard him speaking Polish with his friend in Donnington, near Telford.[7] It is probable that the people who perpetrated these acts 'want their country back' and think that Churchill was the greatest ever Englishman. It is unlikely that feeling would be reciprocated.

17

THE MOTHER COUNTRY

Let me ask you to imagine this. Living far from you is a beloved relation whom you have never met, yet this relation is so near a kin that she is known as Mother. Your own mummy talks of her all the time ... Then one day you hear Mother calling. She is troubled, she needs your help. Your mummy your daddy say, 'go, leave home leave families, leave love' ... After all you have heard can you imagine, can you believe, soon soon you will meet Mother?

The filthy tramp that eventually greets you is she. Ragged Old and dusty as the long dead ... This stinking cantankerous hag. She offers you no comfort after your journey. No smile. No welcome. Yet she looks down at you through lordly eyes and says, 'Who the bloody hell are you?'

From *Small Island* by Andrea Levy (2004)[1]

There is no finer literary legacy from the arrival of the *Windrush*, that grey June day in 1948, than the life and works of Andrea Levy, who died between the 2018 seventieth anniversary year and the first annual Windrush Day in 2019. Aged just 62, her absence at such occasions in the decades to come will be deeply felt.

Her novel, *Small Island* – the story of a couple much like her own parents who came from one small island in the Caribbean only to find another small-minded one in Britain – won both the Orange Women's Prize for Fiction and the Whitbread Book of the Year. Andrea was an astute figure at literary festivals and seminars, and she read the passage above in a West Indian lilt, rather beautifully, until she reached the final line. For this she read in an insolent and confrontational London accent: 'Who the bloody hell are you?'

That Andrea's connection to the *Windrush* influenced her writing trajectory was almost inevitable, for whenever the Tilbury arrival newsreel was shown she had a personal connection. As the camera panned across the arriving passengers, standing there, dressed as dapper as any of the many other very dapper men, was Winston Levy. He was her father, a 28-year-old Jamaican on his way to the 'mother country'.

At first it seemed very much as if the mother country wanted to welcome this group of black people from the Caribbean as much as they wanted to bring in the Poles. The clipped-toned newsreel voiceover was very carefully worded. With the usual frenetic, military band soundtrack in the background, the announcer yelled: 'Arrivals at Tilbury! The *Empire Windrush* brings to Britain 500 Jamaicans, many of them ex-servicemen, who know England, citizens of the Empire coming to the mother country with good intent.'

Every one of those thirty words had been carefully selected to convey precise information. First, it implied, as was the case, that many of these Jamaicans were ex-servicemen. Second, they would therefore be familiar with Britain and her ways. Third, they had a right to be here because they were citizens of the Empire. Fourth, they came with a ready-made attachment. Fifth, to reinforce the message, they were coming wanting only the best for all concerned. It was as positive a spin as the Central Information Office could have written.

Once again, there are layers to peel away. The newsreel did not and could not claim that these were the first black people to arrive in Britain. There were, of course, already large populations in port cities such as Liverpool and Cardiff. Neither was the *Windrush* even the first ship carrying black people to arrive in 1948. In January the *Almanazora* had arrived unheralded, docking at Southampton with 150 Jamaicans on board.

Further, although the passing of the British Nationality Act of 1948 (not as a reaction to but still after the *Windrush* had arrived) cleared the way for citizens of the British Empire to come unimpeded on seemingly indefinite leave, there was no sudden rush. Hardly more than 1,000 arrived in the next five years, Caribbean people much preferring the nearer prospect of the United States, where there was plentiful work in the congenial Florida climate on fruit farms and in canning factories.

It was only after the US Congress passed the McCarran Walter Act in 1952 that migration to the USA was restricted. Only then did what became known as the Windrush generation begin to arrive in significant numbers to Britain – the next best option where many had relatives and friends who had made the first journeys in 1948.

So, what made those 1948 men and women wish to set out from the West Indies? Sam King, passenger on the *Windrush*, became a legendary black campaigner and future Mayor of Southwark. He explained why it was worth paying the huge fare of £28 10s for the trip: 'In 1948, Jamaica was in a bad shape; it's still recovering from a hurricane a few years earlier and things were very bad because the coconuts were destroyed in '44 and it takes five years for the crop to recover. Things were very bad in farming.'[2]

Sam was just 22 but had already served in the RAF during the war, only returning to the hills of eastern Jamaica when peace broke out. He spotted a chance:

It was in the daily Jamaican newspaper, the *Gleaner*, that this troop ship would call and go back to England. I arrived shortly at the office of the agent, and I was shocked. There was a great queue … Well, the average Jamaican who came on the *SS Empire Windrush* was not a destitute. The destitute man did not have £28.10. In my case it cost three cows. The average Jamaican did not have three cows. And I think you'll find, in statistics, the people who are destitute, he might stow away … But to the best of my knowledge, let's say 500 people were on the boat, also including the stowaways, I would say three-quarters of these people were tradespersons. Again about a third were ex-service.

I'd worked on an aircraft, I've worked on all propeller driven aircraft that you can think. So three-quarters of us I would say are skilled.[3]

But before Sam and his friends had even stepped on board, a hostile environment was being brewed up by newspapers like the *Daily Express* on 8 June 1948 under the banner headline, 'I DON'T KNOW WHO SENT THEM'. The report stated that questions were already being raised in the House of Commons. The Conservative MP for Bristol West, Oliver Stanley, demanded of the Minister of Labour, 'Will you find out who is responsible for the extraordinary action?'

George Isaacs, a Labour MP, replied:

That is already being done. I wish I knew, but I do not. Those who organised the movement of these people to Britain did them a disservice in not contacting the Labour Ministry and giving it a chance to take care of them … I hope no encouragement will be given for others to follow them.

The hoo-hah over the feared arrival of Caribbean immigrants caused a flurry of anxious correspondence between ministries and politicians for the next few weeks, some even suggesting that the *Windrush* should be prevented from docking. It was only calmed down by the firm hand of the Prime Minister, Clement Attlee. He wrote a letter to a group of eleven backbenchers:

I am replying to the letter signed by yourself and ten other Members of Parliament in 22 June about the West Indians who arrived in the country on that day aboard the *Empire Windrush*. I note what you say, but think it would be a great mistake to take the emigration of this Jamaican party to the United Kingdom too seriously.

It is traditional that British subjects, whether of Dominion of Colonial origin (and of whatever race or colour), should be freely admissible to the United Kingdom. That tradition is not, in my view, to be lightly discarded, particularly at a time when we are importing foreign labour in large numbers. It would be fiercely resented in the colonies themselves, and it would be a terrible mistake to take any measure which would tend to weaken the goodwill and loyalty of the colonies towards Great Britain. If our policy were to result in a great influx of undesirables, we might, however unwillingly, have to consider modifying it. But I wouldn't be willing to consider that except on really compelling evidence, which I do not think exists at the present time.[4]

This message of conciliation did not appeal to the *Daily Express*, which was apparently ignorant of the skilled background of the majority of the passengers on board like Sam King. On 21 June 1948, it ran this article:

EMPIRE MEN FLEE NO JOBS LAND:
500 HOPE TO START A NEW LIFE TODAY

Five hundred unwanted people, picked up by the trooper *Empire Windrush* after it had roamed the Caribbean, Mexican Gulf, and Atlantic for 27 days are hoping for a new life. They include 430 Jamaican men … The Jamaicans are fleeing from a land with large unemployment. Many of them recognise the futility of their life at home.

This spin was entirely counter to the precisely worded and accurate voiceover on the newsreel. These were unwanted men leading futile lives. It is possible to imagine the dawning of the first Little Englander that morning opening his newspaper and saying, 'They come over here, they nick our jobs, etc. etc.'

On board the *Windrush* for that voyage was a British man who had already sailed on her many times before, one of the ship's cooks, Arthur Coats. Arthur came from Cardiff and he was a long-time employee of the New Zealand Shipping Company, well aware of the *Windrush*'s background:

'Actual fact it was an ex-German ship. Apparently, from stories we was told, that it was sunk and refloated and brought on as a troop ship.'

Arthur was also well aware why the *Windrush* was bringing such a large contingent from the Caribbean:

Well it's only a personal opinion but how would we have got going again after the war? It wasn't me, I wasn't ashore, I was at sea, but – factories, tubes, railways, nursing. Can't make up all them thousands of dead just like that, can you? So someone had to do it. As I say, to my way of thinking, thank God they come over or else this country would still have been in debit to America.

Arthur's view was widely shared by those who understood Britain's predicament. It wasn't just the death toll from the war. Throughout the late 1940s very large numbers of Britons packed the trains out of London, and the boats out of Liverpool and Southampton, and made their way to Canada, Australia and New Zealand.

In 1947, Winston Churchill blamed two years of socialist rule for 'half a million of our ... most lively and active citizens in the prime of life' wanting to emigrate. 'We cannot spare you,' he said, 'at a time when we are scouring Europe for 20,000 or 30,000 or more of unfortunate displaced persons of the great war to come in and swell out labour force.' His words did not stem the flow, and by the end of the 1950s some 650,000 British people had left for other parts of the Commonwealth.

On the day that the *Windrush* left Kingston, Arthur recalls, the Jamaican men were excited and ready for the voyage. However, for many of them setting out on the high seas proved challenging. He gleefully recalls:

The first morning that they come on board they're all up for breakfast through their mess hall and to see the sight of some of them, their eyes were rolling, you know, they all looked ill, being sea sick and not used to being at sea they wasn't, and that struck me as funny in a sense, you know, that was all … They're nearly all sick and you start rubbing them up the wrong way talking about fatty pork and all that.

He also remembers what had already proved, and would prove many times again, to be the ship's Achilles heel, her engines: 'And then she broke down, coming home she broke down, had to put into Bermuda for repairs.'

There, three men he'd befriended on the ship had found themselves a spot playing in a dance hall during the stopover. He remembers the friendship, and how 'we used to have them down in the cabin, having drinks and all that and then once we got to Tilbury more or less that was it, finished, and I didn't see them anymore'. He doesn't name them, but there is a good chance that the three men were a remarkable trio who went on to be catalysts in their own way in the history of British music: Lord Kitchener, Lord Woodbine and Lord Beginner.

Lord Beginner was responsible in 1950 for writing and recording a song formally titled 'Victory Test Match' but better known as 'Cricket Lovely Cricket'. He wrote it quickly to mark the remarkable win by a West Indies XI against England at Lords in 1950, and it is said that he and Lord Kitchener sang it as they led a crocodile of West Indies fans all the way from Lords in St John's Wood to dance around Eros at Piccadilly Circus.

Lord Kitchener, who became famous instantly when singing 'London is the Place for Me' for the newsreel cameras at Tilbury, remembers the experience of starting the singing off at Lords:

After the match I took my guitar and called a few West Indians, and I went round the cricket field singing and dancing. That was a song I made up. So while we're dancing up come a policeman and arrested me.

And while he was taking me out of the field, the English people boo him, they said 'Leave him alone, let him enjoy himself! They won the match, let him enjoy himself.' And he had to let me loose because he was embarrassed. So I took the crowd with me singing and dancing, from Lords, into Piccadilly in the heart of London.[5]

Lord Kitchener was so inspired by this experience that he later wrote 'The Alec Bedser Calypso' in tribute to the great Surrey and England test bowler, celebrating Bedser's skittling out in a later test of the Australians. Anyone in their mid fifties and over will remember quite how thoroughly calypso penetrated British radio and television stations, sometimes used as a parodic structure for political satire by white comedians such as Lance Percival.

Musicologists take all this melding of society, cricket and music very seriously. Kevin Le Gendre wrote:

> Although the contest reached its conclusion at Lords in London, one of the other matches took place at Old Trafford, in Manchester, which gave Blacks from Liverpool, Manchester, Birmingham and beyond the opportunity to experience this sporting and political event as a collective entity. So the line, 'West Indies voices all blended', refers both to the union of different islands in the West Indian team and the various Caribbean communities in Britain. That single line, so incisive in its simplicity, marks out 'Victory Test match' as one of the seminal tunes to a national manifestation of Blacks living in postwar Britain. Cricket, rather than London, is the place for me.[6]

The third Lord, Lord Woodbine, an ex-RAF man like Sam King, went on to be an edgy and sometimes controversial manager of talent and nightclubs in north-west England who, although a musician like his friends from the *Windrush*, was never recorded. He became famous as a footnote in world music history when, during his time working in Liverpool, he befriended a young group by the name of the Silver Beetles at his Jacaranda nightclub, where they played some of their first gigs.

Woodbine's entrepreneurial drive took him to Hamburg at the invitation of a German sailor with his own outfit, the Royal Caribbean Steel Band. He then negotiated a deal to bring over what were now called The Beatles: Pete Best, George Harrison, John Lennon, Paul McCartney and Stuart Sutcliffe. To get them going, he even drove them to Hamburg in his van.

It was Lord Kitchener, born Aldwyn Roberts, of the three *Windrush* Lords who had the best career, and who gave the best account of that trip from the Caribbean. He had always wanted to go to the 'mother country', as he called it too, and:

> While we're going to Bermuda, a woman stowaway was discovered and she started crying, because she thought they would want to put her in prison, So, the purser of the boat said, Well, if you all get together and get some dollars, some pounds, you can save this lady the embarrassment. Pay the fare for her, and then she'll be free. So we all gather and gave a concert on the boat. And we got the money, paid the money to the purser, and she was free to travel to England ... And the boat reached Tilbury ... Well it's the time I realised that people really are brave. All those stowaways jumped from the ship into the water and started swimming ashore ... About a week later I went to a place called the Paramount and to my surprise many of the stowaways were in [there] jiving, dancing and what-have-you. I had to laugh, I couldn't believe it. A man just stowaway and, after a couple of days, he in is a dance hall jiving and dancing around.[7]

Also on the *Windrush* that day was the Trinidadian singer and actress Mona Baptiste, who a year after her arrival became a cast member of the much-loved BBC radio programme *Variety Bandbox*, and afterwards became the singer for outfits such as Ted Heath's Big Band. She had a hit with a song called 'Calypso Blues' and later became a star in both music and film in Germany, becoming one of many black artists who not only performed in European countries but in European languages too.

So how did the optimism of 1948 become soured in 2018? How did the persecution of this cohort of people begin? In 1968, under Harold Wilson's Labour government, activists were offered a poisoned chalice.

In return for being given stronger powers to challenge discrimination in employment and housing – with a Race Relations Board newly enabled to act on its own behalf rather than always having to go through the Attorney General – immigration laws were strengthened.

There in plain sight in 1968, but somewhat under regarded at the time, is the removal of the rights of Commonwealth citizens to settle in the United Kingdom. It did not occur to any of those arriving in 1948 that, seventy years on, their very right to be British would be challenged by a hostile government taking its cue from the 1968 law. A law, perhaps, of unintended consequences.

THE FORGOTTEN WAR

The *Windrush*'s increasingly wheezy journeys during the late 1940s had been confined mainly to the Mediterranean. In 1950, however, she was obliged to engage once again in longer and more arduous voyages to the Far East, with her engineers maintaining round-the-clock vigilance for her belching number one engine.

The reason for her now being called back to carrying troops to far-flung places was the outbreak of the Korean War. This conflict was a watershed in post-war British history but today it is little known about or understood. Veterans describe themselves as 'the Forgotten Army'.

When it arises on the current A-level history syllabus, it is in the context of essays about the emergence of the new United Nations, American hegemony, studies of the nascent Cold War or the grim irony that after so much effort demilitarising Germany and Japan both nations were then actively encouraged to return to armaments manufacturing to supply the United Nations' forces requirements. Indeed, this partially explains how both experienced such a fast economic resurgence.

Ignorance, though, is pretty universal when compared to what people know of the Second World War, which ended only five years earlier. The over-fifties may recall Korea as the setting for the long-running US comedy, *MASH*,[1] but even when this was transmitting in the early seventies it was taken as a satire on the still-live war in Vietnam.

Yet the significance of the Korean War in both British and world history cannot be overstated. It was the first conflict where forces from sixteen countries came together under the United Nations flag. It was also the first time British and Chinese fighters had engaged in conflict against each other since the Opium Wars, which had ended more than a century earlier.

Those captured by the Chinese – many of them men who'd been ferried to Korea on the *Windrush* – were subjected to the 'Lenient Programme' – a sophisticated brainwashing propaganda scheme depicted later in the film *The Manchurian Candidate*. One captive who required no torture to begin to betray his country was the future British agent turned Soviet spy, George Blake.[2]

Ten years before the Cuban Missile Crisis, Korea was a conflict in which the senior American, General McArthur, Head of UN Command, had to be stopped by colleagues from trying to end it all with nuclear bombs. Even so, the red-hot tension between east and west led to the first deployment of American B-29 bombers to British airbases ready for war with Russia. They are still there.

Perhaps most importantly, Korea was a war that never ended; it still goes on. The current position on the Korean peninsula is one of an unstable ceasefire, but a formal end to war was never declared. That ceasefire was only achieved on the death of Stalin and with the rise of Mao Zedong, Chairman of the Chinese Communist Party, for whom the conflict was an unwanted distraction.

Coincidentally, in the demilitarised zone between the North and South may lie some of the most important evidence on the habitat of plants and animals on Earth. It is an area left devoid of human meddling and pollution for so long that rewilding experts long to penetrate it, if and when it is rid of the thousands of landmines that pepper the whole zone.

On the domestic front the war had two historic effects. In Britain, just at the moment the Labour government, which had recently founded the National Health Service, wanted to turn its efforts to ending austerity, expenditure was diverted away from seeking the elusive peace dividend after the Second World War and was forced into armaments manufacture and the re-expansion of the military. The Conservatives duly won the next election. At the personal level, Korea meant that national servicemen who'd anticipated a quiet eighteen months square-bashing in Aldershot found themselves being marched up the gangplank on to the *Windrush*, many hundreds of them never to return.

Tony Younger, later to become Major General A.E. Younger, was proud to be a professional soldier, but by the time he boarded the *Windrush* in the autumn of 1950 to head for Korea he could be forgiven for thinking he'd already done his bit.

When Younger had passed his officer's exams back in 1937, with war still odds-against, what seemed to lie ahead for him was a well-resourced military training with the Royal Engineers, followed by an army-sponsored education at Cambridge. 'But Hitler invaded Poland just before we were due to start there, and our lives were changed.'[3]

So, for the next decade, instead of idly punting down the Cam, Younger went to war. First he blew up bridges in north-east France, then helped organise the evacuation of the British army from Dunkirk, after which he was seconded to take a role in the anthrax experiments on the western Scottish island of Gruinard, commissioned by Porton Down.

As the inevitable invasion of Europe beckoned, he took a leading role adapting the Royal Engineers assault vehicle (AVRE) into a landing craft, with which he practised by invading the Isle of Wight. Then he actually invaded Europe in an AVRE on D-Day, near Courseulles.

After a brief intermission having treatment in Portsmouth on an eardrum that he had damaged in the invasion, he was flown back out to the front, crossing the Rhine with the British army towards the miraculously undamaged medieval village of Celle. From Celle he drove just a few miles out of the village to find himself confronted by the concentration camp at nearby Belsen. There, he encountered 'a huge pit filled with hundreds of naked corpses. I have heard it said that soldiers in wartime become casual about seeing dead bodies and about suffering. In my experience nothing could be further from the truth.'

After the war he was sent to Burma, now with his family by his side, where he helped organise the repatriation of approximately a quarter of a million servicemen to Britain and other parts of the Commonwealth. From there he was despatched to Malaya where the first skirmishes of the insurgency were just beginning.

Only thereafter did Tony Younger return to take up his place at Christ's College, Cambridge, in the autumn of 1948, nine years later than intended and now married with two young children. Perhaps too worldly to fall for the dreaming spires, he found the standard of instruction in his chosen subject of engineering 'not just bad, it was appalling'.

It was with some relief that Younger completed his Cambridge course and rejoined the army at Perham Down, near Tidworth, on Salisbury Plain. Like the rest of the country, both Younger and the army were hoping to quietly rebuild their lives and the nation's fabric in the hard-won peace. However, for him that peace lasted just weeks. He wrote:

In 1950, when North Korea suddenly invaded South Korea, the British people and their Army, were more concerned with recovering from the Second World War than with preparing to fight again. The Army in England was not in a particularly healthy state, in spite of the high quality of its leaders. NATO had just been forced into existence by the autocratic policies of Stalin's government in Moscow, and priority had to be given to British units in Germany both for equipment and manpower.

Younger was now given command of 55 Squadron, 29 Brigade, Royal Engineers, which should have stood 350 strong but was depleted to just 150. His attention turned to who would be supplementing this number on the chosen troop ship, which was to be the *Windrush*, but when he met the first reservists off a 3-ton truck from Salisbury railway station just three men climbed out: a policeman with a letter from his station commander requesting his immediate return, a refrigeration mechanic with no home whose wife had just given birth to twins and a veteran with only one leg.

Soon, though, this unpromising trickle of recalled men became a river, and 150 were selected from the 450 possibles who passed through the brigade's hands. With only six weeks before they had to board the *Windrush* at Southampton, they trained hard and drank hard, but their principal personal difficulty was financial: 'Many were good tradesmen who had been earning up to three times what the Army would give them. Nearly all were married with young children and many were faced with rents or mortgage payments attuned to their civilian pay scale, so their problems were real.'

Younger did his best to ensure that all his men were in good mental and physical condition, but he knew from hard-won experience that 'true battle-worthiness would only come from experience … of conditions in the theatre of war … we evolved a full training programme for the voyage ahead.'

Yet although Younger was an officer, when he boarded the *Windrush* he was as worried about the personal financial cost as any of his men. It might seem highly unjust today, but in 1950 when a soldier was posted overseas he immediately lost his army accommodation in Britain. Younger's wife and their two children were now homeless, and with money an issue in expensive Wiltshire, they had to settle across the Solent on the Isle of Wight.

On the day of his departure on the *Windrush* he found his quarters below and made ready to execute the plan he'd hatched to see his family one last time as he sailed away for Pusan. As the ship left port and headed down the east side of the Isle of Wight he'd calculated that he'd be close enough to shore to be able to wave at them as they hung out of their top window in their new seaside home. Yet, extraordinarily for this calm and rational man, the entire occasion spooked him to his core.

He was unsettled first when he realised it was time to get over to the starboard, island side of the ship, only for the master, Captain Wilson, to announce a surprise safety drill: 'All ranks proceed to emergency boat stations immediately.'

Younger's muster point was on the port side, so he was pulled in exactly the opposite direction to where he needed to be. He endured precious passing minutes while heads were counted before he slipped away prematurely and found a window on the starboard side. On the shore he saw a great white sheet flapping in the air from his family's bedroom window. He frantically waved a handkerchief back, optimistically hoping that they'd see him and know that he appreciated their efforts. Yet in that single moment he was overwhelmed by feelings he had never known before: 'Quite suddenly it hit me. I had a clear presentiment that I was heading for death and that I would never see my family again.'

Younger was utterly perplexed. In five years of serious warfare he had never felt anything more than rational fear in a dangerous spot. His morale had been high of late, the hectic six weeks of training had gone well and the initial news from Korea had been good: 'There just seemed to be no logical reason why such a thought should enter my head. My musings were interrupted by a quiet voice: "Hello; are you all right?"'

The speaker was Captain Pat Angier, soon to become Major P.A. Angier. Younger was calmed by this friendly intervention, and by Angier's explaining that, as Younger had asked earlier, air blowers had been arranged for what would soon be the stiflingly warm troop decks below.

But this sense of foreboding stayed with Younger for the entire journey – a voyage during which he became particularly attuned to death after a most peculiar occurrence akin to something out of a nautical horror story. It all began when the usually implacable Captain Wilson had flown into a rare rage on being told that a group of infantrymen, firing off their elderly Lee–Enfield rifles from the bow of the ship into the Red Sea, had committed an act which in effect cursed the ship.

The men's routine had been for their sergeant to set a target for them by creating a splash in the sea with a single round, and then for the other four men to shoot quickly to see how close they could land their own bullet before the ripples disappeared. But that afternoon a report reached the bridge that the men had hit and killed a dolphin.

Pat Angier came into the officers' dining room, where Younger and his fellow officers were eating, and relayed the news. "'The Captain is furious," Angier said. "One of our men who was shooting over the stern was seen by a member of crew to shoot a dolphin. He says this is inexcusable and that all shooting must stop at once."'

Younger countered that the shooting practice was vital training and must go on, but Angier said absolutely not. The fact it was a dolphin that had been hit was an utter disaster. In the passionate opinion of Captain Wilson – and according to nautical superstition – this would inevitably mean there would be a death on board.

Horrifically, this irrational prediction came to pass within twenty-four hours. A 19-year-old sapper who'd been ashore in Port Said, unused to the region's tradition of bartering, had grown angry with an Arab stallholder, and in his fury had turned over a table of trinkets in the bazaar. A fight broke out, and the sapper was hit heavily on the back with a heavy stick. The prognosis was grim.

Pat Angier recorded, 'He may die before we reach Aden. Poor chap, what a place to be ill! He was hit by an Egyptian Policeman and has a punctured spleen. We called for blood donors and had forty in half a minute.'[4]

The operation on the sapper's spleen took place the evening after the dolphin had been shot, and only after the heat of the day had passed. The air blowers on the *Windrush* had to be switched off for fear of dirt being blown into the open wound, and it was judged this could only happen as dusk fell and the temperature dropped. However, the young man died on the operating table, and was buried at Aden, the next port.

Younger was devastated to have to write home to the man's parents in Northern Ireland about their son's senseless death:

This occasion hit me very hard, I felt it was all so pointless. The argument had been about a few shillings and nothing more. Who should take the blame? The Egyptian police certainly over-reacted, but why? Had they suffered under some officious Englishman who threw his petty authority about, leaving a sullen resentment in those under him?

A sense of resentment could easily have been the overriding emotion for another young soldier as the *Windrush* progressed east. The 18-year-old Private Dave Green of the Glo'sters had been conscripted as a national serviceman just a few months before on the understanding that he had eighteen months of barrack-bound tedium ahead of him. Almost immediately he was told he was bound for the war in Korea, but he was happy that at least he had the compensation of an associated pay rise.

However, by the time he'd reached the Mediterranean he'd learned that the government had increased the mandatory length of national service from eighteen months to two years. At that time, any serviceman electing to stay on beyond the obligatory year and a half was signed up as a professional, with associated better terms. Now, the government had stretched the lower rate period to two years instead. He wouldn't be getting a pay rise after all. He'd already doubled the 9s a week he'd been sending back to his mother in Cheltenham and didn't have the heart to reduce it. Therefore, life on board for him was very tight.

But Dave Green didn't care. Not for him was the presentiment of death felt by Tony Younger. These last few months of training had transformed him, and the *Windrush* completed the job – a genuine example of the rites of passage.

Green had come from an unpromising background: a poor family in which he was one of seven, with an elder brother, Eric, whose life was overshadowed by drink since being torpedoed in the Royal Navy during twenty-two years at sea. His father was a poorly paid but content local gardener for hire in Cheltenham – a principled man who'd been a conscientious objector in the First World War for which he served time in prison.

Green remembered:

I'm afraid it caused a good deal of turmoil in his family as two of his brothers went to war, one being killed in France when he was only nineteen years old. So perhaps it was hardly surprising that dad was a bit bothered about my going to Korea. He told me that I didn't have to go and I said don't worry dad, it'll be all over by the time we get there.[5]

Green had struggled to find direction in life, and he too had served time in jail – for a petty theft committed by a friend for which he was erroneously charged. But his army training at Bulford Camp, near Amesbury, beginning in the spring of 1950, gave him a feeling of comradeship 'that would leave an indelible mark with us for the rest of our lives'. Like many of his new pals, the army represented opportunity.

When he was unable to take part in the passing out parade because of a minor injury, he watched instead from the hospital ward as his comrades marched by, with the band playing 'To Be a Farmer's Boy', bayonets fixed, arms swinging in unison: 'A great lump came to my throat and to my astonishment a torrent of tears rolled down my cheeks. Now at last I understood … how much the comradeship of my mates meant to me.'

While some boarding the *Windrush* on that warm autumn evening had done so with apprehension, Green had stood enthralled on the stern looking out over Southampton Water: 'To say I was elated would be an understatement. I would not have missed this for the world – the smell of the sea, the harbour lights and the hooting of the seagoing ships.'[6]

His sleeping quarters were on G deck, the lowest of all, which also housed the brig (prison cell). There were no portholes and the sea continuously pounded the steel plates of the hull. Hammocks were slung in two tiers from steel poles and the entire set-up was a recipe for seasickness. Green wasn't afflicted, and would have chosen to sleep on deck when possible anyway, and besides 'quite apart from my natural love of fresh air, the appalling smell of vomit on the troop decks kept me on the upper decks. At night I would creep up the iron stairway with my blankets in search of a suitable roost.'

One night he was mistaken for a pile of rubbish by the early morning crew washing the decks with a firehose, which cost him two days' pay. The rougher the sea he encountered the more he enjoyed standing on the foredeck as 40ft waves crashed over the bow rails. He wrote:

It gave me a feeling of belonging, made me wish that I'd lived in the days of sail, climbing barefooted up the rigging, body in tune with the roll of the ship, to the crow's nest, just as we youngsters used to climb up to the rook's nest in the tall swaying elms, throwing out eggs for our mates to catch in their jackets held below … The sea, and especially the porpoises which now followed us constantly, often racing ahead of the ship, and the flying fish, all fascinated me. There was an atmosphere of a pleasure cruise about the whole ship, officers and men making the most of everything and getting a good tan. Korea was furthermost from our minds. Discipline eased. The nights were warm with slight breezes in clear, star-studded skies, encouraging the lads to come up on the upper deck to witness the beauty of the planet – something most of them had overlooked until then, having been too busy trying to earn a living.

With the Egyptian coast on the starboard side, heading for Suez at Port Said, the *Windrush* passed within sight of Alexandria. For Green this was a seminal moment. During his intensive training with the Glo'sters he had learned why only this regiment wore cap badges on both the front and back of their berets. It was because of a battle between the French and the British fought on 21 March 1801 in which the Glo'sters 28th Foot were attacked from both front and rear in the sand dunes facing the coast. They found themselves fighting on two flanks simultaneously in what was said to have been a great victory. This had happened at Alexandria.

Their gallant actions won them the honour of wearing the Egyptian sphinx on their cap badge and a regimental badge front and rear. It is easy to imagine the surge of pride and adventure in the heart of an 18-year-old 150 years later as the *Windrush* sailed past the battleground.

When the *Windrush* docked in Port Said on 12 October 1950, ten days out of Southampton, Green was greatly looking forward to an assortment of stereotypical pleasures he imagined might be available in the Middle East. However, previous troop ships had allegedly behaved with such abandon in the city that most of it was now declared out of bounds, and he was not allowed to disembark.[7]

Nevertheless, this young man was captivated by the call to prayer from the minaret of a nearby mosque and, defying the prohibition on alcohol amongst the local people, sat on deck in the sun watching the world go by with a beer. The nearest he and his great friend Pete Hone got to sensual delight was a pineapple bought from a trader's boat. Familiar only with pineapple in a can, they attempted to gnaw through the husk and were left highly frustrated.

As the *Windrush* approached the southern end of the Suez Canal, Green had the opportunity to vent these frustrations when he saw a notice announcing that a boxing tournament was being arranged. Green had received his first boxing lessons as a boy back in Gloucestershire during the Second World War, taught by 'coloured American soldiers … when I got myself as a general errand boy, boot cleaner and kitchen hand in their anti-aircraft camp outside Cheltenham. Often playing truant in school for days on end I earned more in a day than poor old dad earned in a week.' Green had become a decent regional boxer in the south-west, only losing in various finals.

On board the *Windrush* he was entered as a welterweight. He won both of his first two fights on technical knockouts before:

As is the story of my life, I was beaten narrowly on points in the final. I was not altogether surprised to learn later that he [my opponent] was the referee's batman. After these two fights many of my comrades had reassessed their opinions of me and I'd become 'the blonde bomber'.

The last fight on the card that evening was between what Green describes as two men, 'one from the forest proper'. This refers to the Forest of Dean, an area west of Gloucester that had – perhaps still has – a reputation for being something of a backwoods. This contest made the crowd hoot with laughter:

The shorter forest man was a real country boy, a reservist in his early forties but without much between the ears. However, what he lacked in brains he made up for in guts. It was comic to watch as the two of them eventually jumped on each other's backs, flailed fists and refused to separate – so much so that the referee jumped out of the ring and left them to it.

As the *Windrush* left the Red Sea and turned east towards Aden and the Indian Ocean, the stratifications of the British class system were fully evident. The night-time temperature was in the nineties and as many ordinary soldiers as could grab a space on the hatches lay in their boxer shorts on the open deck. Above them, a group of similarly raw national service officers:

> Fresh-faced and straight from college, would appear at the rail above our heads accompanied by the nurses coming out to Korea with us, and ladies from the ship staff. The gentle breeze, which blew after dark, blowing up their skirts [was] putting all sorts of ideas into the minds of our watching lads below.

The first port of call in Asia was Colombo in Ceylon where, despite the searing heat, it was decided the men should march through the capital.[8] Then, crossing the Bay of Bengal and on into the Straits of Malacca, Green and his friends anticipated the pleasures of Singapore, only to find that the very same troops who had caused Port Said's pleasure havens to be forbidden had caused similar chaos in Singapore too. But the city was a much bigger canvas than Port Said, and with Korea now on their mind the men were determined to have some fun:

> Singapore gave us our first taste of the mysterious East though we would find that as in every other port of call the two other battalions of our 29th Brigade, the Ulster Rifles and the Northumberland Fusiliers, had queered our pitch by painting the town red on their way through. Nevertheless, we were able to get around much more than we had in Port Said. Warm, tranquil air breezed through the busy streets, neon signs flashing invitingly, and beautiful girls with split skirts adorning their slim bodies slipped past us, giving Pete

and I shy smiles. We, who had shared a bottle of Tiger beer were anybody's. Unfortunately, girls of the night in Singapore had seen many good-looking servicemen and seamen from the big wide world, most of them with far thicker wallets than ours – and money was the number one priority. We ended up in the Raffles hotel, named after the founder of Singapore. There we enjoyed a splendid evening with a lot of our mates, sipping our beer and singing the good old army songs with the whole place joining in.

We finished the night with a chariot race back to the ship in half a dozen rickshaws, pulled by equally enthusiastic, athletic rickshaw wallahs. Well rewarded and praised for their efforts, they stood with us as, each propping the other up as we sang 'Now is the Hour', joined by the Empire Windrush Male voice choir, who lined the ship's rails. A good night had been had by all!

19

A COLD PREMONITION

It is fortunate for historians that if they look hard enough they can find the transformative voyages on the *Windrush*, such as those made by Tony Younger and Dave Green, tucked away in books about far wider subjects – even if half a century had passed before they gathered their thoughts for publication. Also travelling, on what is recorded in the *Windrush* voyage record book as number fifteen of the twenty-nine voyages she would eventually make in the decade since she was captured in Kiel, was Major Pat Angier, the deliverer of Captain Wilson's fatal prognosis after the shooting of the dolphin.

It is highly significant that Angier's name arises in others' accounts too, for although his narrative of that time has not yet been published, it is a remarkable contemporaneous volume of letters and diaries, collated and edited by his wife, Diana, soon after the Korean War was fought.[1] In its wit, courage and the elegance of his story-telling – with no bluster or hyperbole – it is as vital a piece of British war writing and social history as any other, and deserves to be more widely read.

Pat Angier's writing epitomises an emotional restraint familiar perhaps to those who have seen films from that period such as *Brief Encounter*, and it is all the more moving for it. Emerging from a heartrending series of events comes a portrait of a very young couple and the mere decade they had together. The life Pat and Diana Angier led was not unique in twentieth-century history, but in the familiarity of its domestic rhythms amidst the casual horrors of war it stands as proud as any other testimony of the times. More than any other it depicts the awful sense of six vivid weeks on the *Windrush* slipping through the hourglass while a possibly terminal destiny awaits on a peninsula very few troops could even find on a map.

Diana and Pat Angier's romance had begun in September 1941 when he was billeted at her family home on the Cathedral Close, Gloucester. At first, these opposites did not attract. She was fascinated with music and art, of which he was more or less ignorant, while he loved anything practical, from the workings of an engine to the science and practicalities of agriculture. Soon, however, they were so caught up in one another that in June 1942 they married in Gloucester Cathedral. Diana was astonished by this life's turn: 'In all my wildest dreams, I had never thought I would marry in the Regular Army. I had never liked the thought of the kind of life I was now facing. Similarly, Patrick told me he had never dreamed of marrying a person like me.'

It was a time of many dark paradoxes. On their honeymoon near Stratford-upon-Avon they watched bombers winging their way to Germany. 'It seemed strange and infinitely sad that in this beautiful warm scented dusk, death and horror should be on their way, and for us, fulfilment and peace,' she wrote.

With world war raging, Pat Angier decided to train as a paratrooper with the 4th Battalion Parachute Regiment, while his younger brother David began to train as a pilot in the RAF. Pat's last leave before being posted overseas was in Burford in the Cotswolds, the very village through which the River Windrush runs. Diana wrote, 'I can never hear *The Lark Ascending* by Vaughan Williams without thinking of that leave, the Spring, the clouds passing in shadows across the field, but above all the feeling that a door was closing: slowly, inevitably, the day was dawning when the parting had to be faced.'

With his young wife due to give birth that August, Angier was posted to north-west Algeria, until in mid August he became part of Montgomery's Eighth Army preparing for the invasion of Italy. But while he waited for the signal to invade, Diana gave birth on 18 August 1943 to a baby boy who survived for just three days. Angier wrote to her:

I thought of you lying there, weak from giving birth, and now deprived of your reward. I cannot bear to think of leaving you to face the world, perhaps for many years, alone … Try to feel that Julian has surely been accepted into the hand of God, with his little life of innocence, and he waits there to greet us one day.

Diana wrote in her volume, 'For me that letter became one of my most treasured possessions.'

At a time of war, finer feelings are soon trampled under the feet of aggression. Just two days after hearing of the loss of his child, Angier embarked for Taranto in southern Italy, before his battalion moved further up the Adriatic coast. Back in Gloucestershire, Diana had a chilling foreboding and within days, on the night of 12–13 December 1943, this proved prophetic. When a sergeant next to Angier was killed by a mine, some of the shrapnel flew into Angier's head just above his left ear and into his brain. He was evacuated via Bari and back to Algiers, until he was reunited with Diana at a hospital in Southport, Lancashire, on 12 February 1944.

For a while, his brain injury caused serious impairments of literacy and speech, and his letters from that time read like a deliberately misspelled comedy sketch. Neither could he remember the names of his closest friends nor read the menu when he went out for his first dinner with Diana. Slowly, though, he recovered, and that November the Angiers had a daughter, Rosalind. As if happiness could not be trusted, within days of her christening at Gloucester Cathedral in February 1945, news came that Angier's brother David was 'missing'. His remains were not located until 1948.

With all of the above taken into consideration, it might be thought that by now the Angier family, rather like Tony Younger's, had served its country sufficiently. That is not what the fates had in store for them. Angier now had the opportunity to leave the army on grounds of disability, but tenaciously fought his way back to A1 fitness. After a brief posting to South Africa, the family moved to Mulberry Tree Farm, Brookthorpe, near Gloucester, where Pat became adjutant to the

5th (Territorial) Battalion Gloucestershire Regiment. Diana wrote, 'The two and a half years at Brookthorpe were the longest consecutive time we had ever been together.'

By May 1950, the two young daughters they already had were added to by a son, Philip. Happiness awaited, yet just a few weeks later Diana heard the news on the radio that there was to be war in Korea. 'A cold premonition gripped me,' she wrote.

A few days later, she collected Pat from Stroud railway station after he had been sent away for a secret briefing. He had not been able to tell her before, but he placed his hand on hers and said, 'My poor darling, once more it falls on you.'

They then endured a strange latent period in Norfolk while the battalion trained for war by day and came home to loved ones in billets by night: 'I wanted to be happy for Pat's sake and yet I felt stunned with dread at the thought of the coming goodbye.'

Apparently, Pat Angier did not like to use the telephone, but nevertheless on 1 October 1950 he phoned Diana at their new home in Gloucestershire from a temporary brigade office in Southampton. The next day, he told her, he was to set sail on the *Windrush* as ship's adjutant, assistant to the commanding officer Lieutenant-Colonel J. P. 'Fred' Carne.

Of this last phone call, Diana wrote:

I had no idea of the intensity of feeling I could experience at suddenly speaking to him once more. I said very little and tried to get him to do all the talking … praying, 'Oh God, please let my voice work, help me to speak', as I felt I could not force a word out … Pat sensed the strain I felt and tried to cheer me up. 'Well,' he said 'Think of the maximum time it will be, it can't be more than three years, it may be less, so see you in two or three years!' I put down the phone for the last time.

Diana would never hear Pat's voice again.

❖

Pat Angier did not have a presentiment of death as Tony Younger had, but from the start of his voyage on the *Windrush* one can almost hear the calculations in his mind, and the discreet effort he put in to conceal his worst fears. Unlike Dave Green, Angier's journey began with seasickness in a force-8 gale even before the ship had rounded Ushant.[2]

Soon, though, he was distracted by his duties as adjutant on board working under Lieutenant Colonel Alistair MacLaine, a 20-stoner nicknamed 'Mother', who had been the officer in charge of troops aboard the *Windrush* for a number of voyages. Angier's role gave him a place for dinner at Captain Wilson's table, who was already unhappy that 1,500 troops were breaking in snow boots on his polished decks.

Entering the warmer waters of the Mediterranean, Angier found that his romantic sense of lives past was piqued: 'I have read so often of the histories of these waters that I could almost see the Galleons burning in Cadiz beside the little white houses on the coast. Nelson's Fleet passing through on an expedition, and another time the great rock under siege.'

Although his dream on leaving the army was to become an agriculturalist, his sharp mind was well attuned to the more worldly manipulations of the mass media: 'We have had masses of newspaper cuttings sent out, including *The Daily Worker*, who said we were fighting "America's dirty war etc.!". The hero of all the Press seems to be a man who the War Office called up in error!'

This comedy of errors was running under the headline 'MRS WAGSTAFF MAKES WAR OFFICE CHANGE ITS MIND' in the *Daily Mail*,[3] with other newspapers lapping it up too. Reading between the exaggerations, it seems that Private Sidney Wagstaff was a French-born bandsman in the Glo'sters and should never have been sent off on the *Windrush* in the first place. He had joined aged 14 as a boy musician years before and had already done thirteen years of army service, his duties completed. It was only after Mrs Wagstaff ('25-year-old mother of two') marched into the War Office at Whitehall to confront a major in civilian clothes that the alarmed officer became aware of the error. He telephoned Southampton to get Frank Wagstaff off the *Windrush* thirty-five minutes before she sailed.[4]

The press were making merry with what, for those who could not simply get off the ship, was a pretty mirthless subject. The *Dundee Courier* and many other papers ran with a half-page picture of the grinning Frank Wagstaff, with his knapsack over his right shoulder and his Lee–Enfield in his right hand, walking towards the camera, leaving the *Windrush* which was pulling away from the quayside behind him.[5] Given Angier's state of mind, and his evident rational tendency to doubt the whole purpose of the war in Korea – and his role in it – that the mocking press was choosing only to cover Korea in either patronising or oppositional tones, while the ship slowly ate the miles at 12 knots, was becoming hard for him to ignore.

Before long, his responsibilities became more onerous. Anthony Farrar-Hockley had to fly home after the death of his son and Angier was obliged to take on extra roles. He endured a typhoid injection, which made him feel very ill, and a separate cholera injection which he said made him feel rather 'blue'. At least, unlike Dave Green, he was permitted as an officer to go ashore at Port Said, where he had some relief on 'a nice trip round the harbour in an R.A.S.C [Royal Army Service Corps] launch, like the faster type we saw at Yarmouth. The place is like a Clapham Junction for ships and it is fascinating to watch.'

Angier was as affected by the death of the young sapper at the hands of the Egyptian police, as had been Tony Younger:

Thank God we are passing through these hellish climates and on to something cooler. Today has been one of sweat and short tempers, relieved for me by one thing of beauty only. I saw the sea full of porpoises (so they say, although even their appearance was more like that of a shark than the English channel porpoise) but even they found pleasure in the shade of the ship where they leapt like salmon going up a waterfall.

In Aden he seemed more impressed by spider crabs on the foreshore – sending a shell home for his children to examine – than by the expensive, volcanic British Protectorate. He was beguiled by the dhows, 'exactly the same in every respect as those sent there by the Queen of Sheba', and didn't mind paying off a local cab driver with £2 for damage caused by a soldier, as this was the only misbehaviour recorded ashore. He and his great friend Major Cedric Bath watched as the younger officers escorted nurses into Aden for free-spirited nights out, leaving the older men to enjoy the harbour lights as they sank 'more whisky than was good for us'. They determined to lay off it until Colombo.

The *Windrush* maintained a good lending library, and between Aden and Colombo, Angier completed *Villette* by Charlotte Brontë, again poeticising about the sea seeming glassy under a full moon: 'The wake is as snow and the mild air has all the properties necessary for romance. And how is it being employed? In the preliminary rounds for the boxing competition.' Angier too set his book aside to enjoy watching the ludicrously mismatched contest witnessed by Dave Green between the punchy Forest of Dean man and his mighty opponent. Angier's voracious reading then took him to Laurence Sterne's *A Sentimental Journey*, which 'certainly bears as yet no possible resemblance to the experiences of my present voyage', by now carrying the *Windrush* into port at Colombo.

Ceylon was a curious dominion. It had been colonised first by the Portuguese, then by the British. The importation of south Indian Tamils by the British to work the tea plantations was good for profits but created ethnic divisions that later led to Sri Lanka's terrible civil war from 1983 to 2009.[6] As an aspiring farmer, Angier might have greatly enjoyed a trip inland to the magnificent tropical garden at Kandy but he had no such luck. As the *Windrush* arrived in Colombo harbour he was suffering from prickly heat with the weight of the world on his only just 30-year-old shoulders.

He dealt with 'everything in this ship now from courts martial to china mugs, smells from socks in cabins, ironing room allocations, inspections, showers, discipline, training, cinemas, mail, orders, lavatories, shore leave and filling in forms! In this heat it is very trying.' There was to be no relief ashore, no train trip to Kandy or visits to the Reclining Buddha at Pollonawura. Instead, as Dave Green recorded earlier, Angier and the Glo'sters marched.

They rose at 5 a.m. on 26 October 1950, Angier wrote, and, over a thousand strong:

> Covered seven miles altogether, passing first the Parliament buildings, white and set in vivid shrubs and trees, where the Duke of Gloucester recently proclaimed Ceylon's dominion status. A very successful status it would seem to be. There is poverty to be seen but not glaring like in India or Egypt, but there is an over all atmosphere of peace and contentment. Indeed it would be difficult to be an agitator in this sultry clime … On the way I noticed many interesting shrubs, including some fine white magnolias and coconuts. Every back garden sports banana trees and every tree, so it seemed, sports a cheeky little jackdaw.

Perhaps this enervating walk affected the general mood. Another Glo'sters soldier, Private Harry Chalke, like so many of the men, was very annoyed to be on the *Windrush* at all. He too had an arduous Second World War (also entering Belsen) and only had two weeks left as a reservist when he was called up for Korea. He had to give up a good job with a builders in Essex and leave his wife and two very young children behind. But in Colombo he received the news that the army had written to the council and 'she was now in a lovely new house, thank you sir! At least something good had come out of all this upheaval for me.'[7]

Also in Colombo, Harry Chalke:

> Heard the good news, the Yanks, under new boss General MacArthur, had landed behind the North Koreans at Inchon and had cut their army in half and they were in full retreat towards the Yalu River, the border between Korea and China. The rumour was we would be home again just after Christmas and it was not a war but a police action.

Apart from the good news about his new council house, everything else that Harry was told in Colombo would prove to be horribly wide of the mark. Three days later, as if in a Conrad novel, the *Windrush* was passing the coast of Sumatra to starboard, where Angier witnessed a sunset the likes of which he had not seen even in his time in Africa:

> The spectacle was glorious for fully half an hour. The whole changing scene had a tall mountain, with graceful slopes on either side of its flat summit, as a background, and the rippling sea as its frame and mirror. I was made to think that it will be in such a view as this that 'The Glory of the Lord shall be revealed and all flesh shall see it together'. It has been Sunday and treated as a day of rest and I have thought of you [Diana] so much and prayed for you and the children to be blessed.

Shortly after the next Easter, Patrick Angier would be dead.

20

A CELTIC CROSS

With the *Windrush* coming within days of Singapore, the mood on the ship darkened. Dave Green recalled that:

> The luxury cruise atmosphere had gone, yielding reluctantly to thoughts of Korea and the challenges we would soon be facing. Our wills were now drawn up – something to which I, for one, had never given a thought but now made me realise for the first time that all of this was for real and that war was no longer for us just a word. It was a little thing but when I heard one man being asked for details of his next of kin by the officer and he replied 'none sir' I felt all of a sudden that I now understood him much better, his toughness and his drinking, and I realised that perhaps the mutual mate who had pinched his girl some years back may have done something more significant than he realised at the time.

Pat Angier, with every passing mile, was becoming more determined that he would never leave his family to fight again, and with comrades he thought about other employment prospects once they were back on Civvy Street. Like Dave Green, he ended up at Raffles in Singapore, only to read in a copy of the *Straits Times* there that 'the enemy was counter-attacking, and thus to be filled with an even stronger desire to eat, drink and be merry. Over our first drink Richard Reeve-Tucker and I declared that we would strive to be civilians when this job was done.'[1]

It was at this time that Green was taught by a veteran to remember the soldier's prayer, which he would be very grateful for within a few weeks:

Stay with me God, the night is dark
The night is cold, my little spark of courage dims,
The nightmare road is long
Be with me God and make me strong

The word spread that the *Windrush* was now under conditions of radio silence. On 2 November 1950, Angier recorded her entering the South China Sea, keeping out of the main shipping routes and trying to stay out of sight of land. Charts were now kept secret, and some officers on board who were trained in ju-jitsu were teaching others for a display. Seeing a large white bird with white wings and black markings, Angier told Captain Wilson that he had spotted an albatross, but the captain said that they were not to be found in these seas.

Next the *Windrush* ran into the north-east monsoon, which caused the ship to pitch heavily all day. What awaited them on land seemed no smoother. 'Bad news from the Front,' Angier recorded. 'All rather too serious. Nearer to Korea we are to black out. We shall have no dead-lights and so the fuses will be taken out and we shall stagger about.' By 4 November there was more 'news from the Front of seven Enemy Divisions attacking. Looks as if we are in for a winter campaign.'

On 6 November, Wilson ordered his staff to prepare a full Christmas dinner for the Glo'sters. No matter the weather, this huge catering operation could not be postponed, and the fare included soup, salmon, asparagus, turkey, ham, Christmas pudding and herring roes. With the ship violently lurching up and down, only 60 per cent of the Glo'sters even made it to the table.

An atmosphere of tension prevailed. Then on 8 November the *Windrush* passed Okinawa. The Battle of Okinawa had been a decisive conflict just five years earlier, fought across April, May and June 1945. It left at least 12,000 American servicemen and 110,000 Japanese dead.[2] Only in the twenty-first century have Japanese education authorities allowed it to be taught that 300,000 civilians died too, many forced by the indoctrination or coercion inflicted by Japanese forces to commit suicide, with methods including death by hand grenade. Historians today[3] argue that the grotesque loss of human life at Okinawa persuaded the Americans of the moral case for attacking Hiroshima and Nagasaki a month later with atomic bombs.

Angier would have known some if not all of this by 1950, yet in his final diary entry on the *Windrush* he described Okinawa as:

> A flat island with some low hills in the centre. It has a green aspect and is surrounded by a pleasant blue sea. The cloud effects were pleasant today and the temperature like that of an English May … Well, a lot of sweat has passed through these pores since we cast off at Southampton and now I must close this tale. We disembark at Pusan tomorrow. Many happy returns to Rosalind.

Arriving in Korea at Pusan, David Green's transformation seemed to him to be complete as he packed away his shorts and donned a string-vest, a heavy sweater and gloves. He wrote that the last few miles had been heavy going:

> Into the teeth of that increasingly bad weather, the good old *Windrush* battled on. I had got really fond of that old tub. She had a lot of character and standing in my favourite place in the forepeak, as she rolled and pitched into the waves, my now longish blonde hair blowing in the wind, I developed a real sense of belonging. I would miss after we disembarked … 2nd November was my 19th birthday, though I kept that to myself. We have never made any fuss about birthdays in our family and in any case, much as I enjoy the company of my mates,

I kept myself to myself. Now, musing about the all too often mis-spent days of my youth I had come to realise that in many ways I have become a different person. I now belonged to a military family with a tremendous family spirit which we were all intensely proud that wonderful Glo'sters' spirit was going to carry us through, no matter what was demanded of us.

According to Pat Angier, as the *Windrush* docked, the mountains behind Pusan were covered in low cloud. He watched from the ship as Captain Wilson went ashore with Lieutenant Colonel J.P. Carne, the 44-year-old Glo'sters commander who was about to be at the helm of one of the most awful episodes in the history of the British army.

The British were astonished by the reception awaiting them. Harry Chalke remembers:

We landed at Pusan to the music of an American band … some of the Yanks on the docks thought we were the grand-daddy brigade and I did not blame them. Most of us were in our early 30s, some with grey and balding hair, and I was one of the youngest, getting on for 29. Nearly all the Americans in Korea were still in their teens, just virgin babies to us.[4]

It seemed an odd arrival to Tony Younger too:

Surprisingly we were greeted by an American Army band. The gang-plank was lowered and Fred Carne descended first, to the salutes of the Port Commander and some of his staff. This seemed a rather light-hearted way to start the serious business of going to war, but we appreciated the gesture and the obvious trouble that had been taken on our behalf. One by one we all stepped down onto the dry land of a country about which we knew virtually nothing, saying goodbye to the kindly crew who had watched over our needs for six long weeks. The voyage was finished at last and a new chapter in the lives of each one of us was opened.[5]

During the Second World War, American periodicals in particular began to commission lengthy front-line reports from embedded correspondents; this was the most significant beginning of the phenomenon we see today when journalists spend months in flak jackets trying to sneak back reports that will not have their accreditation removed. These reports, especially from the first Gulf War in 1991 to the present day, always need to be approached with care.

However, one great *New Yorker* journalist, E.J. Kahn Jr, was renowned for writing it as he saw it. He'd left Harvard in the early 1940s and after he was drafted wrote *The Army Life*, which narrated his experience from boot camp to battles in the Pacific. When the Americans and their allies went off to Korea, Kahn followed and in 1951 found himself at the Battle of Gloster Hill, in which the surviving members of the outgunned Glo'sters crawled to safety beneath machine-gun fire in 'a ditch about a foot deep'.

This was the report he filed to be published in May 1951, a month after the Battle of the Imjin River:

It is hard to tell at this date which battle of the Korean war military historians will ultimately single out for special mentions, but it is doubtful whether they can overlook a recent two-and-a-half-day engagement that, whatever name the historians may settle for it, is now known to those who went thorough it as the Battle of the Imjin, and that has already been characterised as 'epic' by the Eighth Army. The battle began just south of the Imjin River and some twenty-five miles northwest of Seoul on the night of April 22nd. The great majority of the United Nations troops who participated in it were British, of the 29th Brigade, but it was nonetheless a fittingly multinational affair, involving Belgians, South Koreans, and Filipinos, as well as Americans from both the continental United States and Puerto Rico. The 29th Brigade, with a total strength of sixty-six hundred and a front-line fighting strength of four thousand, suffered more than a thousand casualties during that bloody span of time.

Out of something like sixty thousand Chinese who assaulted the seventeen-thousand-yard sector the brigade was holding when the battle started, it is widely, if unofficially, believed that between ten and fifteen thousand were dispatched. And what is perhaps more important, since hordes of dead Chinese were almost as commonplace as hordes of live ones in Korea that particular week – is that the steadfast resistance of the British to this massive assault was very likely the most influential single factor in the dashing of the Communists' probable hope of celebrating May Day in the capital city of the Republic of Korea.

The entire 29th Brigade saw action in the Battle of the Imjin, but the worst assault fell upon one unit, the 1st battalion of the Gloucestershire Regiment, informally called the Glo'sters. Of the six hundred and twenty-two Glo'sters who were in the most advanced of the brigade's three echelons when the fight got under way, just five officers and thirty-four other ranks were available for duty three days afterward, and they only because they had made a near-miraculous withdrawal through enemy fire so intense and enveloping that they subsequently said they felt like human targets in a shooting gallery.[6]

Kahn's contemporaneous account vividly and accurately captured what soldiers of the Glo'sters felt after the war about what was inflicted upon them for those few days in April 1951. The United Nations forces had been surprised and then overwhelmed by the strength in numbers of the Chinese 63rd Army, and a retreat was ordered. The Glo'sters found themselves cut off on what was known as Hill 235 overlooking the Imjin River. There were attempts to reinforce them with supplies and arms by air, but these dropped behind Chinese lines, and the Glo'sters were left to hold out until, on the morning of 25 April, they were forced to surrender.

Military historians agree, however, that without those few days' delay, the Chinese would have been able to sweep south into Seoul and shatter the UN operation. There might then have been no such country as South Korea. It was heroic, and yet their veterans have always recognised that their suffering sits in a context of appalling loss.

It is now reckoned that a total of 1.2 million Korean civilians, Korean fighters, Chinese and UN forces lost their lives. Thousands of women were raped and many were also forced into prostitution, being used by troops from both sides. Its ultimate outcome has yet to be determined, but for the moment 50 million people live in the area of the mega-city of Seoul, just 35 miles south of the 38th Parallel, on the other side of which is a demilitarised zone and one of the most psychotic dictators apparently in the world, who is developing a nuclear arms capacity.

Yet despite the magnitude of all this, the personal still has a great effect. The courage and sacrifice of those Glo'sters who travelled out on the *Windrush* deserves the deepest consideration. There were undoubtedly men of profound character involved, some of whom paid the ultimate price. Tony Younger was a huge admirer of Pat Angier, and remembers Angier hearing the news that a reconnaissance plane had just reported hundreds of thousands of Chinese troops spotted unexpectedly a few miles north, before the Battle of the Imjin River commenced.

Younger wrote that an unusually serious Pat was affected by the news:

By then he had been promoted to command a company in his battalion … 'I am sure there was nobody there yesterday,' he said. 'We sent a patrol deep into that area. They must have moved up last night and have been lying quiet all day.' I tried to press him to another drink, but he refused. Showing obvious gratitude for the little chance he had had to relax with us, he excused himself. But that ready smile had left his lips.[7]

Just a page later, Younger writes of the blizzard of gunfire against the Glo'sters: 'one of its platoons was overwhelmed by great numbers of Chinese infantry. The stalwart Pat Angier organised a counter-attack to redress the situation, at the cost of his life.'[8]

'At the cost of his life': six words to describe the loss of a complex man and a potentially superb writer. As with so many who have written partial accounts of war, only to be unable to complete them because of their deaths, we are left with a sense of 'what if'. Yet, wonderfully,

Angier's daughter Tabby Angier keeps his memory alive today, raising money for veterans' charities, and she remains a visitor, as the guest of the South Korean government, to the battle site, including the features that will always be known as 'Gloster Hill' and 'Castle Hill'. Now living in Scotland, she has become a piper, and she has played the pipes at many commemorative events for British forces, wearing her late father's medals. Her father would have been proud.

❖

Gloucester Cathedral has its origins in a monastery that was one of an active chain running the length of the Welsh Marches, including Hereford, Worcester, Shrewsbury and Chester. Its elevation to cathedral status was a matter of politics. When Edward II was infamously murdered at nearby Berkeley Castle, supposedly by means of a red-hot poker inserted into his anus, his son made the burial at Gloucester into a glorifying occasion.

Designed to bury his father's infamy by this process, it was the founding act of what would become the fifty-year reign of Edward III. With the prestige of a king interred under its flagstones, Gloucester Cathedral underwent a lavish, centuries-long building programme, leaving us today with 'the most exciting of England's smaller cathedrals … the epitome of late gothic harmony'.[9] More recently, it has regularly lent this gothic grandeur to feature-filmmakers, notably two *Harry Potter* movies, *The Chamber of Secrets* and *The Philosopher's Stone*.[10]

Over the centuries since, the cathedral has acquired many rich artefacts, but few are as steeped in human suffering and nobility as the tiny Carne Cross, carved by Lieutenant Colonel James Carne, who was one of the captured Glo'sters at the Battle of the Imjin River. No sooner had he crafted it than he was taken from his men into solitary confinement by the Chinese, where he stayed from January 1952 to August 1953. A few months after the ceasefire, Carne had the satisfaction of leading 300 survivors through the heart of Gloucester with a look of grim determination to the west door of the cathedral. Less than a month earlier, on 27 October 1953, he had been awarded the Victoria Cross by the Queen.

Once they'd marched inside, Carne's cross was presented to the Dean and Chapter for safekeeping. Today, it stands in one of many display cabinets in the cathedral's treasury. It lies behind secure glass but looks as if, were someone to grasp it, it would possess an extraordinary power – the very symbol of bloody-minded resistance to bullying and an implacable adherence to a given faith.

S.J. Davies, the regimental chaplain, wrote to *The Times* in advance of the event, his letter published on 20 November 1953:

Sir – On Saturday, November 21, during the Gloucestershire Regiment's thanksgiving service in Gloucester Cathedral, the Dean and Chapter will receive into their keeping from the 1st Battalion a small, beautifully carved cross made from grey Korean stone. It is a Celtic cross, because its maker is a Cornishman. For all who were with Colonel Carne during the stirring times in which he won the Victoria Cross, and were later in the P.O.W Camp 2, North Korea, this little stone is a treasured thing.

Colonel Carne carved it in captivity using only a couple of nails and a primitive hammer, and I have a vivid recollection of him during the bitter December weather of 1951 patiently, day after day, rubbing smooth the sides of the cross on the concrete steps of the Korean schoolhouse in which we were imprisoned. He presented it to me for use in our religious services, and it first graced our crude altar that Christmas at the Holy Communion in the drab camp lecture-room, the temperature below zero, with the portraits of Marx, Lenin, Stalin, Mao Tse-Tunng, and the rest gazing down.

It was at this service, the first Eucharist of the five we were able to celebrate during the two and a half years, that Colonel Carne made his first and last Communion of his captivity, for he was taken from us on January 28, 1952, and after his 'trial' by the Chinese Communists went into the long period of solitary confinement which did not end until we saw him again three weeks after the Armistice this year.

At this service our chalice was a Chinese metal cup, our paten a British mess-tin. Vestments had I none. But we had the essential matter – wine, bread, a pocket Book of Common Prayer, and the intention to consecrate and offer the Eucharist in accordance with the rites of the Holy Church. More than 100 British and American officers received the Sacrament. I was not allowed to visit the other ranks.

Colonel Carne's cross stands some 10in. high, rising sturdily from its rough-hewn plinth. The arms of the cross, at the top of their small column, are embraced, after the manner of a Cornish cross, by a circle of stone. When Colonel Carne was invested recently by her Majesty with this great award, there were those of us who were thinking also of this other cross, so patiently and so beautifully carved under somewhat bizarre circumstances. In my prayer of blessing of this cross in the prison camp these words occurred: 'May all who look to it with faith and love be given grace to endure unto the end.' Now, in Gloucester Cathedral, this sturdy symbol of redemption and endurance carved from Korean stone, will find, it is our hope, a resting place for centuries to come.

Yours obediently

S.J. Davies, Chaplain

1st Bn., the Gloucestershire Regiment

The Glo'sters regimental museum today is down by the city's remarkable inland wharfs. These were once at the epicentre of world trade, manufactured goods and minerals coming down the Severn canal from the Midlands to be loaded on to ocean-going sailing ships bound for Bristol to the south, and on across the globe. The museum, as is appropriate for this century, is a fine and thoughtful record of the Glo'sters throughout history but without glorification of war.

On a tape loop, without any vainglory, is a short film featuring the words of General Matthew Ridgway, the United Nations commander-in-chief in Korea. In that non-media-coached speaking manner of the middle of the last century, somehow more authentic than the finessed platitudes of our own time, Ridgeway simply says this of the Glo'sters' suffering at the Imjin River:

> It was an unforgettable action executed in the best traditions of sheer doggedness and personal courage. The blackened hills of Gloster Valley are silent these days. There is no need for me to recount in detail the glory of that battle; it is well known in Gloucestershire, England, indeed everywhere in the free world. The memory of it is more than just one additional battle honour added to the history of a famous regiment. The bravery of the Glo'sters demonstrated the power of collective security, a power recruited in farms, in villages, and an ancient cathedral city.

The Forgotten War? In any telling of the story of the *Windrush* it is unforgettable.

THE FINAL VOYAGE

It was 28 December 1953, and at the New Docks in Southampton, now rebuilt after bomb damage, the *Windrush* was tied to a pair of tugs forward and aft. She was ready to be pulled clear through the channel, carefully steering through the many other craft on the waters, before heading out to sea. These were the final days of the Korean War, and she was loaded with 1,500 troops, military families, government officials and crew.

At 11 a.m., Captain Wilson nodded to the port's pilot standing next to him on the bridge, who gave the signal to the tugs to take the strain. The ship was listing a little to starboard with the weight of passengers leaning over the rails waving to family and friends on the dockside. A regimental band struck up with 'Pack Up Your Troubles in Your Old Kit Bag … and Smile, Smile, Smile'.

Outwardly the *Windrush* was in good shape, her white hull surrounded by the broad blue band denoting a troop ship. But she was not quite what she seemed. Although a fully commissioned troop ship, she was still privately run by the P&O subsidiary, the New Zealand Shipping Company. Therein lay a problem. The chain of command from a Ministry of Defence civil servant who wanted to move troops at short notice, through a private company, down to the crew, all involving refitting work at Harland and Wolff, left plenty of possibility for errors.

The pilot on the bridge was about to find this out for himself. With kisses blown over the starboard side and tears falling below, the *Windrush* began to be pulled away from the dock and down the channel. The last of the coloured streamers which had tenuously linked parting lovers broke away and, accompanied by the band in full roar, the cheers could be heard over the water on the fringes of the New Forest.

Now it was time for the pilot to give his final order before handing over to Captain Wilson. 'Dead slow astern,' he said. The crew on the bridge stood tensely, having known this moment would come.

No sound came from the engines. He gave the order again. Nothing. He turned to the captain and asked what was going on.

'We haven't got any engines,' came the reply. The pilot wanted to know more. 'Well, engine repairs are still underway, you see, Pilot, but nobody ashore will believe that we're not yet ready to sail.'

With no radio available, the pilot gave a complicated series of signals to the two tugs to carry on around a bend in the channel, out of sight of the still performing band, and reberth her further along the quay-side. The gangplank was lowered again, and a team of engineers from Harland and Wolff came aboard. With the crew, they worked solidly for the next twenty-four hours until finally the engines turned over.

This time, and with no fanfare, the *Windrush* slipped quietly out into the English Channel. It was hardly a propitious beginning to the voyage.

Captain Wilson had been given the nickname 'Tug' so long ago that nobody knew who'd invented it. All his crew, who are recorded to have adored him, could see why.[1] He was medium height, barrel-chested and usually on departure from port could be seen at the prow rather than the bridge overseeing the work of the tugs taking him out of port. The young fourth officer on this final voyage, W.N. 'Wally' Seybold, later wrote:

By now the *Windrush* was an old ship with a chequered past. Captain Wilson was a fine Master and seaman. He was a strict disciplinarian but always had a twinkle in his eye and a quiet sense of humour. He constantly had the welfare of his crew and passengers at heart but circumstances were sometimes well beyond his control. This voyage started and ended with two of them.

Unusually for a merchant master at the time, Wilson's full title was suffixed with an OBE. At sea since before the First World War, he had spent most of his career with P&O engaged in bringing refrigerated meat from Australia and New Zealand to Britain. But in the Second World War he became embroiled in an international incident arising from the detention by neutral Sweden of ten Norwegian merchant ships, under lease when war broke out to the British government. For a year, litigation had progressed in Sweden's Supreme Court, until in March 1942 the detention order was lifted.

Ten brave British shipmasters volunteered to fetch the ships and were flown to Gothenburg in Sweden, where they took command of the Norwegian crews. Captain Wilson was assigned the *Skytteren* – more than 12,000 tons of whale factory ship and formerly a White Star liner. Under cover of snow on the night of 31 March 1942 she left Gothenburg for the Skagerrak, the strip of water with Sweden to the east, Norway to the north and Denmark's Jutland peninsular to the south. It was blockaded by the Germans but under international law, reinforced by the decision of the Swedish courts, the captain's convoy had the right of free passage.

The Germans paid no heed to this. As soon as the *Skytteren* was out of neutral Swedish waters they attacked, but the ten vessels refused to surrender; seven of them, including Captain Wilson's, were sunk. Many died but 234 survivors were picked up.

The captain was badly treated at first, beaten up and forced into solitary confinement, but in the end, he was sent to a prison camp near Bremen where he spent the next three years. He was awarded an OBE shortly after his release in 1945. 'Tug' Wilson knew what it was like to lose a ship.

❖

As the *Windrush* passed by the Cotentin peninsula and the port of Cherbourg to the south, Captain Wilson gave the order for the full ship's complement to take part in the 'Emergency and Boat Stations' drill. These were held once a week at sea, usually at 4 p.m. on Fridays, and were understandably considered a bore by the crew. They would later be performed on the way back from the Far East too with a different passenger complement. Wilson's ingrained habit would save many hundreds of lives.

The journey east stopped over in Suez, Mombasa and Aden, disembarking troops in under twelve hours. Most were being despatched overland to the Kenyan hotspots of the Mau Mau uprising. After ten days crossing the Indian Ocean the last troops went ashore in Singapore and the *Windrush* anchored in the Singapore Roads to be cleaned and revictualled. The expectation was that in due course 1,200 service personnel would be ready at the docks to return to Britain.

These balmy days in Singapore were popular with the crew topside, maintaining decks and lifeboats, correcting charts and finishing paperwork from the journey out. The catering staff were kept busy cleaning the accommodation and doing laundry, in somewhat warmer conditions below, with every porthole open wide.

Down in the engine room, however, the engineers were plagued by the heat. Yet again they were patching up boilers and repairing shafts in nothing but their underwear. Wilson came down to see them, and even though he was used to their complaints, he took seriously their expressed relief that soon they would be on their way back to Southampton. This time, they told him, the repairs needed to be urgent.

When had she last been in for a proper overhaul rather than a patch-up? Nobody knew, although the captain confirmed it had not happened in the four years under his command.

But then a wholly unexpected message arrived from the Ministry of Defence. Up anchor and make sail, not for Southampton, but for Hong Kong, and thence even further east to Kure in Japan. Wilson did not reveal his concerns, but the second and third officers wondered aloud to themselves if it was wise to almost double *Windrush's* time at sea in this way by making a rare trip to Japan. They did not know that there the *Windrush* was destined to see the sites of some awful events, perhaps the worst the crew would ever see.

She touched shore only briefly in Hong Kong, refuelling and taking on fresh food, and three days later was entering Japanese waters in the Bungo Suido – the sound between the island of Shikoku to the east and Kyushu to the west.

A ladder was lowered and a pilot, described by Seybold as 'an ancient Japanese mariner, small, and wholly exhausted by his climb', came aboard. He guided them around a large island to starboard and as she turned towards land the crew saw something of which they all spoke for the rest of their lives. Many left written accounts, Seybold capturing their collective experience:

> Abeam to port, what we saw was appalling. A distant view of Hiroshima, or what was left of it. Through my binoculars the scene resembled the aftermath of a forest fire. The remains of a few stunted trees and blackened buildings poking up like burned trees. The rest of the land looked quite level from a distance, but similar to burned undergrowth because most of the city buildings and homes had been of wooden construction. Although this happened some nine years earlier it appeared to me as though it had taken place only the previous day.
>
> Certainly, I felt a wave of nausea and it seemed incomprehensible that man could do this to man. It was the ultimate in destruction.

The ship passed on and the darkness deepened for her crew. On arrival at Kure they found the British army contingent of national servicemen on their way back from Korea ready to be demobbed. They had amongst them amputees, those with head injuries and men who had lost their sight. They all talked openly of the horrors they had seen, first in Korea but latterly in an American-built hospital for the victims of the nuclear attacks nine years earlier.

They were relieved to be on the *Windrush* now sailing south-west, bound for Southampton and home ...

By the time they docked again at Hong Kong, the engines were in trouble once more. *Windrush* had to lay over for two unscheduled days before Wilson felt confident that she wouldn't simply lose power in the Indian Ocean. When Blohm & Voss had launched her in 1931 she was capable of a service speed of 14.5 knots. To squeeze even 13 knots out of her now required full-time nannying from the four engineers below.

Slowly she ploughed her way for two more weeks, refuelling in Colombo and Aden, and just past the south-west tip of Yemen she steered north-west into the Red Sea. Two days later by Sharm Al Sheikh she entered the sea's westerly finger as it approaches the entrance to the Suez Canal. For the troops aboard the excitement mounted. When they reached the Mediterranean, they would finally have left the east behind and be on the final stretch home.

At Port Said, at the mouth of the Suez Canal, she docked again and the complement was swollen by more returning military personnel. There were now 1,276 passengers and 222 crew on board, all looking forward to disembarking at Southampton in ten days' time. It was Saturday 27 March 1954.

Now, it was party time, with a 'Dinner Adieu' arranged by the catering department for first-class passengers. Usually this would be held two days before port in the Bay of Biscay, but the Bay in March is no place for a five-course dinner with dancing. So just as the Glo'sters on their way to Korea two years before had been compelled to eat Christmas dinner weeks early, now as the soldiers returned to England their final night party tempted fate.

Senior deck officers, who were obliged to attend, left accounts behind of the *Windrush's* last supper. Second Officer Jack Cosh wrote:

Lieutenant Commander Austin and his wife were dressed as the Ancient Mariner and Chinese girlfriend. The ship's adjutant turned up dressed in a life jacket and tattered clothing as the survivor of a ship-wreck, prophetically it turned out. I believe he intended to suggest he was actually a survivor of the ship's terrible food, but the point was lost on us. A Royal Navy type arrived as an Alka-Seltzer bottle made up of old charts borrowed from me. There was a ghost train consisting of two officers in white sheets roped together, followed by a guard blow-ing his whistle violently. Then a Brigadier entered amid laughs dressed as a sugar daddy with lipstick marks on his cheeks and bald pate, with a copy of *True Confessions* magazine in one pocket and a bra hanging out of the other.

While the officer and first-class contingent made merry, in the bowels of the ship the engineers, electricians and greasers slaved to keep *Windrush's* engines running. As the dining room clock struck midnight the revel-lers dispersed. It was now Sunday 28 March 1954 and the ship was due north of Algiers. The city lights could be seen clearly twinkling from the port beam. For March, the weather was unusually calm and clear with a fresh westerly force-4 breeze.

At 6.30 the next morning the overnight crew laying the tables for breakfast were surprised to see Captain Wilson in full uniform a good hour before usual, marching towards the bridge. He had been woken by Wally Seybold on the dawn watch. At first, the fourth officer had thought that an unusual amount of smoke coming out of one of the twin funnels (one of which was a dummy) was blow-back from the boiler and that excess fuel had caught alight. It would be fine once it had burned off.

But then he'd seen flames leaping 10ft in the air from the funnel rim and woke Wilson in a hurry. The captain took the bridge, made an assessment, and reached to telephone below. Nothing – the line was dead, although the telephone bell on the bridge kept ringing spontane-ously. He then ordered the alarm bells to be rung. Again, nothing. The *Windrush* was suffering a complete electrical failure.

Now Wilson sensed the terrible urgency of the situation. Before the ship's radio failed too, he needed to send out an SOS. He commanded Chief Radio Officer Fowler, 'Sparks', to send a message to All Ships at once: 'HMT Empire Windrush on fire in position 32 miles NW of Cape Caxine. Request immediate assistance.'

From below, Chief Engineer Christian brought the awful news that the whole of the engine room was in flames: 'The emergency generator has failed, so we have no power or water. It's hopeless.'

Within minutes the engine room fire had burned through the decks and was entering the accommodation areas, and as it climbed up the funnel the paint began blistering off, landing on the deck beneath and setting fire to the wooden and tar caulking. It was time make the call to abandon ship.

The captain realised that many of his crew were still asleep and that the few stewards making breakfast would not be enough to supervise the emergency. He gave the order that the Royal Navy contingent be commanded to take on the role too. Within minutes two dozen men were dashing down corridors waking up passengers.

A then 18-year-old cabin steward, Ray Vincer, recalls taking it upon himself to do one final check of his corridor and, with smoke around his ankles, noticing that the door to cabin 160 was still closed. He knocked, and was told to come in, which he did quickly, to be confronted by a Mrs Mycock.

'What the hell are you doing down here?' he said, all etiquette forgot-ten. 'I can't go yet, Ray,' she said. 'I haven't got my make-up on.'

Both were fortunate enough to survive so that he could apologise to her later for the extreme profanities that fell from his lips as he pushed her upstairs.

As Ray reached the deck he walked straight into the captain. 'Any hopes, sir?'

'None at all, Laddie,' came the reply. 'Get yourself over the side.'

It was just twelve minutes since the alarm was sounded. The lifeboats were stacked in pairs, and the topmost ten – loaded first with children and women, then with service people – had already been winched into the water and were making away from the *Windrush*.

Unfortunately, those same winches needed to be retrieved – a slow process always, but with no power almost impossible. The decision was made to fling the bottom ten boats over the side as elegantly as could be managed. Two smashed into each other and were immediately rendered unseaworthy. Now there were eight, and they needed manning fast.

At first, people descended the ropes thrown over the sides. This came at a cost. Quite a number lowering themselves down were relatively old, unfit men unable to control their descent. By the time they were in the sea, the skin had been burned off their hands and saltwater was stinging their wounds, blood smearing the surface around them. Fortunately, there were no sharks in the area, though many didn't know that and were in fear for their lives.

Young Ray Vincer saw his elderly purser, 'Pickles', in just such a predicament and, flinging as many deck chairs and floats as he could find into the water, took a deep breath and leapt the 60ft below:

> It seemed that I was in the air for hours and then when I hit the water
> I went down for seemingly an eternity. Then I stopped and could
> see the daylight above me. I automatically started ascending with my
> lungs bursting and when at sea level I shot out of the water to the
> height of my waist. Was I glad to breathe again! A lot of seamen know
> the feeling.

He realised that he and 'Pickles' might be dragged beneath the ship, so he grabbed the deck chair the old man was clinging to and began to swim away. He saw a major and a captain who had made the same mess of their hands and, telling them to cling on to the deckchair too, he gripped it with his left arm and swam with his right, until after fifteen minutes a lifeboat was sent out by a Norwegian merchant ship, the *Socotra*.

The three other men were hauled aboard, but exhausted Ray asked to be left alone for a few moments. He put each arm through the grab lines which were looped around the hull of the lifeboat and hung there for ten minutes. Then he was pulled on board.

Back on the *Windrush* Captain Wilson and Fourth Officer Wally Seybold had watched as the last lifeboat put over the side turned like an arrow in mid-air and speared through the hull of the penultimate one. These were meant to be the remaining crew's means of escape.

The ship was now divided in half by the inferno at the centre and as they considered what to do next, one remaining passenger hove into view asking to borrow Seybold's tiepin. He explained that the shutter was stuck in his camera. He did not get the tiepin and was curtly told to jump for his life.

Wilson shouted, 'Every man for himself', and the remaining crew took to the ropes or jumped over the side. Seybold took his last look at the deck. Everything was now black. Twisted steel that had once been the painted sides of first-class cabins only half an hour earlier formed a backdrop to burning window frames.

Flames roared from the accommodation and were coming fast towards him. Above, his master's cabin at the coach top was turning to ash. He was overwhelmed by the terrible noise of an air siren, which would not be turned off, by the heat and by the smell of burning paint, varnish and oil.

Now it was just him and the captain. Thanking his lucky stars for the regular maintenance work on every point of safety, he released the same pilot rope that the exhausted Japanese pilot had ascended days before.

Wilson went four rungs down, then immediately climbed back up. 'We'd better do this properly, Fourth,' he said. 'You go first and I'll come last.'

'As I climbed onto the ladder to this day I shall always remember his eyes,' recalled Seybold. 'They were moist and full, his usual unmistakable twinkle dimmed as he was fighting back the tears.'

Yet the captain and his fourth officer were not, as they thought, the last men off after all. Chief Radio Officer F.W. Fowler, who had radioed the initial distress call, remained in his position at the key, ensuring that the distress calls had been received.

One signal was picked up hundreds of miles away in the Atlantic on the cargo vessel *Thorpe Granger* near Madeira steaming northwards en route from Buenos Aires to Liverpool. The captain, A.D. Seybold, was Wally's father.

Satisfied that he had done his duty, and in the nick of time, Fowler made his way through a burning corridor, bounded through the flames on deck, and hurled himself over the side. He lived to tell the tale.

Four ships had come to the rescue, with the majority of passengers and crew picked up by the *Socotra*. Immediately the British stiff upper lip was apparent in both humour and pathos. A tale was already doing the rounds of four soldiers clinging to one float in danger of being sucked beneath the *Windrush*. Others yelled at them to head away, but with one soldier on each of the four-sided float they went around in circles. All men of action, they worked out that they must go two a side, canoe fashion. Still they got nowhere, like a silent movie comedy caper. A remaining crewman observing from the ship above shouted down that this might be because a rope on the float was still connected to the *Windrush*.

On the *Socotra* the decks and hatch covers could not be seen for humanity, many still in night attire, although not the four stark-naked soldiers puffing cigarettes, crouching over number three hatch playing cards.

The last lifeboat to arrive at her gangplank carried the war-wounded. Survivors watched as a young man who had lost his right leg in Korea three weeks earlier made his way up, unaided, on his crutches. The throng remained silent and got on with squeezing water from their clothes.

By 10.30 a.m. all four ships involved in the rescue were steaming away towards Algiers and began to arrive there from 2 p.m. Second Officer Jack Cosh was on the first ship back, the *Mentor*, a Dutch vessel, where the chief officer lent him clothes, a Philishave razor and a bottle of Bols gin:

> What is more important is that after leaving Algiers he sent off a cable to my wife Jill. I have read about and had occasion during the war to find out how people do rally in Christian help at times of trouble, but he was an outstanding example of kindness. I took his address and later Jill sent him – or rather his family – *The Picture Book of Britain*.

First back to Algiers on the *Mentor*, Jack Cosh was eager to get off early. He was carrying a waterproofed file of secret papers from the Royal Marines and wanted to find their regimental sergeant major as soon as possible to hand them over. But, coming down the gangplank relatively smartly dressed, he was mistaken by the French military reception committee for Captain Wilson. He was kissed by all three dignitaries on both cheeks:

> I soon realised that our *Entente Cordiale* was to be brief and that misapprehension was rife among us. My admission that I was not the captain ended my few moments of glory. They left me with diverse, less beribboned, but more practical types who wanted to know how many troops we had, how many lorries would be needed and so on.

Jack Cosh then sat on a tarpaulin-covered pile of boxes in the hot sun, where he was joined by two of his favourite stewardesses:

> Hetty, a gorgeous, dyed-ginger bombshell in her near seventies and Hannah, a dark-haired ex-barmaid possessed of her own distinctive charm and also avoiding retiring age. Actually both 'girls' were rather pleasant human beings full of cheerful Cockney courage. Both had lost their all accumulated after years of service on the *Empire Windrush*

and both were laughing and joking as if they'd been back at the *Star and Garter*. But what Captain Wilson thought when he saw us, looking from the *Socotra*'s bridge as she arrived in port, I know not.

Soon all the ships had disembarked. A head count was taken which involved everyone standing stock still in the midday heat for ten minutes. 1,276 passengers, servicemen, wives and children, and 218 ship's crew accounted for.

Missing and never to be found were: Senior Third Engineer G.W. Stockwell, First Electrician J.W. Graves, Seventh Engineer A. Webster and Eighth Engineer L. Pendleton. The men had almost certainly died in the first few minutes of the incident.

But as Captain Wilson and the other 1,493 people headed to all parts of Algiers to recover and stay the night, he was wondering what caused this. He had executed a near-perfect evacuation at sea, but to his mind the engines should never have failed as catastrophically as they did.

They were all still a long way from home and were about to have a night in Algiers they would remember with fond amazement their whole lives.

Back in London, though, the cover-up was already under way.

LETTERS TO FATHER

For the press back in Britain, this was a perfect victory-seized-from-the-jaws-of-defeat story. Everyone who had landed in Algiers had been treated splendidly at the French-governed port, with passengers and crew billeted at schools, holiday camps and even with the French Foreign Legion. Austerity-era survivors enjoyed eating foreign food and drinking French wine, if only for a few nights, and a model operation was then mounted to evacuate them four days later by ship to Gibraltar, where Lady Edwina Mountbatten was there to welcome them.

They were all flown home within days, except the four with a fear of flying, mostly to RAF Northolt in Middlesex and Blackbushe Airport in Hampshire. Cameras were present to record it all. In every local newspaper in the country, stories were run of any survivor with even the most tenuous connection to the area. It was sold as a thoroughly good news story.

Love and romance were the favourite themes. The *Edinburgh Evening News* reported on 3 April 1954:

SURPRISE FOR MARINE FROM THE WINDRUSH
Two of the happiest people in Edinburgh today are Miss Caroline Mounsey (21) and Royal Marine Pete Drysdale Cornwall (21) – his friends call him Dale. He is one of the survivors of the SS. *Empire Windrush* which caught fire in the Mediterranean last Sunday.

He arrived in Edinburgh this morning and made for Caroline's house at 17 Lutton Place. The couple who will be married on Saturday were engaged over two and a half years ago when Drysdale left for his tour of duty abroad.

Yards of newspaper were filled for weeks with such happy tales, and only rarely was a negative story printed to spoil it all. At the bottom of a column in the *Daily Telegraph*, on 30 March 1954, there was another human interest story, this one devoid of joy:

FIANCE KILLED

The only officer to die in the *Empire Windrush* disaster, Senior Third Engineer George Stockwell, 25, of Southdown Road, Newhaven, was to have been married on Saturday week at St Peter's, Brighton. His fiancée is Miss Jeanne Gander, 23, of Bevendean Crescent, Brighton.

It must have been a difficult time for the relatives of the four young men who died as the country celebrated a Dunkirk-style story, newsreel of the still burning ship shot from a helicopter showing in cinemas throughout the spring. But in Parliament there were those who wanted to know what had really happened.

It was unfortunate for the directors of the New Zealand Shipping Company, the Ministry of Transport civil servants who dealt with them and the government minsters responsible that one of the crew who died in the fire was Leslie Pendleton, a 21-year-old from Bootle in Liverpool. His Member of Parliament was Bessie Braddock, who would always merit being described as indomitable. A leading light in the British Professional Boxers' Association, she was similarly pugilistic on her feet in the House of Commons.

Within days of the *Windrush*'s sinking, she was demanding written answers to tough questions about the history of the ship. These urgent questions had been provoked by Leslie Pendleton's father, Thomas, contacting her with a bundle of correspondence from his son written during the extended voyage, which at first was only meant to go as far as Singapore but stretched – in the vessel's longest trip in years – all the way to Kure in Japan.

The *Manchester Guardian* reported the matter thus on 5 April 1954:

ANXIETY OF MAN IN EMPIRE WINDRUSH
Letters to Father

In five letters written to his father before the troop ship was burnt out, the ship's eighth engineer expressed anxiety about her condition.

Extracts from the letters are now in the possession of Mrs E.M. Braddock, M.P. for Exchange, Liverpool, who said last night she will put down these questions to the Minister of Transport on Wednesday:

'What reports were made to you about engine trouble in the ship and what action was taken: when was the last occasion when fire was reported aboard the ship: and will the relatives of the four young men receive compensation?'

The eighth engineer, Mr Leslie Pendleton, aged 21, of Haworth Street, Bootle, Lancashire, was one of the men killed. He wrote to his father, Mr Thomas Pendleton: 'There are going to be some anxious moments on the trip home.' Mr Thomas Pendleton has offered five of the letters as evidence in the inquiry into the loss of his ship.

The first of these letters, dated September 29 last year, says: 'It's a hell of a ship. Damn thing keeps breaking down.' On October 30, Mr Pendleton wrote: 'I have never known so many things to go wrong with one trip. There will be fun and games on the home trip.'

On November 3 he wrote: 'Had a fire on the ship just after leaving Hong Kong, which caused some amusement.' On January 29 he wrote: 'No. 4 generator has blown its top again. No one here seems to know how to fix it.' His last letter, dated March 8, said:

'Just over three weeks to go if all goes well. We had a scare the other day. The forward compressor blew up, and it was debatable whether we would have to lay up at Colombo for a while. The Chief went to see the Old Man but it was decided to carry on. As it is now, there are going to be some anxious moments on the trip home. The after compressor[1] has become the most precious thing in the ship.'[2]

Through her Parliamentary question, Bessie Braddock managed to elicit an admission from the New Zealand Shipping Company's assistant superintendent engineer, a Mr Strachan, that there was indeed what he clearly intended to portray as a minor history of just two safety incidents on the ship. In a letter dated 6 April 1954,[3] he first admitted to:

Fire in the boiler room 8.5.49
Put into Gibraltar 9.5.49
Sailed Gibraltar 13.5.49

If Braddock had taken this brief account at face value, it might all have seemed like a storm in a teacup on that 1949 trip five years earlier, bound for Malta, Port Said, Famagusta in Cyprus and Thessaloniki in Greece. Yet in the holdings of the Imperial War Museum are the private papers of Sergeant Derek Burnand, an army education officer, which tell a different tale.

Burnand was destined for Port Said on that voyage, and was already delivering lessons on board the *Windrush* to children of servicemen as the ship travelled south from Southampton. His letters, which include seeing Hitler's yacht *Grille* adrift at sea and teaching children and mothers about Hereward the Wake, are an invaluable source about life on the ship.

Due to the May 1949 fire, Burnand had spent many days more than was expected in Gibraltar, taking the long climb: 'As we beheld the whole of the Rock, the air strip, harbour, international zone, bull ring in La Linea, the Atlantic, Mediterranean, and Africa's mountains across the Straits – really worth the hot climb.'

That 1949 'Fire in the boiler room' might appear, in Strachan's cursory terms, to have been a task for one man and a hand-held extinguisher. That is not how Burnand wrote about it on 12 May 1949:

This is now the fourth day of our stay here whereas we should have had twelve hours … The trouble started last Sunday night, when, having made a detour – we were due in Gibraltar Monday 6 a.m. and were ahead of time – fire broke out in the engine room for some unexplained reason. Every available member of the crew was put down to fight it, and it became so serious at one time – this again is all hearsay but fairly true – that the captain gave them five minutes to get it under control or we would abandon ship. The oil tanks were getting too warm apparently.

Thank heaven we were able to sleep on undisturbed, and only caught snatches of information from the crew and guard next morning. The only recollection I have is of men dashing around our deck during the night (looking for extinguishers I believe), not knowing what it was about.[4]

Thus, the New Zealand Shipping Company's Strachan gave Bessie Braddock little honest idea of the seriousness of the 1949 incident, when the captain had been on the cusp of abandoning ship. It cannot be ascertained if Captain Wilson, who only became the *Windrush's* master in 1950, had been fully acquainted with the gravity of this incident by his predecessor, Captain Maltby, either, or indeed by the company itself.

Strachan then refers to problems earlier in the final 1954 voyage, after being questioned by Braddock, in these terms:

A small fire occurred in boiler room at Hong Kong on the last voyage of the vessel 25.2.54. It was due to a slight oil leak from a manhole door, on to lagging. It was mopped up but it was anticipated a fire might start on lagging when engines were started. All was prepared for this and precautions taken and it was extinguished immediately.

Again, Strachan is downplaying the significance of this. It has been established that even at the earlier time, when his company was saying that no British engineers really understood the German engines and the Ministry was signalling not to worry because they needed a troop carrier, there had been a massive fire in Glasgow in the winter of 1946–47. It had destroyed all the *Windrush*'s insulation. What he was saying now in 1954 was that, with one oil leak on to some lagging, the whole ship was a potential tinder box, as it had been in Glasgow.

Yet Leslie Pendleton's letters establish that the chief engineer was so worried about the condition of the engines after the first 1954 fire on the final journey back from Kure – which the voyage cards confirm was in Hong Kong – that by the time the *Windrush* had sailed for another eight days, laying over yet again in the Singapore Roads for more patching up, he had approached Captain Wilson about it. We cannot be sure what was said, but it is likely he gave his opinion that the ship was no longer safe. It is worth noting that none of the recollections in Wally Seybold's excellent volume came from any of the engineers.

Today, the inquiry into the sinking of the *Windrush* might follow on from a coroner's verdict into the causes of the four engineers' deaths.[5] It may even have become a trial of the New Zealand Shipping Company and the Ministry of Transport for corporate manslaughter.

However, 1954 was a different time. Even then, though, there were still huge political risks for the government, and reputational risks for the company – especially if any inquiry found that when the *Windrush* was put to sea for her final voyage she was unfit for service.

Fortunately for them, the press were quickly seduced by some out-of-context evidence that created a perfect distraction. Was it terrorism?

The most ludicrous candidates for this were so-called 'Nazi terror cells' said to be still roaming the Middle East nine years after the end of the war, like the Japanese soldier who hid on the island of Guam until 1972. More plausible, if ill-considered, suspects were a team of Egyptian fitters and labourers, who had come aboard at her final stop in Port Said.

The QC of the New Zealand Shipping Company, Roland Adams, teed up the second engineer, Jack Tozer, to speculate about this. Tozer was encouraged to say that there was the opportunity for 'mischief' by the Egyptians if they were 'so-minded'. He said he had about a dozen Egyptian workers under his command, but when they went for water or tea they were not under observation. When Adams asked him if he had any view as to what started the fire, he replied, 'Not really, no.'

The terrorism red herring was inflamed by Captain Wilson himself, who clearly misspoke when asked if he considered sabotage 'a probability' and said yes, when he had genuinely intended to use the word 'possibly'. Adams was not about to let this go, and pursued the point with Mr J. Graham, a senior engineer and surveyor to the Ministry of Transport, who was at first forthright that he found the prospect that it was terrorism 'improbable'.

Adams demanded to know whether he had instituted any technical inquiries to find out what sort of sabotage instruments existed. Graham replied, 'No such inquiry was made to my knowledge.' Adams continued with the 'When did you stop beating your wife?' line of questioning and offered the court his own unsought speculation:

> The negative results of the security inquiry may mean no more than that the security services were unable to find any clue in their sphere – that is to say you were unable to find somebody who talked unwisely about such things at the cafes of Port Said … When a fire of very great heat and intensity comes, so to speak, all of a sudden and with a flash, it is at least possible, is it not, since it is very difficult to find an explanation otherwise, that some outside agency might be the explanation, if that was studied?

Graham had little alternative but to answer, 'It is possible but I think improbable.'

Therefore, beyond the responsible technical and factual reporting of record in Lloyd's List, the press coverage of the first few days of the trial were dominated by the absurd 'possibility' that this was either the handiwork of Egyptian nationalists or Nazi terrorism, and coverage was deflected away from what was already perfectly well known by the Ministry, the company and the senior crew. The *Windrush* had been an inferno waiting to happen ever since she was captured in Kiel.

A VERY BRITISH INQUIRY

As soon as she had met the families of the crew who had died Bessie Braddock urged them to appoint their own lawyer at the inquiry, and she recommended Sydney Silverman MP. Short, very blond, as pugnacious as Braddock, Silverman might be suspected today of grandstanding at a nationally reported event – an opportunist backbencher and lawyer looking to make headlines. However, Silverman's bona fides were beyond reproach.

As a conscientious objector, he spent the First World War in Wormwood Scrubs prison. Later he became a leading Parliamentary opponent of Oswald Mosley and his British Fascists, and co-piloted the 1936 Public Order Act which prohibited the public wearing of their neo-Nazi uniforms. In 1948, the year that the Windrush generation arrived in Britain, he was the country's leading proponent of the abolition of capital punishment, winning a motion in the House of Commons for a five-year suspension, which was then vetoed in the House of Lords.

He persisted for many years, leading the outcry after the hanging of Derek Bentley for being present at the murder of a police officer, and in 1965 successfully piloted the Murder (Abolition of Death Penalty) Bill through Parliament, abolishing capital punishment for murder in Britain for a period of five years, with provision for abolition to be made permanent by affirmative resolutions of both Houses of Parliament before the end of that period. The appropriate resolutions were passed in 1969.

Twelve years before he was hired to represent two of the dead engineers on the *Windrush*, Silverman was a central figure in the darkest event in human history through contact with a German industrialist. Eduard Schulte was disaffected with Hitler and all his works, and had been doing all he could to bring information out of Germany to Switzerland under cover of his regular business trips. He was the CEO of Giesche, Germany's leading producer of non-ferrous metals, with interests in both mining and refining.

Thus, Schulte had contacts across German industry and government. Before his historic actions in July 1942, he had already advised the Allies, amongst much other useful intelligence, about the crisis in German gasoline supplies. He'd also leaked the design of the new Ju 52 transport plane, and been able to give chapter and verse on the terrible relationship between Hitler and many of his generals.[1]

Eduard Schulte's Giesche company was headquartered in Breslau, then a great Prussian city, now the Polish city of Wrocław. As an industrialist, Schulte sat at the heart of a web of practical intelligence in Upper Silesia, and as CEO he was worried. The Nazis were showing interest in seizing Giesche-owned land (rich in zinc) for what Himmler described as agricultural experiments. But Schulte heard of barracks being hurriedly built, and of the chemical giant IG Farben erecting buildings. Finally, in early July 1942, Schulte heard that 449 Jews had been gassed in what was known as Bunker 2.

This place, just a hundred miles from Breslau, was Auschwitz. It was the beginning of the Final Solution and to well-informed and intelligent Germans, such as Schulte, it was nothing more than what Hitler had explicitly promised.[2]

At great risk, Schulte crossed the border to Switzerland once more, and fed what he knew through to his contacts there. He was convinced that this must come to the personal attention of President Roosevelt, and that, through Swiss Jewish lines of communication, the best person to tell him was Rabbi Stephen Wise, the president of the World Jewish Congress based in New York. Both the British and the American consulates in Zurich were briefed, but the first reaction of the US State

Department was that this was a 'wild rumour inspired by Jewish fears'. Their view was that Rabbi Wise was a private citizen, and they had no duty to pass on mere rumour. They did not tell Roosevelt.

In Britain, the circumstances were different. Sydney Silverman was already a renowned barrister and the British representative of the World Jewish Congress. In those capacities, his 'private' status was no greater than Rabbi Wise. However, constitutionally, he was also a Member of Parliament (Labour). For a Foreign Office bureaucrat to withhold such information from an MP would have been a serious breach of convention, even in wartime.

So, Silverman was given Schulte's intelligence from Auschwitz, and he wasted no time in telegramming it via Western Union to Rabbi Wise. After much procrastination, in December 1942 the USA, Britain and eleven other countries made a joint declaration condemning the Nazi killing of Jews, four months after Silverman had blown the story open.

Schulte had hoped that the Allies would attack the death camps, but nothing further was done until 1944, by which time most of the Jews of Europe were dead, including those brought to Auschwitz on the *Windrush*.

So, when Sydney Silverman began to tear into the *Windrush* inquiry ten years after that, he was no grandstander; he was, in the best sense, a conviction politician.

The *Windrush* inquiry began on Monday 21 June at the heart of the clubland establishment, the Junior United Services Club, at 11–12 Charles II Street, London, SW1. It was led by the Wreck Commissioner, Mr J.V. Naisby QC, and was billed as 'A Formal Investigation into the Circumstances attending the Loss by fire of the *MV Empire Windrush*'.

On a table at the front of the inquiry room was a scale model of the *Windrush*, and a series of immaculate blueprint drawings showing every deck, the electrical circuits, fire extinguishers, water pipes, lifeboats and so on. These too were on full display, and they were all referred to constantly.

Sydney Silverman had negotiated his way in as the crewmen's representative, and set out his stall on his first day. He said that he had three main propositions to put before the court:

That the *Empire Windrush* was on voyage 29 (her last) unlawfully at sea in that it was not provided with the proper certificates or safety certificates under the Merchant Shipping (Safety Convention) Act 1949.

That the *Empire Windrush* did not comply with all the safety regulations laid down by the Minister under that Act, had not been validly exempted from any of them, and in all the circumstances, was not entitled to such an exemption.

That the *Empire Windrush* was, in any event, unseaworthy by reason of the condition of its engines and machinery, of its consequent undue liability to catch fire, and the fact that its means of fighting or containing such a fire were inadequate and unreliable.

Silverman's angle would have led to a disastrous admission of liability from both the New Zealand Shipping Company and the Ministry of Transport if conceded. From the start, he was unable to get clear answers from anyone.

He began with Captain 'Tug' Wilson, seen by many as a decent man in an impossible position, who had already been coached in sessions prior to the inquiry. We do not know what, if anything, he was advised to say, but even for a forensic barrister like Silverman he was pretty much a clam. Silverman knew that he needed to get Wilson to admit that the ship had a history of fires, which made her final disaster almost inevitable.

Silverman's questions (Q.) to Wilson (A.) are revealed in the inquiry transcript:

Q. There had been previous fires on the ship, had there not? A. One fire that I remember five years ago.

Q. 5 years ago? A. Yes.

Q. I do not profess to be sure about the date; no doubt you are; but was not there one in the vicinity of Gibraltar? A. That is the one I am alluding to.

Q. Was it five years before? A. Practically five years, I think.

Q. I had not gathered that it was quite so long ago as that, but I'm sure you must be right. A. Yes.

Q. How did that occur? A. I believe it started through an electrical fault.

Q. In the engine room? A. In the boiler room.

Q. In the boiler room? Of course, we do not know exactly what happened on this occasion, but this fire too started in the boiler room, did it not? A. I could not say.

Q. What? A. This fire?

Q. The one that resulted in the loss of the ship? A. I should say in the engine room.

Q. In the engine room? A. Yes.

Q. What exactly happened in the fire outside Gibraltar? It occurred in the boiler room, you say that; what happened exactly? A. Well, we successfully dealt with it and went to Gibraltar.

Q. I know you did, but how did it happen, how did it break out? A. I understand it was an electrical fault.

Q. Yes, but what did the electrical fault cause? A. It started a spark and ignited something, probably.

Q. What did it ignite? A. I do not know.

Q. How long did it take you to put it out? A. About two hours.

Q. You know, the deceased Mr Pendleton said in one of his letters that it took the best part of three nights to get it out? A. Well I do not think so, Sir. The chief engineer is here with me now and he could probably tell you the approximate time; but as far as I know, it was about two hours.

Q. Did it break out at night, in fact? A. Yes, it did.

Q. It is a fairly substantial fire, in any case, that takes two hours to put out, is it not? A. I suppose it was, yes.

Q. Was there ever any inquiry into that one? A. No, sir.

Q. Did the gentleman who gave evidence yesterday about the giving of a certificate of exemption or not giving a certificate of exemption – I'm sorry I've forgotten his name – know about this occurrence when he examined the ship in April 1953? A. Well, a fire was reported at the time, and we went to Gibraltar to do our temporary repairs, so that must they must have known about it.

Q. You would say by inference he must have known? A. Yes.

Q. But you do not know whether he knew or not? A. I do not know.

Wilson was playing a dead bat, and might indeed have simply advised Silverman that he had not been the captain in 1949. This was how the entire inquiry went. Silverman did manage to engage Boatswain Birch, one of the ship's emergency 'flying squad' describing the firefighting on the day of the sinking, in the matter of the 1949 fire. Birch agreed that in fact it had taken three days to put the fire out, not the two hours his captain had said.

Silverman had even less success with both Captain Wilson and James Tozer when he put to them the force of the concerns of Leslie Pendleton's file of correspondence, which he had persuaded Naisby QC to admit as evidence. Both men agreed, on different days of the inquiry, that Pendleton had been 'exaggerating', though they offered no reason as to what might possibly have motivated him to do so.

After four weeks of taking evidence and due consideration, a verdict was announced on 27 July 1954. It left nothing in doubt. Naisby began with a series of paeans of praise to all concerned on the day of the sinking:

In the alarming emergency which arose, the conduct of both passengers and crew is beyond all praise. Despite the failure of the aids which would normally be expected to be available in controlling the embarkation of such numbers, the abandonment of the vessel proceeded smoothly. In the words of one witness, everybody in the ship seems to be doing exactly the right thing. Perhaps no higher tribute can be paid to the organisation both by the ship's company and the military officers on board, or to the discipline, coolness and courage of the passengers.

The court also desires to acknowledge with gratitude the assistance given by the masters and crews of the four vessels, the *Socatra*, *Mentor*, *Hemsefjell*, and the *Taygete*.

Then he turned to substantive matters:

The *Empire Windrush* was by no means a new ship and there was considerable criticism of her engines and auxiliary machinery, but the court sees no reason to doubt that the *Empire Windrush* was, as far as could be ascertained, fit to proceed to and be at sea. While employed as a troop ship the *Empire Windrush* had been surveyed by the surveyors of the Ministry of Transport on several occasions and had received a passenger and safety certificate for numbers in excess of those carried on the voyage in question. In several respects the *Empire Windrush* did not comply with the standards laid down in the Merchant Shipping (Construction) Rules, 1952. With one small exception however, she did comply with the Merchant Shipping (Life Saving Appliance) Rules 1952, and she did comply with the Merchant Shipping (Fire Appliance) Rules 1952.

Various possible causes of the fire were considered. In the opinion of the court it is improbable that the origin of the fire was due to a crank-case explosion either in the main engines or the generators. Smoking, electrical fault and sabotage were also considered improbable.

Two more probable causes are: (1) the collapse of a plate in the main uptake causing incandescent material at a high temperature to be deposited at the forward end of the engine-room probably towards the starboard side. Most of this material would probably fall on the platform just inside the entrance to the engine room at 'E' deck level. This platform was of chequered plate with two openings on the centreline but the forward end was a grating under which fuel and lubricating oil pipes were led in a thwart ship direction. Such material on exposure to the air would burst into flame and either by physical contact, or by heat cause a pipe to give way and vaporise and ignite the oil therefrom. There was no evidence given at the enquiry as to whether the upper part of the main uptake had ever been renewed or repaired since the vessel was built, and it did not seem that there was any requirement that the uptake should be inspected internally or that there was any practice to make such an examination. The uptake was lagged so external examination of the plates which must've been liable to corrosion was impossible.

(2) The spraying, dripping or splashing of oil, probably fuel oil, onto a hot exhaust Y piece or pipe. There were a number of fuel supply lines of various diameters passing above or adjacent to the main engines. In order to get the fuel to the engines it is inevitable that at least a certain number of those supply lines must be in some such position. If one of those pipes fractured or became adrift it would have been possible for oil therefrom to spray, drip or splash in comparatively small quantities onto a hot exhaust Y piece or possibly some part of the exhaust pipe where the lagging of that pipe was not perfect. According to the evidence in such event that oil would vaporise and might ignite. Had that happened such ignition might well provide a sufficient 'batch' to set light to the main flow of oil from the pipe and create almost instantaneously a fire of the intensity spoken in evidence and also produce a large quantity of dense acrid smoke.

Having carefully considered the above causes of the origin of the fire I have come to the conclusion that on the evidence given there is no such balance of probability in favour of any one as to justify me in finding that it was the probable cause of this fire.

RECOMMENDATIONS

The court recommends that consideration should be given: (1) To an alteration in the requirements for firefighting appliances by a considerable increase in the number of smoke helmets provided and to their distribution. (2) To the question of making it imperative that there should be a proper periodical examination and inspection of uptakes and funnels in all vessels. (3) To the question of the dispersal of emergency controls and connections. The annex contains Mr H.A. Lyndsay's opinion that he considers that by far the most probable cause of the fire was a failure of a portion of the combined uptake from the main engines, main generators and composite boilers, which thereby released a quantity of burning.

And that was it. A ship now lay at the bottom of the sea off the coast of Algeria. If the incident had happened at night or in bad weather, a thousand or more civilians and service people may have been in the deep too. But the finding was, in essence, 'we don't know'.

Next to no consideration was made of her terrible mechanical history. And to round it off, a series of limp recommendations was proffered to adopt better oxygen masks, send men with clipboards on to ships slightly more regularly and to check the alarm systems. In later years, the shipping industry argued and resisted all of these recommendations.

At the end of his statement Naseby referred to an application by Silverman with regard to costs and said the court could make no order with respect to his clients. Silverman had applied for costs affecting the parents of two of the four members of the crew who'd lost their lives. No costs were awarded, no compensation was ever offered and no apology given.

The job was done. The next day *The Times* headline said:

CAUSE OF SHIP'S FIRE UNKNOWN

———————

EMPIRE WINDRUSH 'FIT TO SAIL'

———————

COURT OF INQUIRY'S RECOMMENDATIONS

Bessie Braddock and Sydney Silverman went to the end of their days telling anyone who was interested that what hurt the families most was not the tragic loss of their loved ones' lives, but the cover-up. It was an ignominious climax to the story of a ship.

Another reading for Captain Wilson's dead bat responses at the inquiry is that, although these partially arose from New Zealand Shipping Company orders, they were exacerbated by what the captain would have made of Sydney Silverman. Wilson is described by his family as 'a dour Yorkshireman' whose family was 'steeped in Conservatism'.[3] He was a stoic figure whose father and brother died at sea in the First World War, and who was at sea himself from the age of 14.

He'd endured three years as a POW in Bremen during the Second World War, having scuttled his own ship *Skyterren* to prevent it falling to the enemy. All that before being ordered to skipper the *Windrush* from 1950 to 1954, a ship he knew full well was not seaworthy. For a tight-lipped pragmatist such as him, the spectacle of Silverman, a Labour politician – and a showman in the courtroom – would have been alienating. His granddaughter said, 'Granpoppy was not going to open up there.' The irony is profound: Silverman could have been the brave captain's best chance of being allowed to tell the whole truth.

In the end, Wilson's suffering only worsened. He was very bitter about the inquiry's outcome, and within two years his wife, Ethel, died. His mental health badly affected, and with no support mechanisms that might be available today, he disappeared from the family radar.

Ten years after the sinking, in 1964, the War Office notified Wilson's family that he was dying in Chichester. He had lost everything and been living alone on a disused 60ft coastal patrol vessel moored on the mudflats of Hayling Island to the east of Portsmouth. It's a Dickensian image: one of self-reliance by the ocean's edge to a lonely end. Despite his valiant efforts, the last captain of the *Windrush* was yet another in the tragic line of those who ultimately had suffered in her name.

AFTERWORD

AT 37°00'N 02°11'E

It is a wonderful irony that the only British people alive today who would have once been taught the most famous poem anthropomorphising ships will either be over 40 or the beneficiaries of an outstanding Caribbean education focussed on the literature and language of the 'mother country'. John Masefield's 1903 *Cargoes* was traditionally used to introduce generations of 9- and 10-year-olds to the way rhythm can be played with in poetry. It has three verses, but only two are usually quoted:

Stately Spanish galleon coming from the Isthmus,
Dipping through the Tropics by the palm-green shores,
With a cargo of diamonds,
Emeralds, amethysts,
Topazes, and cinnamon, and gold moidores.

Dirty British coaster with a salt-caked smoke stack,
Butting through the Channel in the mad March days,
With a cargo of Tyne coal,
Road-rails, pig-lead,
Firewood, iron-ware, and cheap tin trays.

Children used to relate especially to the dirty British coaster, butting through the Channel in the mad March days. There was character in this ship – plucky and downtrodden. Like the horse in *Black Beauty*, we could imagine she'd had better days and could hope that one day better may yet come.

The *Windrush* too was quite some ship. Born German, adopted British, perishing off the coast of Africa, her entire life was both one mass migration after another and a metaphor for migration throughout time.

Some of what she did was awful. Seeding South America with future Nazis, laying the ratlines of a few years later. Invading Norway, bringing her Lebensborn children and their mothers to Germany, many trapped there for another forty years. The unforgivable transportation of Norway's Jews to Auschwitz. Retreating from what many see as the imperial shame of abandoning India, carrying thousands of brave British soldiers to a pointless and never-ended war in Korea. Then, the deaths of the crewmen when she finally sank, and the shoddy and predictable obfuscation at the inquiry of what had truly happened.

And yet, there is one redeeming aspect to her story: the legacy of the Caribbean men and women who arrived at Tilbury on 22 June 1948. Black Britain did not begin then, but that one voyage certainly did the country proud. All the nurses, writers, musicians, industrial workers, servicemen, teachers *et al.* who stepped off the ship and down the gangplank to touch British ground, the majority for the first time, most planning to stay only for a few years but nearly all of whom made it their home.

Today, inadvertently and unhappily, this cohort and their 'generation' have put a mirror up to the British self: who and what the nation thinks it is. The forced banishment of some of them to islands they can hardly remember, or the denial of their paid-for health and employment rights in the present day – this injustice makes a sentient nation wonder how it came to this.

These were a people who were enslaved by the British, forced from Africa by them, who lived after slavery was ended on islands that were ruled from thousands of miles away by distant kings and queens. When war came, they rattled tins in the Caribbean to help the war effort, a million pounds raised in the islands during the Second World War (more than £6 million in today's prices). Thousands of Caribbean men lost their lives in both wars.

Then, in 1948, invited to Britain, asked to come to help, they gladly came to serve 'mother'. And finally in the twenty-first century, kicked in the teeth. Not just by the Conservatives. Many legal experts think that it was the Labour Home Secretary, John Reid, passing the UK Borders Act in 2007 that upped the ante, dialling up ideas of 'criminality' offering justification for deportation, retrospectively applied. Then Theresa May, her hostile environment and, as former Conservative MP Anna Soubry put it in February 2019, her 'obsession with immigration'.

Yet senior figures from a Caribbean background wonder if this presents an opportunity. Speaking off the record on an anonymous basis, one lawyer whose parents were *Windrush* immigrants, and who now works in a central role determining the future of compensation for those so badly treated, sees grounds for hope.

The crisis has presented an opportunity, he suggests, for British Caribbean people to work together, setting to one side the island rivalries that white people are deaf to, but which are a significant social factor still in Britain. A white person sees a black person. A black person may see an Antiguan, a Jamaican or a Trinidadian. Now, they all have a common cause, and perhaps there is a realisation that it is time to move on: time to organise as one to stop this ever happening again.

And he sees hope for the education of the white British too. When the story of the Windrush generation's persecution is finally resolved, there will have to be a reckoning. There will have to be education around it. Will this at last be a chance for the British to confront and properly digest the legacy of slavery, to learn and deeply consider what a nation had done?

Millions will say, 'that wasn't me'. Finding the language to negotiate beyond that reflex defensiveness is a challenge in itself. If that challenge is met, the United Kingdom will be a kinder and better country in which to live.

❖

As to the *Windrush* herself, she is absolved now. Rusting 1½ miles deep in the western Mediterranean off the coast of Algeria at a position 37°00′N 02°11′E, even the most obtuse television commissioner wouldn't send a minor celebrity down in a mini-sub to gawk at her remains. She needs to live on in our imaginations now; there is no point trying to see her again. We need to think about what she once meant, and what she may mean to us again, if only we can think about all the good and bad that was done in her name over a profound twenty-three-year engagement in the most turbulent years of the twentieth century.

If we can imagine her for a few moments in her glory, in the Thames at Greenwich with the Royal Naval College behind her, in the lagoon at Venice or lowering her gangplank to the portside at Kingston, Jamaica, on 24 May 1948 to welcome a generation aboard in the burning sun, perhaps that's a start.

NOTES

Introduction: A Hostile Environment

1   Formerly editor of *The Independent* newspaper and BBC News
    political editor.
2   Younge, Gary, *The Guardian*, 20 April 2018.
3   Video interview, *The Guardian*, 26 March 2018.
4   *The Guardian*, 22 April 2018, p. 43. David Olusoga is professor of
    public history at the University of Manchester.

Chapter 1

1   Philips, Mike and Philips, Trevor, *Windrush: The Irresistible Rise of
    Multi-Racial Britain* (London: HarperCollins, 1998).
2   Leading article, *The Times*, 30 July 2012.
3   *The Voice*, 30 October 1982.
4   Interview with Simon Israel, Channel Four News, 18 December
    2018.
5   Joseph Goebbels, 12 January 1941. Goebbels, Joseph, *Die Zeit ohne
    Beispiel* (Munich: Zentralverlag der NSDAP, 1941), pp. 364–9.
6   Stevenson, Robert Louis, *Treasure Island* (London: Cassell and Co.,
    1883), first published in instalments during 1881 and 1882. Jim
    Hawkins was enlisted on Squire Trelawney's ship, the *Hispaniola*,
    to be captained by Alexander Smollett. Most notorious of the

crew was a Bristol pub landlord who had lost his leg in the same piratical skirmish in which 'Blind' Pew lost his sight, Long John Silver.

7   Kershaw, Robert, *Landing on the Edge of Eternity: 24 Hours at Omaha* (London: Pegasus, 2018).

8   Nelson, Fraser, 'Did Andrew Cooper's polls lose the referendum?', *The Spectator*, 2 July 2016.

9   See Arnott, Paul, *A Good Likeness* (London: Little Brown, 2000). The author was born 'Rory Brennan' in November 1961 and then, after his adoption, christened 'Paul Arnott' in February 1962.

Chapter 2

1   Napoleon III died in exile in Chislehurst, Kent, on 9 November 1873.

2   Adolf Hitler draped the Niederwalddenkmal in swastikas on 28 August 1933 at a mass rally demanding the return of the Saarland.

3   Pye, Michael, *The Edge of the World: How the North Sea Made Us Who We Are* (London: Viking, 2014), p. 21.

4   Schwerdtner, Nils, *German Luxury Ocean Liners: From Kaiser Wilhelm der Grosse to AIDAstella* (Stroud: Amberley Publishing, 2013), p. 181.

5   Miller, William H., *German Ocean Liners of the 20th Century* (Yeovil: Patrick Stephens Limited, 1989), p. 142.

6   Willoughby, Jeffrey, *The KdF Fleet in Historic Photographs* (UK: Maritime Publishing Concepts, 2011), p. 83.

7   *Ibid.*, p. 141.

8   Overy, Richard, *The Bombing War: Europe 1939–1945* (London: Allen Lane, 2013), pp. 436–72.

9   Tonnage should not be confused with weight in tonnes. Tonnage measures the capacity of a ship. Gross tonnage is a measure of the ships interior volume. Net tonnage is a measure of the volume within designated to cargo, passenger, machinery and other used spaces.

10   National Archives TS 52/136.

Chapter 3

1 See Lloyd's of London voyage cards derived from *Lloyd's List*, Guildhall Library, City of London.

2 Hoerder, Dirk, *Germany and the Americas: Culture, Politics, History*, Vol. 1, ed. Thomas Adam (Santa Barbara: ABC-CLIO, 2005), p. 33.

3 Peters, H.F., *Zarathustra: The Case of Elisabeth and Friedrich Nietzsche* (New York: Crown Publishers, 1977), p. 87.

4 Usually, the term *Lebensraum* refers to the expanded Reich thought necessary to house and feed the Germanic peoples. Its borders varied according to the times, and imperialist Germans, envying the British Empire, considered that it could carry to other continents. Historian Alan Bullock makes a clear differentiation between Hitler's ideas and Stalin's in this respect: '[Hitler] sought to prove the advantage of "socializing people" over the Marxist method of socializing production; to unite the German people in a *Volksgemeinschaft* in place of liberal individualism and the Marxists' class war; and to revive their readiness to bear arms in the war to capture *Lebensraum* for the German *Herrenvolk* in the East', Bullock, Alan, *Hitler and Stalin: Parallel Lives* (London: HarperCollins, 1991), p. 501.

5 Peters, *Zarathustra*, p. 122.

6 *Ibid.*, p. 111.

7 *Ibid.*, p. 125.

Chapter 4

1 Directed by Chris Weitz.

2 Directed by Lucía Puenzo.

3 Tombs, Robert, *The English and their History* (London: Allen Lane, 2014), p. 650.

4 Von zur Mühlen, Patrik, in ed. Thomas Adam, *Germany and the Americas*, pp. 172–5.

5 Tyvela, Kirk, in *ibid.*, pp. 867–8.

6 Newton, Ronald C., *The 'Nazi Menace' in Argentina 1931–1947* (Stanford: Stanford University Press, 1992), p. 43.

7 For Eichmann's life and escape after the war see Stangneth, Bettina (tr. Ruth Martin), *Eichmann Before Jerusalem* (London: The Bodley Head, 2014).

8 Organization der ehemaligen SS-Angehörigen (Organisation of former SS-Members).

9 Stangneth, *Eichmann Before Jerusalem*, p. 78.

10 Bullough, Oliver, *Moneyland: Why Thieves and Crooks Now Rule the World and How to Take it Back* (London: Profile Books, 2018), p. 41.

11 Leebaert, Derek, *The World After the War: America Confronts the British Superpower, 1945–1957* (London: Oneworld, 2018), pp. 206–7.

Chapter 5

1 Dressler-Andress, Horst, *Three Years of the National-Socialist Community 'Kraftt durch Freude': Aims and Achievements* (Berlin, 1937).

2 Bullock, Alan, *Hitler: A Study in Tyranny* (London: Pelican Books, 1962), pp. 277, 801.

3 Proclamation of the Action Committee for the Protection of German Labour, 2 May 1933. Nuremberg documents 614-PS.

4 Engelman, R., *Dietrich Eckart and the Genesis of Nazism* (Ann Arbor: Washington University AMI Press, 1971), p. 120.

Chapter 6

1 Bayles, William D., *Caesars in Goosestep* (London and New York: Harper & Brothers, 1940), p. 176.

2 Baranowski, Shelley, *Strength Through Joy: Consumerism and Mass Tourism in the Third Reich* (Cambridge: Cambridge University Press, 2004), p. 171.

3 *Ibid.*, p. 173.

4 *Ibid.*, p. 174.

5 *Ibid.*, p. 181.

6 Willoughby, Jeffrey, *The KdF Fleet,* p. 7.

7   Dell, Robert, *Germany Unmasked* (London: Martin Hopkinson Ltd, 1934), p. 15.

8   *Ibid.*, p. 148.

9   *Ibid.*, pp. 148–9.

10 Sachs, Harvey, *Music in Fascist Italy* (London: George Weidenfeld & Nicolson, 1987), p. 201.

Chapter 7

1   Williamson, Henry, *Goodbye West Country* (London: Putnam, 1937).

2   A fine account of the surprising history of fascism in the West Country is Gray, Todd, *Blackshirts in Devon* (Exeter: The Mint Press, 2006).

3   Tate, Tim, *Hitler's British Traitors* (London: Icon, 2018), p. 6.

4   *Ibid.*, p. 108.

5   Intelligence Report C6/10/29, Board of Deputies of British Jews, in Todd, *Blackshirts in Devon*, p. 95.

6   Tate, *Hitler's British Traitors*, p. 103.

7   The Marburg Files captured by the Americans after the war disclose much correspondence and contemporaneous notes revealing the depths of the Duke of Windsor's preparedness to side with Hitler and betray his family and his country.

8   Law, Michael John, *1930s London: The Modern City* (Canterbury: Yellowback Press, 2015), p. 16.

9   Honig, Ruth, *The League of Nations* (London: Haus Histories, 2010), p. 154.

Chapter 8

1   For a sceptical depiction of Churchill's zeal for Narvik and then his volte-face: Kersaudy, François, *Norway 1940* (Lincoln: University of Nebraska Press, 1990), p. 35.

2   Shakespeare, Nicholas, *Six Minutes in May: How Churchill Unexpectedly Became Prime Minister* (London: Harville Secker, 2017), p. 117.

3   *Private Eye*'s edition before Christmas always features a mocked-up TV listing with a fake title, 'They Flew to Bruges', satirising both the obsession with Second World War films and, when first used, the devout Eurosceptics then fantasising about heading from Surrey to give a verbal drubbing to the EU.

4   *Weserübung* means Operation Weser, named after the German river Weser.

5   Petrow, Richard, *The Bitter Years: The Invasion and Occupation of Denmark and Norway April 1940–May 1945* (New York: William Morrow & Company, 1974), p. 47.

6   *Ibid.*, p. 68.

7   Dean, Martin, *Robbing the Jews: The Confiscation of Jewish Property in the Holocaust* (Cambridge: Cambridge University Press, 2008), p. 141.

8   *Ibid.*, p. 287.

9   Hilberg, Raul, *The Destruction of the European Jews* (Chicago: Quadrangle Books, 1961), p. 312.

Chapter 9

1   www.scandanavianjewishblogspot.com/2015/12.

2   Maier, Ruth (ed. Vold, Jan Erick; tr. Bulloch, Jamie), *Ruth Maier's Diary: A Jewish Girl's Life in Nazi Europe* (London, Vintage 2010) p. 102.

3   Hermann Rausching was a German thinker who had joined the Nazis only to repudiate them and flee the country, publishing many anti-Nazi tracts and eventually settling in America in 1941, where he lived until 1982.

4   Maier, *Ruth Maier's Diary*.

5   Norwegian parliament.

6   Levin Berman, Irene, *'We are Going to Pick Potatoes': Norway and the Holocaust, the Untold Story* (Maryland: Hamilton Books, 2010), p. 14.

7   *Ibid.*, p. 61.

8   Rees, Laurence, *Auschwitz: The Nazis and the 'Final Solution'* (London: BBC Books, 2005), p. 225.

9   Petrow, Richard p. 122.

10 *Ibid.*, p. 320.

11 Ottosen, Kristian, *In Such a Night: The Story of the Deportation of the Jews* (Oslo: Aschehaus, 1994), pp. 334–60.

12 Conrad Caplan survived until early 1945 and his death is recorded as coming 'In transport', likely to be a movement from Auschwitz for the purposes of slave labour elsewhere. Aged 22 at his death, he would have been only 19 when on the *Windrush*.

13 Nathan Fein also survived until 1945 but was shot during transportation to Buchenwald.

Chapter 10

1   Knowles, Daniel, *Tirpitz: The Life and Death of Germany's Last Great Battleship* (Stroud: Fonthill, 2018) is an excellent source for technical data concerning the ship, and a comprehensive linear history of her brief life.

2   Organisation Todt was named after Fritz Todt, the civil and military engineer responsible before the war for the vast expansion of 1,900 miles of Autobahn who was later engaged in building the Siegfried Line and the Atlantic Wall. He died in a suspicious plane crash in 1942 after supposedly having been outspoken directly with Hitler, saying the war in the east against Russia was a fool's errand doomed to defeat.

3   Kennedy, Ludovic, *Menace: The Life and Death of the Tirpitz* (London: Sidgwick and Jackson, 1979), pp. 74–6.

Chapter 11

1   Knowles, *Tirpitz*, p. 134.

2   Kennedy, *Menace*, p. 93.

3   Extract from BBC documentary *Target 'Tirpitz'*, producer Edward Mirzoeff (1973).

4   Air Ministry press release featured in many papers including *The Times* and the *Dundee Courier*, 1 April 1944.

5   Various, *The Official History of the Royal Canadian Airforce*, Vol. 3 (Toronto: University of Toronto, 1980), p. 458.

6   Knowles, *Tirpitz*, p. 231.

7   Jackson, John, *Ultra's Arctic War: The Bletchley Archive*, Vol. 2 (Milton Keynes: The Military Press, 2003), pp. 111–5.

8   ADM 234/350, p. 56.

9   The rank is equivalent to warrant officer second class in the British navy. Zetterling, N. and Tamelander, M., *Tirpitz: The Life and Death of Germany's Last Super Battleship* (Oxford: Casemate Publishers, 2009), p. 314.

10   Kennedy, *op. cit.*, p. 16.

11   Dönitz, Karl, *Memoirs: Ten Years and Twenty Days* (London: George Weidenfeld and Nicolson Ltd, 1959), p. 386.

Chapter 12

1   Alfred Rosenberg was the Baltic German Nazi apparatchik and go-between for the Nazis with occupied Norway.

2   Manus, Max, *Underwater Saboteur* (London: William Kimber & Co., 1953), p. 20.

3   *Ibid.*, p. 28.

4   *Ibid.*, p. 62.

5   *Ibid.*, p. 66.

6   *Ibid.*, p. 68.

7   *Ibid.*, p. 117.

8   *Ibid.*, p. 118.

9   *Ibid.*, p. 20.

10   *Ibid.*, p. 34.

Chapter 13

1   In 1977, Alfred Haase's son, Peter, Anni-Frid's half-brother, saw an article in German teen magazine *Bravo* discussing this. Anni-Frid had long believed her father to be dead, but a few months later they were reunited in Stockholm. He died in 2009 aged 89.

2 Gildea, Robert, Wieviorka, Olivier & Waring, Anette, *Surviving Hitler and Mussolini: Daily Life in Occupied Europe* (London: Berg Publishers, 2006), p. 92.

3 *The New York Times*, 19 October 2018.

4 *The Guardian*, 7 December 2002.

5 *The Guardian*, 16 October 2018.

Chapter 14

1 Claus, Odd, *Witness to War: A Norwegian Boy's Experiences in Germany* (Oslo: Cappelen Damm, 2008).

2 The National Archives TS13/1853. All the papers cited in this chapter are contained in this file.

3 The Germanischer Lloyd SE was a classification society based in Hamburg, Germany.

4 Telegraph transmitter.

5 Radio direction finder.

6 Spanish ports in the Second World War were, in theory, neutral.

Chapter 15

1 *Daily Mail*, 24 July 1934.

2 National Martime Museum, New Zealand Shipping Company archive in the P&O collection.

3 Churchill's crucial paragraph encapsulated the tragedy of the collapse of a strategic friendship with the former Russian states under the Soviet regime: 'From Stettin in the Baltic to Trieste in the Adriatic, an iron curtain has descended across the Continent. Behind that line lie all the capitals of the ancient states of Central and Eastern Europe. Warsaw, Berlin, Prague, Vienna, Budapest, Belgrade, Bucharest and Sofia, all these famous cities and the populations around them lie in what I must call the Soviet sphere, and all are subject in one form or another, not only to Soviet influence but to a very high and, in many cases, increasing measure of control from Moscow ... An attempt is being made

by the Russians in Berlin to build up a quasi-Communist party in their zone of Occupied Germany by showing special favours to groups of left-wing German leaders. At the end of the fighting last June, the American and British Armies withdrew westwards, in accordance with an earlier agreement, to a depth at some points of 150 miles upon a front of nearly four hundred miles, in order to allow our Russian allies to occupy this vast expanse of territory which the Western Democracies had conquered … Whatever conclusions may be drawn from these facts – and facts they are – this is certainly not the Liberated Europe we fought to build up. Nor is it one which contains the essentials of permanent peace.'

4 *The Guardian*, 5 February 1950.

5 Marshall, Tim, *Prisoners of Geography* (London: Eliot and Thompson, 2015), p. 167.

6 Bew, John, *Citizen Clem: A Biography of Attlee* (London: Riverrun, 2016), p. 453.

7 Hickman, Tom, *The Call-Up: A History of National Service* (London: Headline Book Publishing, 2004), p. 16.

8 Vinen, Richard, *National Service: A Generation in Uniform 1945–1963* (London: Penguin, 2014), p. 63.

9 *The Spectator*, 26 August 2017.

10 Shrabani Basu's *Victoria & Abdul: The Extraordinary Story of the Queen's Closest Confidant* was published by The History Press and was made into a feature film directed by Stephen Frears in 2017.

11 Khar is a suburb of then Bombay, now Mumbai.

Chapter 16

1 Harris, Robert, *Enigma* (London: Hutchinson, 1995), which was adapted to film in 2001 (directed by Michael Apted from a screenplay by Tom Stoppard).

2 Imperial War Museum files, which can be read at www.iwm.org. uk/history/the-polish-pilots-who-flew-in-the-battle-of-britain.

3 Welchman, Gordon, *The Hut Six Story: Breaking the Enigma Codes* (New York: McGraw-Hill, 1982), p. 289.

4 Raca, Jane, 'The Other Windrush Generation: Poles Reunited After Fleeing Soviet Camp', *The Guardian*, 27 June 2018.

5 Home Office, *Hate Crime, England and Wales, 2015/16*, Statistical Bulletin 11/16 (2016) report-it.org.uk/files/hate-crime-1516-hosb1116.pdf.

6 *Cambridge News*, 25 June 2016.

7 *Independent*, 20 September 2016.

Chapter 17

1 Levy, Andrea, *Small Island* (London: Review, 2004).

2 BBC World Service Witness Black History interview with Sam King, 2013.

3 Interview in Philips & Philips, *Windrush*, p. 60.

4 The National Archives, CO 876/88, 5 July 1948.

5 Kynaston, David, *Austerity Britain, 1945–51* (London: Bloomsbury, 2007), p. 516.

6 Le Gendre, Kevin, *Don't Stop the Carnival: Black Music in Britain* (Leeds: Peepal Tree, 2018), p. 193.

7 Philips & Philips, *Windrush*, p. 64.

Chapter 18

1 Mobile Army Surgical Hospital.

2 Hermiston, Roger, *The Secret Lives of Agent George Blake* (London: Aurum Press, 2013), p. 129.

3 Younger, Maj. Gen. A.E., *Blowing Our Bridges: A Memoir from Dunkirk to Korea via Normandy* (Barnsley: Pen & Sword Military, 2004).

4 Angier, Diana, *Pat*, private volume held by Imperial War Museum, London.

5 Green, David, *Captured at the Imjin River: The Korean War Memoirs of a Gloster 1950–1953* (Barnsley: Leo Cooper, 2003).

6 *Ibid*.

7 The Ulster Rifles, the Northumberland Fusiliers and two battalions of the 29th Glo'sters.

8   Between 1948 and 1972 Ceylon was an independent dominion with the British sovereign as head of state in the Commonwealth of Nations. In 1972 it became a republic within the Commonwealth and changed its name to Sri Lanka.

Chapter 19

1   Major Pat Angier's papers (including the loose-bound *Pat*, with unnumbered pages) are held at the Imperial War Museum. One of his grandchildren is preparing a book on Pat's life and experiences.
2   An island at the south-west end of the English Channel near the coast of Brittany. It marks the point where vessels begin to turn south.
3   *Daily Mail*, 3 October 1950.
4   According to the *Daily Mail*, a War Office spokesman said, 'Private Wagstaff was called up as an ordinary soldier. So far as we can find out he did not say he was a bandsman and made no complaint.'
5   *Dundee Courier* (3 October 1950) and other publications ran a half-page photograph.
6   There are still serious human rights issues in Sri Lanka today, and anyone visiting the great sites will be confronted by a macho posse of Buddhist monks. However, the island remains extremely beautiful, and in particular it is possible to imagine how much the nature lover Angier might have adored the botanical gardens at Kandy.
7   Chalke, Harry, *The Diaries of H. Chalke*, ed. J.H. Hills, held at Imperial War Museum, London.

Chapter 20

1   Captain in the Glo'sters.
2   Appleman, Roy E., Burns, James M., Gugeler, Russell A. and Stevens, John, *Okinawa: The Last Battle* (Washington, DC: United States Army Centre of Military History, 2000), p. 489.
3   Hanson, Victor Davis, *Ripples of Battle: How Wars Fought Long Ago Still Determine How We Fight, How We Live, and How We Think* (New York: Doubleday, 2003).

4   Chalke, Harry, *The Diaries of H. Chalke*, ed. J.H. Hills, held at Imperial War Museum, London.

5   Younger, *Blowing Our Bridges* (Barnsley: Pen & Sword Military, 2004).

6   Kahn, E.J., *New Yorker*, 14 June 1951.

7   Younger, *Blowing Our Bridges*, p. 193.

8   *Ibid.*, p. 194.

9   Jenkins, Simon, *England's Cathedrals* (London: Little, Brown, 2016), p. 109.

10 www.bbc.co.uk/gloucestershire/focus/2003/08/potter_more_info. shtml will lead Potter enthusiasts to an extensive list of parts of the building used, including its lavatorium.

Chapter 21

1   This chapter is hugely indebted to a privately published volume of memories of these events collated in 1998 by Captain Wally Seybold, at the time of this trip the fourth officer on SS *Empire Windrush*. It is dedicated to the memory of the four crewmen who died in the engine room, and to the late Captain W. Wilson OBE. *Women and Children First: The Loss of the Troopship 'Empire Windrush'*. The dedication reads, 'The passage of the years has not diminished the survivors' knowledge of the courage and steadfastness shown by all on board that morning of the disaster, 28th March 1954.'

Chapter 22

1   On a ship, the emergency air compressor is used for starting auxiliary engines during an emergency or when the main air compressor has failed for filling up the main air receiver. Without air, fuel will not ignite and there will be no power. This type of compressor can be motor driven or engine driven. If motor driven, it should be supplied from an emergency source of power. With the *Windrush*'s unreliable electrics, this would always have been problematic.

2   *Manchester Guardian*, 5 April 1954.

3   National Maritime Museum, New Zealand Shipping Company Files in the P&O Archive.

4   Private Papers of Derek Burnand, held at the Imperial War Museum Library, catalogue number 12724.

5   All quotations from the inquiry may be found in The National Archives, TCA1/88 and TS52/142.

Chapter 23

1   The outstanding account of Eduard Schulte's life is in Lacquer, W. and Breitman, R., *Breaking the Silence: The Secret Mission of Eduard Schulte, Who Brought the World News of the Final Solution* (London: The Bodley Head, 1986).

2   In a speech at the Reichstag on January 1939, Hitler warned if there was an outbreak of war it would be even worse for the Jews: 'If international finance Jewry within Europe and abroad should succeed once again in plunging the peoples into a world war, then the consequence will not be the Bolshevization of the world and therewith the victory of Jewry, but on the contrary, the destruction of the Jewish race in Europe.'

3   Author's private correspondence and interview with Hilary Wilson, granddaughter of William and Ethel Wilson.

BIBLIOGRAPHY

Angier, Diana, *Pat*, private volume held at the Imperial War Museum, London.

Appleman, Roy E., Burns, James M., Gugeler, Russell A. and Stevens, John, *Okinawa: The Last Battle* (Washington, DC: United States Army Centre of Military History, 2000).

Baranowski, Shelley, *Strength Through Joy: Consumerism and Mass Tourism in the Third Reich* (Cambridge: Cambridge University Press, 2004).

Basu, Shrabani, *Victoria & Abdul: The Extraordinary Story of the Queen's Closest Confidant* (Stroud: The History Press, 2017).

Bayles, William D., *Caesars in Goosestep* (New York: Harper & Brothers, 1940).

Bew, John, *Citizen Clem: A Biography of Attlee* (London: Riverrun, 2016).

Bullock, Alan, *Hitler: A Study in Tyranny* (London: Pelican Books, 1962).

Bullock, Alan, *Hitler and Stalin: Parallel Lives* (London: HarperCollins, 1991).

Bullough, Oliver, *Moneyland: Why Thieves & Crooks Now Rule the World and How to Take it Back* (London: Profile Books, 2018).

Burnand, Derek, Private Papers of Derek Burnand, held at the Imperial War Museum Library, catalogue number 12724.

Chalke, Harry, *The Diaries of H. Chalke*, ed. J.H. Hills, held at the Imperial War Museum, London.

Claus, Odd, *Witness to War: A Norwegian Boy's Experiences in Germany* (Oslo: Cappelen Damm, 2008).

Davies, S.J., *In Spite of Dungeons: The Experience as a Prisoner-of-War in North Korea of the Chaplain to the First Battalion, the Gloucestershire Regiment* (Stroud: Alan Sutton, 1954).

Davis Hanson, Victor, *Ripples of Battle: How Wars Fought Long Ago Still Determine How We Fight, How We Live, and How We Think* (New York: Doubleday, 2003).

Dean, Martin, *Robbing the Jews: The Confiscation of Jewish Property in the Holocaust* (Cambridge: Cambridge University Press, 2008).

Dell, Robert, *Germany Unmasked* (London: Martin Hopkinson Ltd, 1934).

Dressler-Andress, Horst, *Three Years of the National-Socialist Community 'Kraft durch Freude': Aims and Achievements* (Berlin, 1937).

Engelman, R., *Dietrich Eckart and the Genesis of Nazism* (Ann Arbor: Washington University AMI Press, 1971).

Gildea, Robert (ed.), Wieviorka, Olivier and Waring, Anette, *Surviving Hitler and Mussolini: Daily Life in Occupied Europe* (London: Berg Publishers, 2006).

Gray, Todd, *Blackshirts in Devon* (Exeter: The Mint Press, 2006).

Green, David, *Captured at the Imjin River: The Korean War Memoirs of a Gloster 1950–1953* (Barnsley: Leo Cooper, 2003).

Harris, Robert, *Enigma* (London: Hutchison, 1995).

Hermiston, Roger, *The Secret Lives of Agent George Blake* (London: Aurum Press, 2013).

Hickman, Tom, *The Call-Up: A History of National Service* (London: Headline Book Publishing, 2004).

Hilberg, Raul, *The Destruction of the European Jews* (Chicago: Quadrangle Books, 1961).

Hoerder, Dirk, *Germany and the Americas: Culture, Politics, History*, Vol. 1, ed. Thomas Adam (Santa Barbara: ABC-CLIO, 2005).

Honig, Ruth, *The League of Nations* (London: Haus Histories, 2010).

Jackson, John, *Ultra's Arctic War: The Bletchley Archive*, Vol. 2 (Milton Keynes: The Military Press, 2003), pp. 111–15.

Jenkins, Simon, *England's Cathedrals* (London: Little, Brown, 2016).

Kennedy, Ludovic, *Menace: The Life and Death of the Tirpitz* (London: Sidgwick and Jackson, 1979).

Kersaudy, François, *Norway 1940* (Lincoln: University of Nebraska Press, 1990).

Kershaw, Robert, *Landing on the Edge of Eternity: 24 Hours at Omaha* (London: Pegasus, 2018).

Knowles, Daniel, *Tirpitz: The Life and Death of Germany's Last Great Battleship* (Stroud: Fonthill, 2018).

Kynaston, David, *Austerity Britain, 1945–51* (London: Bloomsbury, 2007).

Lacquer, W. and Breitman, R., *Breaking the Silence: The Secret Mission of Eduard Schulte, Who Brought the World News of the Final Solution* (London: The Bodley Head, 1986).

Law, Michael John, *1930s London: The Modern City* (Canterbury: Yellowback Press, 2015).

Leebaert, Derek, *The World After the War: America Confronts the British Superpower* (London: Oneworld, 2018).

Le Gendre, Kevin, *Don't Stop the Carnival: Black Music in Britain* (Leeds: Peepal Tree, 2018).

Levin Berman, Irene, *'We are Going to Pick Potatoes': Norway and the Holocaust, the Untold Story* (Maryland: Hamilton Books 2010).

Levy, Andrea, *Small Island* (London: Review, 2004).

Macdonald, Callum, *Britain and the Korean War* (Oxford: Basil Blackwell, 1990).

Maier, Ruth (ed. Vold, Jan Erick; tr. Bulloch, Jamie), *Ruth Maier's Diary: A Jewish Girl's Life in Nazi Europe* (London, Vintage 2010).

Manus, Max, *Underwater Saboteur* (London: William Kimber & Co., 1953).

Marshall, Tim, *Prisoners of Geography* (London: Eliot and Thompson, 2015).

Miller, William H., *German Ocean Liners: From Kaiser Wilhelm der Grosse to AIDAstella* (Stroud: Amberley Publishing, 2013).

Newton, Ronald C., *The 'Nazi Menace' in Argentina 1931–1947* (Stanford: Stanford University Press, 1992).

Ottoson, Kristian, *In Such a Night: The Story of the Deportation of the Jews* (Oslo: Aschehaus, 1994).

Overy, Richard, *The Bombing War: Europe 1939–1945* (London: Allen Lane, 2013).

Peters, H.F., *Zarathustra: The Case of Elisabeth and Friedrich Nietzsche* (New York: Crown Publishers, 1977).

Petrow, Richard, *The Bitter Years: The Invasion and Occupation of Denmark and Norway April 1940–May 1945* (New York: William Morrow & Company, 1974).

Philips, Mike and Philips, Trevor, *Windrush: The Irresistible Rise of Multi-Racial Britain* (London: HarperCollins, 2008).

Pye, Michael, *The Edge of the World: How the North Sea Made Us Who We Are* (London: Viking, 2014).

Rees, Laurence, *Auschwitz: The Nazis and the 'Final Solution'* (London: BBC Books, 2005).

Sachs, Harvey, *Music in Fascist Italy* (London: George Weidenfeld & Nicolson, 1987).

Schwerdtner, Nils, *German Luxury Ocean Liners of the 20th Century* (Yeovil: Patrick Stephens Ltd, 1989).

Seybold, Captain W.N., *Women and Children First: The Loss of the Troopship 'Empire Windrush'* (privately published, 1998).

Shakespeare, Nicholas, *Six Minutes in May: How Churchill Unexpectedly Became Prime Minister* (London: Harville Secker, 2017).

Stangneth, Bettina, *Eichmann Before Jerusalem* (London: The Bodley Head, 2014).

Stevenson, Robert Louis, *Treasure Island* (London: Cassell & Co., 1883).

Tate, Tim, *Hitler's British Traitors* (London: Icon, 2018).

Tombs, Robert, *The English and their History* (London: Allen Lane, 2014).

Various, *The Official History of the Royal Canadian Airforce*, Vol. 3 (Toronto: University of Toronto Press, 1980).

Vinen, Richard, *National Service: A Generation in Uniform 1945–1963* (London: Penguin, 2014).

Williamson, Henry, *Goodbye West Country* (London: Putnam, 1937).

Willoughby, Jeffrey, *The KdF Fleet in Historic Photographs* (UK: Maritime Publishing Concepts, 2011).

Wills, Clair, *Lovers and Strangers: An Immigrant History of Post-War Britain* (London: Penguin, 2017).

Younger, Maj. Gen. A.E., *Blowing Our Bridges: A Memoir from Dunkirk to Korea via Normandy* (Barnsley: Pen & Sword Military, 2004).

ACKNOWLEDGEMENTS

This book had been planned before we knew there would be a fresh controversy surrounding government policy towards the Windrush generation in the spring of 2018. A brilliant exhibition at the British Library, *Songs in a Strange Land*, had also been planned without fore-knowledge of those national events. I am indebted as ever to that great institution for research, but would like to express further gratitude for its serendipitous curating of a number of talks and seminars associated with the developing story.

I was able to meet many people with particular perspectives on, for example, the underplayed role of Windrush women, the history of race relations legislation in the UK, the effect that the same legislation is having on British citizens whose origin is beyond the Caribbean in the present day, and the enormous living musical and literary benefits to this country of that period of immigration. That may sound a little po-faced, but in fact it was just a privilege to hear so many voices. This book of course covers that 1948 arrival in a linear narrative biography of the ship, but hopefully many more books will come covering the contemporary *Windrush* resonances. Huge congratulations to Amelia Gentleman and *The Guardian* for running with the story in 2018.

For research, in addition to the British Library staff, warm thanks go to the staff of The National Archives in Kew, the National Maritime Museum in Greenwich, the Guildhall Library in the City of London, the

University of Exeter Library and the Soldiers of Gloucestershire Museum in Gloucester. Further thanks are due to the Company Archivist of the Hamburg Süd Shipping Company. I have spoken with dozens of people with either experiences of or knowledge about the *Windrush*'s two and a half decades, too numerous to list, and would like to thank you all here.

Some valued friends have borne with me while I have been immersed in the book. They know who they are, but specifically I'd like to thank my colleagues in the East Devon Alliance of Independents, of which I am the chairman. I succeeded our founder chairman, His Honour Ian McIntosh, a few years ago, who remained as our president. We were devastated to lose him in 2018, and thank Rosie and his family for lending him to us. He was a wise counsel on this book, as with so much else.

Locally, I would also like to thank Mark Mann and Sheila Smith for their support and for unfailingly doing the right thing, and also the many friends in Colyton and the Axe Valley for their kind interest. The 'Colyton Laundry Protest' happened in the middle of the first draft, and I was delighted to be associated with it, and for that I'd like to pay tribute to Claire Mountjoy and her family.

I've spent much time in London researching and would like to thank all those who so kindly let me stay. Thanks to my children Benja Arnott and Sasha Arnott, and to Kate Aylward and Susannah Harker, for your generous hosting. Thank you too to my wife, Lydia Conway, and to Jake Arnott and Tara Arnott, for so much kind support, and to all the family for putting up with my occasional mental absences.

Thank you too to the Cakemaker's Dozen football team as we approach our thirty-fifth anniversary. The game we played in Taunton in -8°C the week I began this book made me feel as alive as a child playing his first game. Our skipper, Crispin Aylett, my best friend of more than four and a half decades, has kept me going with his daily motivational calls.

I am particularly indebted to a wise and kind agent, Charlie Viney, to our mutual friend, Richard Beswick, and to a superb team at The History Press: Chrissy McMorris, Jezz Palmer, Katie Beard and Caitlin Kirkman. It has been wonderful working with you.

Finally, to the people without whom, truly, I would not be here today. I am deeply grateful to the medical staff at the Seaton & Colyton Medical Practice, the Royal Devon and Exeter Hospital, and the Bristol Royal Infirmary, particularly Dr Joe Kent at Seaton & Colyton, Dr Paul Kerr and Neil Toghill at Exeter, and Dr Rachel Protheroe at Bristol. This is my first book since I had a dose of leukaemia that ultimately required a bone marrow transplant. These staff, and our nation's pride, the National Health Service, kept me alive. Literally saving my life was the anonymous 28-year-old donor who kindly gave me a couple of litres of his bone marrow fluid. I'll never know who you are, but thank you; you rebooted me. And all of us must thank the Anthony Nolan Trust, the blood diseases charity that brokers such donations, and does much else. If you are able to register as a blood donor or a bone marrow donor, please do.

INDEX

Abbot, Diane (Labour MP) 11
Adams, Roland (QC of New
    Zealand Shipping Company)
    242–3
Algiers 229, 234–5, 237
Angier, Captain Pat 192–3, 201–9,
    211–14, 217–18
Angier, Diana 201–4
Anglo-German Information
    Service 72
anti-Semitism 54, 87
  in Argentina 40–1
  in Britain 74–5
  in Norway 85, 94, 96
  media 43
  'New Germany' 31–2
Argentina 43–6
  anti-Semitism 40–1
  economy 40
  fascism in 37, 41
  Nazism 39–41
Attlee, Clement 45, 163, 180–1

Auschwitz (Concentration camp)
    43–4, 91–3, 138, 246, 247
  account by Odd Nansen 94–5
  list of prisoners compiled by
    Kristian Ottosen 97–100
  Norwegian Jews 17, 83, 88
  see also Belsen; Grini

Baptiste, Mona (singer and actress)
    185
Battle of Okinawa 212–13
Battle of the Imjin River 215–18,
    221
  see also Korean War
Bayles, William (journalist) 57–8
BBC (British Broadcasting
    Corporation) 7, 101, 133, 185
Belsen (Concentration camp) 131,
    189–90, 208
  see also Auschwitz; Grini
Berman, Irene 91–3
'Big Lie' principle 17

Bismarck ship 101–2, 104, 107

Blohm, Hermann 23

Blohm & Voss (shipbuilders) 23–6, 77, 104, 228

Board of Deputies of British Jews 74

Braddock, Bessie (Labour MP) 238–41, 245, 254

Brazil 30–1, 37–8

Brexit 8, 14–15

British Nationality Act 11, 179

British Union of Fascists 72

Buenos Aires 25, 37, 40

Burley, Adrian (Conservative MP) 13

Burnand, Sergeant Derek (army education officer) 240–1

Cameron, David 19

Caribbean immigrants to UK 13, 20, 169, 174, 177–8, 182–3, 256–7
  Baptiste, Mona (singer and actress) 185
  influence of Caribbean culture on Britain 184
  King, Sam (black campaigner) 179–81, 184
  Kitchener, Lord 183–5
  Lord Beginner 183
  O'Connor, Sarah 8–11
  Vandiel, Vernon 14
  Woodbine, Lord 183–4
  see also Windrush generation

Carne, Lieutenant Colonel James 204, 214
  Carne Cross 218–20

Ceylon 198, 207–8

Chalke, Private Harry 208–9, 214

Chamberlain, Neville 80, 88, 104

Churchill, Winston 80, 161, 182
  and the Polish Resettlement Act 172
  and the *Tirpitz* battleship 102, 106, 109, 111, 113, 117, 119

citizenship
  British 14–15, 178–9, 186
  Norwegian Jews 85
  Tyskerpiger 132, 135–6

class system
  in Britain 19, 63–4, 74, 229
  in Germany 50, 64–5

Claus, Odd 147–8, 157

Coats, Arthur (*Windrush* cook) 181–3

concentration camps 49, 96, 108
  Auschwitz 17, 43–4, 83, 88, 91–5, 97, 138, 246–7
  Belsen 131, 189–90, 208
  Grini 84

Conservative Party 7, 46, 72, 189
  and Windrush 14–16, 257
  see also individual politicians by name

Cooper, Andrew (policy adviser) 19

Cosh, Second Officer, Jack 229, 234–5

cricket 183–4

Daily Express 180–1

Daily Telegraph 63, 238

Dallas, Major Thomas 18

Davies, S. J. (Regimental Chaplain, Gloucester Cathedral) 219–20

Dell, Robert (*Daily Telegraph* foreign correspondent) 63–7, 70

Denmark 115, 124, 132, 134, 149
    Second World War 81

Donau ship 83, 86, 89, 93, 124, 129

Dönitz, Grand Admiral Karl 113, 119

Dowding, Sir Hugh, Air Chief Marshal 171–2

Dressler-Andress, Horst 48, 62

Eckart, Dietrich 54

economy
    Argentina 40
    Germany 25, 29, 50

Edinburgh Evening News 237–8

Egypt 196, 242–3
    Port Said 60, 160–2, 198, 240, 242

Eichmann, Adolf 37, 42–4

Empire Windrush ship
    as cruise liner 34–5
    as migrant ship 30, 69, 169–70, 173–4, 177–80
    as Nazi vessel 39–40, 49–81, 83, 86–7, 93, 131–2
    as support vessel for *Tirpitz* battleship 101, 106–8, 111, 113–16, 172
    attack by Max Manus 121–9, 147

demise of 231–5, 239
    inquiry into ship's demise 238–43, 245, 247–54
    legacy 256–9
    mechanical problems 158, 183, 224, 228–30
    origins and construction 18–21, 23, 27, 29
    role in 'Strength through Joy' scheme 47–55, 57, 59–63, 66, 77, 111, 131
    under British ownership 149–51
    voyage cards 27, 79, 148, 170

Enders, Tom 101–2

Eurobond 44

ex-enemy vessels 154–5

Falklands War 45–6

fascism 62, 122
    in Argentina 37, 41
    in Britain 66–7, 70, 72–4, 126, 245

Fassbender, Captain-lieutenant 117–18

Final Solution 93, 246

First World War 22, 24–5, 29, 194–5
    Norway 82
    South America 38
    United States of America 30

Förster, Bernhard 31–3

Förster-Nietzsche, Elisabeth 31–3, 38–9

Francois, Mark (Conservative MP) 101–2

Franco-Prussian War 22, 24, 32
Frank, Anne 131

German Labour Front 48–9
Germany
  class system 50, 64–5
  economy 29, 50
  Hamburg 23–4, 26–7, 29, 39, 52,
    69, 72, 77, 184
  Hanseatic League 23
  Navy 82, 104–5, 111, 114, 119
  Nuremberg Trials 48–9, 96, 153
  Rüdesheim 21
  unification 22
Gestapo 61, 80, 92
  and Max Manus 122, 128–30
  and women on KdF ('Strength
    Through Joy') cruises
    59–60
  seizing of Jewish assets 83
  spies aboard KdF ('Strength
    Through Joy') cruises 51–2,
    57–8
Glo'sters (British Army,
    Gloucestershire Regiment)
    194, 196, 205, 207–8, 212,
    214–18, 220–1
Gloucester Cathedral 218–20
Goebbels, Joseph
  and Adolf Hitler 48–9, 57, 65
  and 'Big Lie' principle 17
  and 'Strength Through Joy'
    scheme 48, 51, 60–2, 64, 66
Great Britain
  anti-Semitism 74–5

class system 19, 63–4, 74,
    229
  fascism in 66–7, 70, 72–4, 126,
    245
  influence of Caribbean culture
    on 184
  London 71–2, 75–6
  Nazism in 71–3
  racism in 175–6
  Tilbury Docks 69, 169–70,
    173–4, 177–80
Greece 162, 240
Green, Private Dave (Glo'sters
    Regiment) 194–9, 201,
    205–7, 211–14
Grini (Concentration camp) 85
  see also Auschwitz; Belsen
Guardian newspaper 13–14, 162

Haakon VII, King of Norway 82,
    92, 123, 129, 135
Hamburg, Germany 23–4, 26–7,
    29, 39, 52, 69, 72, 77, 184
Hamburg Süd Shipping Line
    Company 24–6, 29, 39, 50,
    52, 69, 71, 158
Hanseatic League 23
Heliand gospels 24
Himmler, Heinrich 42, 93–4, 132,
    134, 246
Hindenberg airship 69–7
Hiroshima 213, 227
Hispaniola ship 17–18
Hitler, Adolf 31–3, 40–1, 63, 72, 74,
    131, 246

and 'Big Lie' principle 17
and Joseph Goebbels 48–9, 57, 65
and Lebensborn 132, 134–5, 136
and the *Tirpitz* battleship 103–5,
    107, 110, 117, 119
Hofmo, Gunvor 89–90
Holocaust 42, 91, 95, 163
Holocaust Centre, Oslo 95–6
Holocaust Memorial Speech (2012)
    91
'hostile environment' policies 8–9,
    11, 180, 257

Imjin River, *see* Battle of Imjin
    River
immigration
    from Poland to UK 171–5
    from West Indies to UK 8, 13–14,
        20, 169, 174, 177–86, 256–7
    Immigration Act 10–11
    policies 8–9, 11, 25, 180, 186, 257
    to South America from Germany
        29–31, 37–8
    to United States of America 179
India 158, 162, 164–6, 256
International American Treaty of
    Reciprocal Assistance 45
International Holocaust
    Remembrance Day 82–3
Isaacs, George (Labour MP) 180

Jamaica 14, 20, 170, 178–9, 181–2,
    258
Jews
    Berman, Irene 91–3

confiscation of Jewish assets 44,
    83, 85–6, 88, 91, 94, 138
in Germany 23–4
in Norway 17, 80, 82–100
Maier, Ruth 89–91, 94, 96, 130
Rabinowitz, Moritz 87–9
see also anti-Semitism;
    concentration camps;
    Holocaust
Jordan, Jessie (German agent) 72

Kahn, E. J. (journalist) 215–16
KdF (Kraft durch Freude) *see*
    'Strength Through Joy' scheme
Keenan, Brigid (author and
    journalist) 164–5
Keynes, John Maynard
    The Economic Consequences of
    Peace 38
King, Sam (black campaigner)
    179–81, 184
Kitchener, Lord 183–5
Klingbeil, Julius (tailor) 32–3
Korean War 187–90, 194, 204, 208,
    212, 217–18, 221, 223
Krigsbarnsutvalget (War Children
    Committee) 135–6
Kuhn, Otto 62–3

Labour Party 163, 180, 185, 188,
    247
    see also individual politicians
        by name
Landmesser, August (shipyard
    worker) 77

Lawrence, Lady Doreen, 15–16
Lawrence, Stephen 11, 15–16
League of Nations 76, 163
Lebensborn project 132, 134–8,
    147–8, 256
    see also Tyskerpiger
Le Gendre, Kevin 184
Levy, Andrea (writer) 177–8
Ley, Robert (Hitler loyalist) 48–9,
    57–8
Lingstad, Anni-Frid 132–3, 137
Lingstad, Synni 132–3
Lloyd's List 27, 79, 243
London 71–2, 75–6
Lord Beginner 183

Maier, Ruth 89–91, 94, 96, 130
Manchester Guardian 64, 239–40
Manus, Max 121, 123–7, 132, 135,
    148, 157, 171
    and Gestapo 122, 128–30
    attack on *Empire Windrush*
    121–9, 147
Marr, Andrew 7–9
Masefield, John
    Cargo 255
May, Theresa 7–11, 14–16, 257
McBeath Leech, Sub Lieutenant
    John 149–51
McCarran Walter Act 179
media 13, 15–16, 181, 237–8
    anti-Semitism 43
    Second World War 215
    see also individual newspapers
    by title

Mengele, Josef (Auschwitz doctor)
    37, 43
Monte Rosa ship 19, 25–6, 114,
    131–2, 149, 152–4, 157
    see also Empire Windrush
Monte sister ships 50
    Monte Cervantes 25
    Monte Olivia 25–6
    Monte Pascoal 25–6
    Monte Rosa see Monte Rosa ship
    Monte Sarmiento 25–6
Mosley, Oswald (British fascist) 64,
    66, 73–4, 126, 245
Mussolini, Benito 66–7, 76

Naisby, J.V., QC 247, 250–3
Nansen, Odd
    account of Auschwitz 94–5
Nasjonal Samling Party 85, 96
National Archives, The 149, 151
National Health Service 8, 161, 188
national service 163–4, 194
Navy
    German 82, 104–5, 111, 114, 119
    Royal 45–6, 229–30
    United States of America 173
Nazism 37, 63–4
    in Argentina 39–41
    in Britain 71–3
    in Norway 85–6, 88
    in Paraguay 39
    'Strength Through Joy' scheme
    47–55, 57, 59–63, 66, 77, 111,
    131
    see also fascism; Third Reich

NDA, Emergency Organisation of German Anti-Fascists 38

'New Germany' (Neue Germania) colony 31–3, 38–9

New Zealand Shipping Company 158–60, 223, 238, 242

Niederwalddenkmal monument 22

Nietzsche, Elisabeth *see* Förster-Nietzsche, Elisabeth

Nietzsche, Friedrich August 7, 32–3

Nordic League 73–4
see also fascism in Britain

Norway 52–5, 61–2
anti-Semitism 85, 94–6
First World War 82
Jews in 17, 80, 82–100
Nazi invasion 81–2, 88
Oslo 82, 86, 90, 92, 122–3, 130, 132
Second World War 79–81

Norwegian Nazi Party 85–6, 88

Notgemeinschaft Deutscher Antifaschisten *see* NDA

Nuremberg Trials 48–9, 96, 153

O'Connor, Sarah 8–11

Okinawa *see* Battle of Okinawa

Øksnevad, Toralv (Norwegian broadcaster) 133–4

Olusoga, David, 11–12

Olympics, 2012 London opening ceremony 13

Operation Paravone 116

Operation Source 110–14

Operation Tungsten 115–16

Operation Weserübung 81

Oslo, Norway 82, 86, 90, 92, 122–3, 130, 132
Grini (Concentration camp) 84
Holocaust Centre 95–6

Ottosen, Kristian (Norwegian resistance leader)
compilation of identities of expelled Norwegian Jews 97–100
In Such a Night: The Story of the Deportation of the Jews 96

'Oxford Groups' 64

Palestine 162–3

Paraguay 31–2, 38–9

Pendleton, Leslie 235, 238–40, 242, 249–50

Peninsular and Oriental Steam Navigation Company (P&O) 158–9, 223, 225

Perón, Juan Domingo 41, 45

Phillips, Mike 13

Phillips, Trevor 13

Poland 104, 171–4
Second World War 175–6

Polish Resettlement Act (1947) 172–3

Port Said, Egypt 60, 160–2, 198, 240, 242

Powell, Enoch 11

PQ.17 convoy 110

propaganda 39, 47–8, 60, 63–6, 72, 188

Quisling, Vidkun 84–6, 94, 96, 121–2

Rabinowitz, Moritz 87–9
Race Relations Board 186
racism 14–15
  in Britain 175–6
  in Germany 23–4
Ramsay, Captain Archibald Henry Maule 74
Ridgway, General Matthew (United Nations commander-in-chief in Korea) 220–1
Right Club 73–4
  see also fascism in Britain
Rio Pact see International American Treaty of Reciprocal Assistance
Rosel, Rudolph (Fifth Column) 72–3
Rosenberg, Alfred 121
Royal Navy 45–6, 229, 230
Rüdesheim, Germany 21

Scandinavia 24, 29, 47, 79, 81, 115, 117
  see also Denmark; Norway; Sweden
Schulte, Eduard (German industrialist) 246–7
seafaring superstitions 17–18
Second World War 25–6, 161
  Denmark 81
  Norway 79–81
  Poland 175–6

Seybold, Officer W.N. 'Wally' 224–5, 227, 229, 232, 242
Silverman, Sidney (Labour MP) 245–50, 253–4
Singapore 198–9
Socotra ship 233
Solberg, Erna (Norwegian Prime Minister) 136–7
South America 24–5, 33–4, 37
  Argentina 39–41, 43–6
  Brazil 30–1, 37–8
  Buenos Aires 25, 37, 40
  Falkland Islands 45–6
  First World War 38
  migration from Germany 29
  Paraguay 31–2, 38–9
  Uruguay 32
Sri Lanka see Ceylon
Stalin, Joseph 171–3, 188, 190, 219
Stoltenberg, Jens 82–3
  Holocaust Memorial speech (2012) 91
Strachan (New Zealand Shipping Company's assistant superintendent engineer) 240–1
Strasser, Gregor (Hitler's ally) 39, 48
'Strength through Joy' scheme 47–50, 55, 61–3, 66, 77, 111, 131
  and Gestapo spies 51–2, 57–8
  and women 58–60
Sweden 83–4, 225
Switzerland 44, 246

terrorism 242–3
Thatcher, Margaret 46
Third Reich 43, 48–9, 52, 61, 75, 104, 132
Tilbury Docks, Essex 69, 169–70, 173–4, 177–80
    50th anniversary celebrations 13
Times newspaper 13, 219–20, 253
Tirpitz, Alfred von 104–5
Tirpitz battleship
    and Adolf Hitler 103–5, 107, 110, 117, 119
    and *Empire Windrush* ship 101, 106–8, 111, 113–16, 172
    and Winston Churchill 102, 106, 109, 111, 113, 117, 119
Tozer, Jack (engineer) 242–3, 250
Treaty of Versailles 30, 38, 103–4
Tyskerpiger 80, 130–8, 147–8
    see also Lebensborn project

UK Borders Act (2007) 257
UKIP (United Kingdom Independence Party) 11
unification of Germany 22
United States of America 45
    First World War 30
    immigration to 179
    Navy 173
Uruguay 32

Vandiel, Vernon (Jamaican immigrant) 14
victim-blaming 15–17
Vilmar, August (theologian) 24

Vincer, Ray (*Windrush* cabin steward) 230–2
Volberg, Heinrich 40–1
von Thermann, Baron Edmund 39–40
Voss, Ernst 23
    see also Blohm & Voss
voyage cards, *Empire Windrush* 27, 79, 148, 170

Wallis, Barnes 116
War Children Committee (Krigsbarnsutvalget) 135–6
Welchman, Gordon (Bletchley cryptologist) 172
Williamson, Henry 69–70, 71
Wilson, Captain (*Windrush* ship's master) 192, 223–6, 229–30, 232, 243, 248–50
Windrush
    generation 8–12, 14
    ship *see Empire Windrush*
    see also Caribbean immigrants to UK
Wodehouse, P.G. 126–7
women
    and Gestapo 59–60
    'Strength Through Joy' scheme 58
    Korean War 217
    see also Tyskerpiger
Woodbine, Lord 183–4

Younger, Tony (soldier) 189–94, 201, 203, 205–6, 214, 217